Software Configuration Management Strategies and Rational ClearCase®

The Addison-Wesley Object Technology Series

Grady Booch, Ivar Jacobson, and James Rumbaugh, Series Editors

For more information check out the series web site [http://www.awl.com/cseng/otseries/].

The Component Software Series

Clemens Szyperski, Series Editor

For more information check out the series web site [http://www.awl.com/cseng/csseries/].

Software Configuration Management Strategies and Rational ClearCase®

A Practical Introduction

Brian A. White

Addison-Wesley

Boston • San Francisco • New York • Toronto • Montreal
London • Munich • Paris • Madrid
Capetown • Sydney • Tokyo • Singapore • Mexico City

Many of the designations used by manufacturers and sellers to distinguish their products are claimed as trademarks. Where those designations appear in this book and we are aware of a trademark claim, the designations have been printed in initial capital letters or all capitals.

The author and publisher have taken care in the preparation of this book, but make no expressed or implied warranty of any kind and assume no responsibility for errors or omissions. No liability is assumed for incidental or consequential damages in connection with or arising out of the use of the information or programs contained herein.

Rational, the e-development company, the Rational logo, Rational ClearCase®, ClearCase MultiSite, and ClearQuest are trademarks or registered trademarks of Rational Software Corporation in the United States and in other countries. All other names are used for identification purposes only and are trademarks or registered trademarks of their respective companies. All rights reserved.

The publisher offers discounts on this book when ordered in quantity for special sales. For more information, please contact:

Pearson Education Corporate Sales Division
One Lake Street
Upper Saddle River, NJ 07458
(800) 382-3419
corpsales@pearsontechgroup.com

Visit us on the Web at *www.awl.com/cseng/*

Library of Congress Cataloging-in-Publication Data

White, Brian A.
    Software configuration management strategies and Rational ClearCase: a practical introduction / Brian White.
        p. cm. — (Addison-Wesley object technology series)
    Includes bibliographical references and index.
    ISBN 0-201-60478-7
        1. Software configuration management.   2. Rational Clearcase.   I. Title.   II. Series.

QA76.76.C69 W54 2000
005.1'5--dc21   00-040628

Text printed on recycled and acid-free paper.

ISBN 0201604787

3 4 5 6 7 8 ML   04 03 02 01

3rd Printing   April 2001

To Shannon and Florann White,
who taught me that through God
all things are possible.

Contents

Foreword

As chief engineer for the Configuration Management business unit of Rational Software, I have the pleasure of focusing on a fascinating problem: how to do software configuration management "right."

My first experience with the rewards and perils of "doing it right" was as an undergraduate in applied mathematics at Harvard University. My freshman mathematics professor turned out to be a 35-year-old graduate student with one goal: solving an elegant little puzzle that had baffled mathematicians for a century, the Four-Color Problem. His reward was that he got up every morning knowing exactly what he was going to do. The peril was that fifteen years later, he was still a graduate student. Happily, any immediate risk of my following that perilous path was eliminated when later that year I had my first encounter with software engineering (back then, we just called it programming). Programming was mathematics with a built-in positive-feedback mechanism. You get the proof (the program) right, and you have not only intellectual gratification, but also something that actually does something interesting and for which companies are eager to pay large sums of money.

But later, in graduate school, the positive-feedback mechanism started to break down. By that time, the software systems I built involved combining large numbers of files from a variety of programmers, some of whom worked even more irregular hours than I did. Instead of composing elegant algorithms, I spent the majority of my time finding out what others had done and letting them know what I planned to do. Not only was this far less intellectually gratifying, but everything took much longer to build, and funding agencies were correspondingly less eager to pay for results that came ever more slowly.

So this would be my Four-Color Problem: discovering the process by which an individual could be a member of a team of programmers but be as productive as when working alone. Attempts to solve the problem by introducing policies and procedures for managing change did make the process more predictable and decrease certain classes of errors, but at the cost of further decreasing both the intellectual gratification and the productivity of the programming process.

One ray of hope came from the cute little program called "make." No policies or procedures were required. With only file system date stamps and an admittedly cryptic "makefile," the work from an arbitrarily large number of programmers could be compiled as reliably and efficiently as that of a single programmer working alone. The challenge was to find an analogous software tool that would reduce or eliminate the overhead of programming in a team environment. (As a side note, around that time, the Four-Color Problem was finally solved, but only with the aid of a computer program. Apparently, even some mathematical problems are tractable only with the aid of software tools.)

During a decade of studying the problem of software configuration management at Inference Corporation, Sun Microsystems, Hewlett-Packard, and Bellcore, I had the opportunity to identify and implement several key components of automated software configuration management. Then, in November of 1995, I was asked to join Atria Software as project lead for "ratbert," the code name for a project to build a process automation layer above ClearCase.

One of my first activities at Atria was to participate in the design of an "out-of-the-box" process for the new process automation product. Initially assigned to implement this process was a soft-spoken sales engineer named Brian White. Although it seemed a bit strange to have someone in the sales organization be responsible for implementing such a key element of a new product, it soon became apparent that sales engineers at Rational were some of the world's experts on SCM processes. Their job was to go to the most sophisticated software development organizations in the world, learn about how those organizations did software development, and then show them how to use Clear-Case to automate that process. We needed the best sales engineer we could get for this project, and Brian was the person we picked.

The initial design meetings for the out-of-the-box process were held off-site at the almost-completed new home of Dave Leblang (the chief architect of Clear-Case). There were occasional interruptions intrinsic to the completion phase of a successful entrepeneur's new home: Irish stonemasons building granite walls for the terrace; 40 loads of earth brought in to level out the back gardens. But, gradually, the out-of-the-box process took shape.

Although we rapidly converged on the key elements of the process, two distinct viewpoints emerged. One viewpoint was that every organization was very different, and any process that we developed was just some initial code that would be modified significantly by every installation. The other viewpoint, shared by Brian and me, was that a wide range of organizations could share a common process if that process was designed to be easily configured. This viewpoint was supported by the fact that ClearCase sales engineers tended over time to develop a set of standard scripts that they would use with little modification at each new organization. This viewpoint was also supported by my experience that most process variations are added to address missing underlying tool support; but when full tool support is provided for the key SCM functions, a remarkably similar set of processes become appropriate for a wide range of organizations.

In the most recent release of ClearCase, the common process viewpoint has been realized in the form of the "unified change management" process. This takes the form of both a process and tool support specifically designed to support that process (e.g., new objects, operations, and GUIs). Although tool support for this process will need to evolve, it is my belief that this common process will become the standard way of performing software configuration management. Brian White's book, *Software Configuration Management Strategies and Rational ClearCase®,* provides the foundation for both understanding and adopting this process.

Geoffrey M. Clemm, Ph.D.
Rational Software Corporation

Preface

What This Book Is About

This book is about the engineering discipline of software configuration management (SCM) and how the widely used SCM product, Rational ClearCase®, automates and supports SCM best practices through a model called unified change management (UCM). This book covers basic SCM concepts, typical SCM problems encountered as projects and software systems grow in size and complexity, and how you can apply SCM tools and processes to solve these problems. Advanced SCM topics are also discussed, such as managing large geographically distributed teams and combining the disciplines of SCM and change request management (or defect tracking).

Specifically, this book discusses SCM in terms of a specific SCM tool called ClearCase. Although the discussion is specific to ClearCase, some of the material covered is SCM-tool-neutral. There are very few new books on software configuration management and even fewer that provide strategies for a specific tool. It is in the application of an SCM tool where projects most often run into problems and fail.

ClearCase is a commercially available SCM tool. It is a good choice of tool for this discussion because it provides an open architecture that is used to implement and automate a wide range of SCM solutions. ClearCase is used in many different development environments on many types of applications, such as mission-critical IT, embedded systems, telecommunication systems, financial applications, Web site content, and other commercial and government software systems. Companies in these diverse industries are successfully using ClearCase as the cornerstone of their SCM environment.

This book is not a step-by-step cookbook for using ClearCase, nor does it serve as a substitute for the ClearCase product documentation. You can use the concepts in this book to improve your application of any SCM tool. However, you will get the most out of this book if you are planning to deploy ClearCase or you want to improve the current way you use ClearCase.

On a personal note, this book is a collection of the experience I've gained by working with some incredible people in the SCM field over the last ten years. After reading it, you should have a better understanding of software configuration management, a better idea of the software development problems solved by using SCM tools and techniques, and a clear understanding of how you can use ClearCase to solve these problems and meet your SCM requirements. I sincerely hope you enjoy the book and find it valuable.

What You Need to Know before Reading This Book

The key to your success is understanding SCM, the requirements for your software project, and how to apply an SCM tool to meet a project's requirements. This book will get you started if you are new to software configuration management. However, you will get the most out of this book if you already have some SCM experience and have used basic version control tools before. This book assumes you are familiar with the software development process. It will also be helpful if you have a specific development project in mind while you are reading.

Who You Are and Why You Should Read This Book

This book is not about the nitty-gritty details of writing ClearCase triggers and scripting home-grown integrations with legacy tools; rather it will give you a high-level view of some common SCM scenarios and how ClearCase can be applied. If you are new to SCM or ClearCase, read this book cover to cover. If you have used ClearCase or have a strong foundation in SCM, look through the table of contents and pick chapters and sections that are of particular interest to you.

For a Software Engineer

The biggest thing an SCM tool can do for a software engineer is to stay out of the way. SCM should perform its function, yet be as transparent as possible. The SCM tool and how it is applied should maximize your ability to make changes to the software. Poor tools or poorly designed processes can add unnecessary time and effort to your work. This book can help you identify the areas in your SCM tools and processes to streamline. It discusses some new advances in the SCM area specifically designed for streamlining development. One of these is the notion of activity-based software configuration management. The idea here is to raise the level of abstraction from files to activities. This makes working with an SCM tool, tracking your changes, and sharing changes with other software engineers more intuitive.

If you're new to SCM, read Chapter 1, What Is Software Configuration Management? For an overview of the objects managed by ClearCase, see chapter 4, A Functional Overview of ClearCase Objects. To gain an understanding of how ClearCase is used on a daily basis from a development perspective, see chapter 8, Development Using the ClearCase UCM Model.

For a Software Project Manager or Technical Leader

As a leader for a software project, you are concerned with deciding what changes to make to a software system and then ensuring that those changes happen. Unplanned changes, made by well-meaning developers, introduce risk into the project schedule and may cause schedule delays and poor product quality. The ability to control and track change is essential to your project's success.

This book should help you gain a solid understanding of SCM, see why you need it, and learn how ClearCase can be used to solve problems you may encounter on projects. Specifically, see chapter 6, Project Management in Clear-Case, and chapter 7, Coordinating Multiple Project Teams and Other Scenarios. If you are managing teams that are not all in one location, see chapter 10, Geographically Distributed Development, for a discussion of the issues and strategies involved.

For a Tools Engineer

The role of tools engineer is often overlooked but is essential to success, particularly in large organizations. Your job is to figure out how to apply a given tool to the people, processes, and organization for which you work. This book will give you information about SCM and ClearCase that you can use to determine the best way to apply ClearCase to projects.

For Those Evaluating ClearCase

This book is a good starting point in the evaluation of ClearCase because it presents a number of common software development scenarios as well as more complex scenarios such as geographically distributed development. It discusses the requirements of SCM processes and tools in terms of a set of SCM best practices and shows how to apply ClearCase to support them. Included are overviews of ClearCase's out-of-the-box process, unified change management, and ClearCase objects.

Use chapter 1, What Is Software Configuration Management?, and chapter 2, Growing into Your SCM Solution, to help determine the SCM tool requirements for your project. Look to the remaining chapters to determine whether ClearCase will meet your needs.

For Experienced ClearCase Users

If you are a long-time ClearCase user, this book is interesting from a general software configuration management perspective and may offer some insights into how to approach SCM solutions on your projects. It also offers some advice if you are being asked to support geographically distributed development teams (see chapter 10, Geographically Distributed Development).

The book contains an overview of ClearCase's out-of-the-box usage model called unified change management, which is a recent addition (see chapter 3, An Overview of the Unified Change Management Model). If you are curious about integrating change request management with ClearCase, then look at chapter 11, Change Request Management and ClearQuest. Look also through the table of contents and pick chapters and sections that are of particular interest to you.

How the Book Is Laid Out

Here is a brief summary of all the chapters.

- Chapter 1, What Is Software Configuration Management, provides a general introduction to software configuration management and the key best practices behind it. It answers the questions: what is software configuration management?, what are SCM tools?, and what is the SCM process?

- Chapter 2, Growing into Your SCM Solution, discusses the growing complexity of software development projects and proposes that as projects grow in complexity so does their need for richer SCM support. It covers the history of SCM tool evolution using five categories of software projects ranging from software developed by a single individual to projects with many geographically distributed project teams.

- Chapter 3, An Overview of the Unified Change Management Model, provides an overview of ClearCase's out-of-the-box usage model, unified change management, which automates and supports a particular SCM process. The material is discussed in terms of the roles and responsibilities of the various team members, such as the architect, project manager, developer, and integrator.

- Chapter 4, A Functional Overview of ClearCase Objects, provides a functional overview of ClearCase objects and concepts. This chapter serves as a bridge between general SCM terminology and ClearCase-specific terminology.

- Chapter 5, Establishing the Initial SCM Environment, provides information on setting up an initial SCM environment. It discusses the basics of ClearCase architecture. The chapter also covers mapping the software architecture to the physical components in the SCM tool and briefly discusses creating the SCM repositories and importing existing software.

- Chapter 6, Project Management in ClearCase, focuses on the role of the project manager with respect to SCM. Particular attention is paid to automation and functionality in ClearCase that specifically supports the project manager. It presents an example of creating a ClearCase project.

- Chapter 7, Coordinating Multiple Project Teams and Other Scenarios, discusses the issues of coordinating parallel work. It also covers the scenarios involving multiple teams cooperating on a common release, development of multiple releases in parallel with multiple teams, coordination of IS/IT–style projects, and coordination of documentation-oriented projects.

- Chapter 8, Development Using the ClearCase UCM Model, provides an introduction to using ClearCase, specifically focusing on the role of the developer. It shows you how to find and join an existing project, how to make changes to files to accomplish an activity, how to deliver the changes associated with the activity, and how to update the development workspace with changes made by other developers on the project.

- Chapter 9, Integration, Build, and Release, focuses on the role of the integrator and discusses approaches to software integration. This chapter briefly covers building, baselining, and how baselines are promoted. It provides an overview of how components are staged in a separate repository that is used for delivery and version control of the "built" deliverable files and directories. It also discusses how software is released by comparing different types of software systems.

- Chapter 10, Geographically Distributed Development, discusses the organizational, communication, and technical challenges that need to be overcome to be successful in distributed development. It looks at three common scenarios of distributed development and the issues associated with each. Finally, this chapter discusses the technology provided by ClearCase MultiSite and how to apply MultiSite to the three scenarios.

- Chapter 11, Change Request Management and ClearQuest, covers the area of change request management (CRM), a subset of which is defect tracking. SCM and CRM are two closely related disciplines, which together form comprehensive change management support. This chapter also discusses a product called Rational ClearQuest and how it works in concert with ClearCase to provide the foundation technology for the unified change management model.

Conventions Used

Commands and Emphasized Text

Command line operations are called out with a different font and prompt, for example:

```
prompt> command -flag1 -flag2
```

Long commands are written on multiple lines for clarity (as shown here), but should be typed on one line, for example:

```
prompt> longcommand longobject-identifier
    -flag1 //machine/pathname
    -flag
```

▶ **Note:** Particular points that need to be emphasized appear in the text in this font with an arrow to alert you.

WARNING: The screened warning box is used to emphasize an issue or concern that might be encountered and should be avoided.

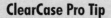

ClearCase Pro Tip

A screened box labeled with the above denotes information that is specifically useful for people who are already using ClearCase. If you have not used ClearCase, you can skip the tips.

UML Diagram Format

This book includes diagrams that use a graphical modeling language called the unified modeling language, or UML. For more information on UML, see *The Unified Modeling Language User Guide* by Grady Booch, James Rumbaugh, and Ivar Jacobson [Booch 1999].

Here is a description of the small subset of UML used in this book: An object is shown as a box, with text that describes the object. Lines represent associations between the objects, with text that describes the association. For example, "a house has a roof":

The association can be annotated to provide additional information, such as how many objects can be connected. This is called the "multiplicity" of the association. For example, any given house has only one roof and any given roof can be associated with only one house. Any given house can have many windows or no windows. Any given window can be associated with no house (before it is installed) or one house. These annotations would be represented as shown here:

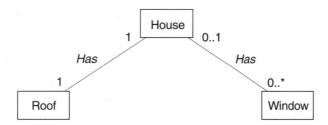

Is it really a house if there are no windows? If not, then you would use "1..*n*" for the windows rather than "0..*n*."

A black diamond is another association annotation that is used to show composition. Composition means one object is composed of another. Important semantics are implied by this type of association. One object "owns" the other. That is, owned objects can be created and removed, but once created they live forever with the owning object. If the owning object is destroyed, its parts are also destroyed. For example, a database has database tables. When the database is destroyed, all the tables are also destroyed. This would be represented in UML as shown here:

Finally, a UML relationship called "generalization" occurs between a general thing and a more specific kind of that thing. For example, the general thing could be a shoe, and specific types of shoes are running shoes, hiking shoes, and tennis shoes. Generalization is represented by an open arrow pointing toward the general object as shown here:

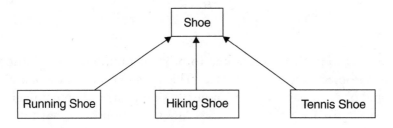

Acknowledgments

I could never have even begun this book without the help of some key people who shaped my career and me. For that I would like to thank Larry Hull, Larry Oslund, Edward Ely, John Leary, and Claudia Dent. After I tossed the idea around for quite a few years, Steve Yost was the catalyst that actually started the project by putting me in touch with someone at Addison-Wesley. I would also like to thank Lorie Stull for her encouragement to take on this challenge.

This book would never have been completed without the help of many others. I would like to thank Kimberly Stamm for her support and encouragement through many long weekends; Claudia Dent for allowing me the flexibility and time I required; the staff of Addison-Wesley—particularly my editor, Debbie Lafferty, and Marilyn Rash; and the production team—Judy Strakalaitis, Hilary Selby Polk, and Doug Leavitt—for walking a new author through the process; Brad Appleton for sharing his depth of knowledge in SCM and for the time spent providing detailed comments throughout many drafts; Arte Kenyon, who was of great assistance in the writing process; and Geoff Clemm, Peter Klenk, Alan Tate, and Nat Mishkin for the finishing touches. I'd also like to extend my thanks to the reviewers: David Bellagio, Ralph Capasso, David Cuka, Elfriede Dustin, Doug Fierro, Susan Goetcheus, Michael Harris, Bill Hasling, Philippe Kruchten, Dean Larsen, Jeff Leyser, Jas Madhur, Linda Okoniewski, Brett Schuchert, Ken Tessier, and all the others who provided invaluable input.

Without ClearCase, this book would not have been written, and without David Leblang ClearCase would never have been built. I would like to sincerely thank the original 10 people who took their fate in their hands and started a company that resulted in the birth of ClearCase: David Leblang, Howard Spilke, Bob Chase, Paul Levine, Dave Jabs, Debbie Minard, Bryan Douros, Gordon McLean, Peter Hack, and Jim Herron. It has been a privilege to have worked directly with most of these incredibly talented individuals who helped set the standard of excellence for SCM tools.

Unified change management would not have been born without the ideas and support of a number of people at Rational Software and at a number of companies using ClearCase. I would like to thank Geoff Clemm, David Leblang, Debbie Minard, and the many ClearCase users I've had the pleasure to work with for formulating the basic ideas behind the UCM model; Peter Klenk for turning those ideas into reality and leading the UCM development effort; Jonathan Aibel, Howard Bernstein, Brian Douros, Hans Heilman, Shirley Hui, Mark Karuzis, Matt Lennon, Nat Mishkin, Brian Morris, Ken Tessier and Mary Utt for the attention to detail and leadership in the design, documentation, implementation, and testing of UCM; Dave Bernstein, Claudia Dent, and Hugh Scandrett for their management leadership; and everyone at Rational Software who is involved with the UCM efforts. Keep up the good work.

Chapter 1 What Is Software Configuration Management?

Software configuration management (SCM) is a software engineering discipline comprising the tools and techniques (processes or methodology) that a company uses to manage change to its software assets. The introduction to the IEEE "Standard for Software Configuration Management Plans" [IEEE 828-1998] says this about SCM:

> SCM constitutes good engineering practice for all software projects, whether phased development, rapid prototyping, or ongoing maintenance. It enhances the reliability and quality of software by:
> - Providing structure for identifying and controlling documentation, code, interfaces, and databases to support all life cycle phases
> - Supporting a chosen development/maintenance methodology that fits the requirements, standards, policies, organization, and management philosophy
> - Producing management and product information concerning the status of baselines, change control, tests, releases, audits, etc.

One thing is clear: software is easy to change—too easy. Here is about as short a definition of SCM as you will find: SCM is about managing change to software.

Today, most software project teams understand the need for SCM to manage change to their software systems. However, even with the best of intentions, software projects continue to fail because of problems that could have been avoided through the use of an SCM tool and appropriate processes. These failures are reflected in poor quality, late delivery, cost overruns, and the inability to meet customer demands.

In order to understand software configuration management, you may find it easier to look first at configuration management in a hardware development environment. Hardware systems have physical characteristics that make the problems caused by the lack of sound configuration management easier to see.

For example, take a personal computer. A computer has a processor, some memory, a hard drive, a monitor, and a keyboard. Each of these hardware items has an interface that connects it to other hardware items. Your mouse has a plug, and your computer has a port into which you plug your mouse, and, voilà, everything works.

If the plug on the mouse was not compatible with the port on the computer, there would be no way to connect the two pieces of hardware into a working system. Throughout the computer, there are many other similar interfaces. The processor and memory plug into the motherboard; the hard drive plugs into the computer; and the printer, monitor, and keyboard all have interfaces.

When the hardware is manufactured, the interfaces that are essential for the operation of the final system are easily seen. Therefore, they are well known and are carefully examined whenever changes are made to the hardware design.

For a hardware system, configuration management has the following aspects. Each part is numbered or identified and also has a version number. Each version number identifies different designs of the same part. For example, the model year for a car is a version number of that car. It is a 1999 Ford Explorer, a 2000 Ford Explorer, and so on. When the design of a specific part is changed, the part gets a new version number.

A hardware system may be made up of hundreds, thousands, or tens of thousands of parts. The next thing that must be recorded is which versions of these parts go together. In manufacturing terms, this is often called a "bill of materials." The bill of materials lists all the parts and specifies which version of each part should be used.

Parts are assembled into bigger parts, which simplifies the manufacturing process for large systems. In our personal computer example, you can say what version of the mouse, hard drive, processor, and monitor go together to make a complete system. Each of these parts, for example, a hard drive, is made of many, many subparts, all of which must go together to have a working unit.

Software configuration management deals with all of the same problems as hardware configuration management. Each software part has an interface, and software "parts" are plugged together to form a software system. These software "parts" are referred to by different names, such as subsystems, modules, or components. They must be identified and must have a version number. They must have compatible interfaces. You need a bill of materials to see which versions of which components make up the entire software system.

However, software is not exactly like hardware. Software configuration management is much harder to get right because software is much easier to change. A few keystrokes and the click of the save button and you've created a new version of the software. Unlike hardware, software manufacturing is very fast and could be performed hundreds of times a day by individuals on a software team. This is usually referred to as "performing a software build," or "building the software."

It is in this dynamic, changing environment that the discipline of SCM is brought to bear to ensure that when a final version of the entire software system is produced, all of the system's component parts can be plugged together to work as required. While most software project teams understand that they need SCM, many fail to get it right because SCM is complex. The rest of this chapter discusses key best practices of SCM in detail.

1.1   SCM Best Practices

When implementing SCM tools and processes, you must define what practices and policies to employ in order to avoid common configuration problems and maximize team productivity. Many years of practical experience have shown that the following best practices are essential to successful software development:

1. Identify and store artifacts in a secure repository.
2. Control and audit changes to artifacts.
3. Organize artifacts into versioned components.
4. Create baselines at project milestones.
5. Record and track requests for change.
6. Organize and integrate consistent sets of versions using activities.
7. Maintain stable and consistent workspaces.
8. Support concurrent changes to artifacts and components.
9. Integrate early and often.
10. Ensure reproducibility of software builds.

1.1.1   Identify and Store Artifacts in a Secure Repository

To do configuration management, you must identify which artifacts should be placed under version control. These artifacts should include both those used to manage and design a system (e.g., project plans and design models) and those that instantiate the system design itself (e.g., source files, libraries, and executables). IEEE calls this *configuration identification:* "an element of configuration management, consisting of selecting the configuration items for a system and recording their functional and physical characteristics in technical documentation" [IEEE Glossary 1990].

In terms of an SCM tool, identification means being able to find and identify any project or system artifact quickly and easily. Anyone who has managed a development project with no SCM or poor SCM can attest to the difficulty of finding the "right" version of the "right" file when copies are floating around all over the place. Ultimately, losing or misidentifying artifact versions can lead to the failure of a project either by hindering delivery of the system because of missing parts or by lowering the quality of the system because of incorrect parts.

Organizing artifacts and being able to locate them are not enough. You also need fault-tolerant, scalable, distributable, and replicable repositories for these critical assets. The repository is a potential central point of failure for all your assets; therefore, it must be fault-tolerant and reliable. As your organization grows, you will add data and repositories, so scalability and distributability are required to maintain high system performance.

Another means of growth in today's software market is through acquisition, which affects many companies by resulting in the geographical distribution of development groups. The SCM tool, therefore, must be able to support teams collaborating across these geographically distributed sites.

Finally, the repositories should be backed up with appropriate backup and disaster-recovery procedures. Sadly, many companies overlook this last step, which can lead to severe problems.

1.1.2   Control and Audit Changes to Artifacts

Once the artifacts are identified and stored in a repository, you must be able to control who is allowed to modify them, as well as keep a record of what the modifications were, who made them, when were they made, and why they were made. We refer to this as the "audit information." This best practice is related to the IEEE configuration management topics *configuration control* and *configuration status accounting,* defined, respectively, as "the evaluation, coordination, approval or disapproval, and implementation of changes to configuration items" and "the recording and reporting of information needed to manage a configuration effectively" [IEEE Glossary 1990].

Using both control and audit best practices, an organization can determine how strictly to enforce change control policies. Without control, anyone can change the system. Without audit, you never really know what went into the system. With audit information, even if you don't restrict changes, you can see at any time what was changed, by whom, and why. The audit information also allows you to more easily make corrections if errors are introduced. Using control and audit in balance allows you to tune your change control approach to best fit your organization. Ideally, you want to optimize for development productivity while eliminating known security risks.

1.1.3 Organize Artifacts into Versioned Components

Once there are more than a few hundred files and directories in a system, it becomes necessary to group these files and directories into objects representing a larger granularity in order to ease management and organization problems. These single objects, made up of sets of files and directories, have a number of different names in the software industry, including "packages," "modules," "subsystems," and "development components." For the purposes of this book, they are referred to as "SCM components," or just "components." An *SCM component* is a set of related files and directories that are versioned, shared, built, and baselined as a single unit.

To implement a component-based approach to SCM, you organize the files and directories into a single SCM component that physically implements a logical system design component. The Rational Unified Process refers to the SCM component as a *component subsystem* [RUP 5.5 1999].[1]

A component-based approach to SCM offers many benefits, as follows:

■ *Components reduce complexity.*

Use of a higher level of abstraction reduces complexity and makes any problem more manageable. Using components, you can discuss the six that make up a system rather than the 5,000 files subsumed under them. When producing a system, you only need to select six baselines, one from each component, rather than having to select the right 5,000 versions of 5,000 files. It is easier to assemble consistent systems from consistent component baselines rather than individual file versions. Inconsistencies result in unnecessary rebuilding and errors discovered late in the development cycle.

---

1. The Rational Unified Process (RUP) is a software engineering process developed and marketed by Rational Software.

■ *It is easier to identify the quality level of a particular component baseline than that of numerous individual files.*

A component baseline identifies one and only one version of each file and directory that makes up that component. Because a component baseline contains a consistent set of versions, these can be integration-tested as a unit. It is then possible to mark the level of testing that has been performed on each component baseline.

This method improves communication and reduces errors when two or more project teams share components. For example, a project team produces a database component, and another team uses it as part of an end-user application. If the application project team can easily determine the newest database component baseline that has passed integration testing, then they are less likely to use a defective set of files.

■ *Instantiating a physical component object in a tool helps institutionalize component sharing and reuse.*

Once component baselines are created and the quality level is identified, project teams can look at the various component baselines and choose one that can be referenced or reused from one project to the next. Component sharing and reuse is practically impossible if you cannot determine which versions of which files make up a component. Component sharing between projects is not practical if you cannot determine the level of quality and stability for any given component baseline.

■ *Mapping logical design components to physical SCM components helps preserve the integrity of software architectures.*

In an iterative development process, pieces of the software architecture are built and tested early in the software lifecycle to drive out risk. By mapping the logical architectural components to the physical SCM components, you gain the ability to build and test individual pieces of the architecture. This mapping between architecture and the implementation of the architecture leads to higher-quality code and cleaner interfaces between the components by preserving the integrity of the original architecture in the SCM tool.

1.1.4   Create Baselines at Project Milestones

At key milestones in a project, all the artifacts should be baselined together. In other words, you should record the versions of all the artifacts and components that make up a system at specific times in the project. At a minimum, artifacts should be baselined at each major project milestone. In an iterative development process as prescribed by the Rational Unified Process [RUP 5.5], at a minimum baselines should be created at the end of each project iteration. Typically, new baselines are created more frequently (sometimes daily) near the end of an iteration or release cycle. It can be useful to create baselines before each nightly build. This allows you to reproduce any project build, query what has changed between builds, and indicate the stability of a build using baseline quality attributes.

There are three main reasons to baseline: reproducibility, traceability, and reporting. Reproducibility is the ability to go back in time and reproduce a given release of a software system or a development environment that existed earlier. Traceability ties the requirements, project plans, test cases, and software artifacts together. To implement it, you should baseline not only the system artifacts, but also the project management artifacts. Reporting allows you to query the content of any baseline and to compare baselines. Baseline comparison can assist in debugging errors and generating release notes.

Good traceability, reproducibility, and reporting are necessary for solving process problems. They enable you to fix defects in released products, facilitate ISO-9000 and SEI audits, and ultimately ensure that the design fulfills the requirements, the code implements the design, and the correct code is used to build the executables.

1.1.5 Record and Track Requests for Change

Change request management involves tracking requests for changes to a software system. These requests may result from defects found by a testing organization, defects reported by customers, enhancement requests from the field or customers, or new ideas produced internally.

Recording and tracking change requests support configuration and change control as defined by IEEE (see the Control and Audit Changes to Artifacts section in this chapter). The critical points are that change requests are recorded and that the progress, be it through implementation or a decision never to implement, is tracked. Chapter 11, Change Request Management and ClearQuest, covers this best practice in more detail.

1.1.6 Organize and Integrate Consistent Sets of Versions Using Activities

While all SCM systems provide version control at the file level, it is left to the software developer to keep track of which versions of which files go together in order to implement a logical, consistent change and to ensure that this change is integrated as a unit. This is a tedious, manual, and error-prone process. Mistakes are easy to make, especially if a developer is working on more than one change at a time, leading to build errors and lost development time. Mistakes also show up as run-time defects that can't be reproduced by the developer in his or her working environment.

Some SCM tools provide a way for developers to record which change request or defect they are working on. This information is used to track which file and directory changes make up a single logical change. Often this information is not used by the SCM tool, but is instead maintained only for reporting and auditing purposes. The key advantage of collecting this change information is to streamline the integration process and to ensure consistency of the configuration in any given working or build environment.

The grouping of file and directory versions is called a *change set,* or change package.[2] This grouping is mostly useful when the change set contains a single logical change. The change set approach has been around for a long time. In 1991, Peter Feiler wrote an excellent paper, "Configuration Management Models in Commercial Environments" [Feiler 1991], that describes the change set model.

Change sets are only the glue. There must be a linkage between the versions that are changed and the activity that is the "why" for the change. An *activity* represents a unit of work being performed. Activities can be of different types. For example, a defect, enhancement request, or issue are all activities. This unit of work ties directly into the change request management system and processes. An activity may also be a child of another activity that appears in the project management system. The ability of the change set to tie together the disciplines of configuration management, change request management, and project management is where the power of the activity-based approach really becomes visible.

The key idea of activity-based SCM is to increase the level of abstraction from dealing with files and versions to dealing with activities. This is done first by collecting versions created during development into a change set and associating that change set with an activity. Activities are then presented throughout the user interface and used by SCM operations as the way to operate on a consistent set of versions.

---

2. Some in the SCM industry distinguish between these two terms. The difference is subtle and has to do with the implementation. A change set is defined as the actual delta that comprises the change even if it spans files. A change package is a grouping together of a set of file versions. In this book, I use the ClearCase term change set to refer to the grouping and manipulation of a change.

The benefits of activity-based SCM are as follows:

■ *Consistent changes cause fewer build and integration problems.*
Integrating a consistent change set (single logical change) reduces build and integration errors caused by developers forgetting about files when delivering their changes. It also ensures that the testing was performed against the same versions being integrated, making integration errors less frequent.

■ *Activities are logically how people group what they do.*
Generally, developers think about what feature, request for enhancement, or defect they are working on, which are all types of activities. By conforming to this activity-centric approach in the SCM tool and by using automation, developers are not required to know many details of the SCM implementation.

Activities are a level of abstraction that all project members can use in common, enabling project leaders, testers, developers, and customer support personnel to communicate more effectively.

■ *Activities provide a natural link to change request management.*
Change request management (a subset of which is defect tracking) is an essential part of most software development organizations, and tracking change requests is one of the key best practices of SCM. Rather than being a collection of versions in meaningless bundles, the change set should be tied to the change request stored in the change request management system. This combining of the change request and the change set allows accurate reporting of what defects were fixed and what files were changed between project baselines.

■ *Activities provide a natural link to project management.*
Project managers are interested not only in what is being changed but also in the status of the change, who is assigned to it, and how much effort is estimated to be needed to implement the change. The change set links the project management data for an activity to the files and versions that are changed. This link supports better automation, bringing advantages to the project leader without requiring extra effort on the part of the developer. For example, when a developer completes a change in the SCM tool, a change of status in the activity could be made automatically and would show up on a project report.

■ *Activities facilitate reporting.*
Activity-based SCM allows all reports and tools to display information in terms of the changes made rather than the files and versions that went into making the change. This is more natural for everyone involved with a project.

■ *Activities streamline code reviews.*

Traditionally, when performing code reviews a reviewer receives a list of files and which versions of these files to review. The trick is determining which version to compare against when doing the review. Should you compare the latest version against the immediate predecessor, the last baseline, or some other version? It is unclear.

With the change set information, it is possible for the SCM tool to provide the developer with the predecessor version of the change set automatically. This makes performing code reviews easier and less error-prone.

■ *Activities streamline testing efforts.*

Testing organizations often work with software builds "thrown over the wall" by development organizations. They must determine what went into the build or what was different from the previous build to decide what needs to be tested and what level of testing is required.

Most testing organizations do not have the resources to run the full test suite on every software build that development delivers. So, automatic reporting between two baselines that provides a list of the activities included in the new baseline is far easier to work with than a list of the hundreds of file versions that were modified from one baseline to the next.

1.1.7   Maintain Stable and Consistent Workspaces

The developer requires tools and automation to create and maintain a stable working environment. This maintenance involves periodically synchronizing changes with other team members in a way that results in a consistent set of shared changes that are of a known stability.

Consistency and stability in the developer's working environment maximizes the developer's productivity. Without stable and consistent workspaces—private file areas where developers can implement and test code in relative isolation—developers spend significant time investigating erroneous build problems and are sometimes unable to build the software in their own workspaces. These problems can quietly sap time and available effort out of any project.

A stable model allows developers to isolate themselves easily from disruptive changes going on in other parts of the project. A consistent model means that when developers update their workspace these updates will consist of a buildable, tested set of versions.

1.1.8   Support Concurrent Changes to Artifacts and Components

Ideally, you would have only one person making changes to any single file at a time or only one team working on any single component at a time. Unfortunately, this is not always efficient or practical. The most obvious case is when maintaining a release in the field while developing the next release.

Early SCM tools forced users to serialize changes to files. This was inefficient in that some developers were blocked waiting for other developers to complete their changes. It was also a problem from a quality standpoint. Blocked developers would often work around the system by getting a copy of the file without checking it out and modifying it outside SCM control. After the original developer checked in his or her changes, other developers would check out the file, copy their changes in place, and check the file back in, unknowingly removing the previous developer's changes from the latest version of the file (see Figure 1-1). This problem is usually exposed when a bug reappears in the latest build of a system. Since the assumption is made that the bug has been fixed and already verified, full regression tests may not be run. If so, the reintroduced bug could make its way into released software.

One of the key things a SCM tool must support is the ability to modify the same files concurrently and to integrate or merge the changes made in parallel at the appropriate time. This may mean integrating at checkin time for two developers working on the same project, or it may mean scheduling an integration action when merging maintenance changes into the latest development work. By providing this support, developers won't be forced to work around the system or be blocked.

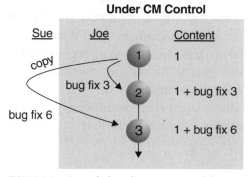

FIGURE 1-1   Serial development problems

1.1.9   Integrate Early and Often

During integration you will discover problems with interfaces and misunderstandings in the design. Both of these problems can have a major impact on the development schedule, so early discovery is essential. Plan integration points early in the development lifecycle and continue integrating often over the course of a software development project.

If you do too good a job at developer isolation (see the Maintain Stable and Consistent Workspaces section in this chapter), you may establish a model in which it is easy to remain too isolated. This problem can occur regardless of the tool you use since it is more often related to how you use a tool rather than the tool itself.

Development workspaces should be under the developer's control; however, project managers and integrators must have an automated and enforceable way to ensure that developers keep current with ongoing project changes. This is the classic developer-isolation-versus-project-integration dilemma. The balance to be maintained here is to integrate as early and as often as possible without negatively impacting productivity (see the Isolation and Integration with ClearCase section in chapter 9).

1.1.10   Ensure Reproducibility of Software Builds

It is often necessary to find out how a software build was constructed and what went into its construction in order to debug a problem or reproduce the same build. You must establish the proper procedures and provide sufficient automation to record who did the build, what went into each executable or library that was built, which machine it was built on, what OS version was running on that machine, and what command-line options were specified in the build step. Once you have this build audit information, it is useful to have tools that allow you to do reporting. In particular, being able to compare two builds can often help debug problems. Sometimes bugs can be introduced simply by changing the optimization switches to the compiler.

Without being able to reproduce a software build, you will be unable to perform system maintenance and, therefore, to support a system distributed to your customers.

1.2   SCM Tools and SCM Process

SCM best practices are achieved through the application of both processes and tools to a software development project. This section briefly discusses both.

1.2.1   SCM Tools

SCM tools are software tools that automate and facilitate the application of the SCM best practices. Like a compiler, debugger, and editor, an SCM tool is an essential part of every software engineer's tool kit today.

It is unrealistic to try to maintain effective SCM without an SCM tool. In early SCM project environments, one or more individuals acted as the CM librarians. These librarians handed out pieces of software for people to work on, diligently recorded who had which pieces, and logged in new versions as people turned in changes. This approach is not competitive today because it is too slow, too prone to error, and does not scale.

The goal of successful SCM is to allow as much change as possible while still maintaining control of the software. SCM tools help automate tedious, manual, and error-prone pieces of the SCM process and can ensure that your project is able to support all of the SCM best practices.

1.2.2   SCM Process

A process defines the steps by which you perform a specific task or set of tasks. An SCM process is the way SCM is performed on your project, specifically how an SCM tool is applied to accomplish a set of tasks.

A key mistake most people make is to assume that an SCM tool will, in and of itself, solve their SCM problems or support their SCM requirements. This is wrong! The picture will not hang itself if you buy a hammer and nails. It is not the tool itself that solves a problem but rather the application of that tool. How the SCM tool is applied is the "usage model," or SCM process.

Chapter 2   Growing into Your SCM Solution

Once you understand the best practices behind software configuration management (SCM), you need to understand how to apply SCM processes and tools successfully. One of the biggest mistakes that people make is assuming that one size fits all or that one solution is the "right" solution. In reality, different software projects have different requirements and varying degrees of complexity. These requirements are not fixed but rather change all the time. Thus an SCM tool and process that works well one day might be woefully inadequate the next.

The key to successful SCM on any project is to allow as much change to occur to the software as possible without losing control over the software. Like a race car driver in a race, in order to win you must speed up software development to the extreme limit while still staying on the "track." You must constantly tune the SCM process, like a race car engine or suspension, so that the overhead involved with the SCM tool meets the changing project requirements. In a nutshell, you must have an SCM tool that is highly customizable and flexible. You must be able to perform SCM tool customizations quickly and easily.

This chapter discusses the changes software projects undergo that influence the project's SCM process and tool requirements. It also discusses how SCM tools have evolved to solve SCM-related development problems in the context of five software project categories.

2.1   Dealing with Changing Project Requirements

The tooling and process requirements for any software project change over time. For example, suppose you are a software developer for a small integrated system vendor (ISV). You have developed a prototype of a new tool. A lunch-time demonstration of the prototype has caught the attention of one of the company's vice presidents, who decides that it is worth further development.

You form a team consisting of yourself, two more software developers, a technical writer, and a tester. As its first job, the team completes the first version of the product, which turns out to be very popular and a best seller.

For the second release, you grow the team size to 12 members. The current requirements are to incorporate some complementary third-party components and expand the number of platforms on which the product will run. The team immediately begins work after finalizing the first release.

While the second release is being developed, a key customer reports some critical defects in the first release that must be fixed. A patch for the first release of the product is produced in parallel while the second release is being developed. This patch also must be incorporated into the second release.

At this point, the product catches the attention of a larger, well-established company. This company believes that the product will complement its existing product line, so it acquires the small ISV. The major development center for the new parent company is located in a different part of the country. The development team grows again to 25 members. The new team includes, among others, three more software developers located locally and five developers located remotely. Management decides to test the product using the parent company's testing group. Thus your team needs to find a way to deliver software builds to the remote testing team.

Release 3 is full of new features and includes a number of integrations with the parent company's existing product line. As if this was not enough, a new project manager is assigned from the parent company. This manager has a different approach to change management and begins asking for more detailed reports on what changes are being made to the product and the status of those changes. And so it goes. Success breeds complexity.

Do you think that the SCM tools and processes used to implement release 3 are the best choice to manage the development of the prototype? Do you think that the tools and processes used for release 1 would readily support the development environment for release 3? How do you think that your SCM tools and processes will scale as your projects and your company grow?

The changes that any software project will undergo over time fall roughly into four categories:

1. increasing complexity of the software system being developed;
2. increasing complexity of the project environment needed to develop the software system;

3. changing requirements based on the development lifecycle phase; and

4. changes to an organization's management processes and/or personnel.

The first two categories of change require scalability in tools and process. The second two change over time and are not easily predicted. They, therefore, require flexibility in both tools and process. The following subsections discuss these categories in detail.

2.1.1   Increasing Software System Complexity

As a software product evolves, it typically increases in complexity, usually with the addition of more features and functions after the initial design. Thus more areas of the product must interact with each other, more things must be tested, and more possibilities for failure arise. This increase in complexity can be a big concern if steps are not taken to maintain the architectural integrity of the system while it evolves.[1]

From a configuration management standpoint, the increase in complexity takes several forms:

- Increase in the size of the software that is being managed
- Increase in the complexity of the problems that are to be solved
- Increase in the complexity of a maturing architecture
- Inclusion of third-party software components
- Increase in the number of platforms to support

Increasing Software Size and Architectural Complexity

Solving more complex problems with an existing software system requires more features. This increases the complexity of the system architecture and thus the size of the software system, both in terms of lines of code and the number of files being managed by the SCM tool. Thus when considering a SCM tool, you need two primary capabilities. First, you need to be able to add new files to a SCM repository easily. If it is not easy to add new files, you might tend to add new functions to existing files, which might not make sense architecturally.

Second, you must be able to version-control directories. Version control is as important for directories as it is for files. Directories, like files, have contents,

---

1. See in *The Rational Unified Process: An Introduction, Second Edition,* the chapter entitled "An Architecture-centric Process" for more information on the importance of software system architecture [Kruchten 2000].

which are files and other directories. These contents evolve over time (e.g., a file can be added, renamed, or removed). Versioning the directory structure allows you to easily rebuild previous releases of a software system or quickly roll back a Web site to a previous state.

Inclusion of Third-Party Components and Software Reuse

Component sharing, software reuse, and the use of third-party components all are essential elements of meeting the schedule demands of developing software systems today. This approach has been applied to hardware systems for a long time; the days when a company developed all of the pieces of a hardware system itself are no more. Software is experiencing a similar trend.

Use of third-party components and reuse of internally developed components among projects or organizations add complexity that SCM tools and processes must support. The key factor is ensuring that the components (regardless of their sources) are placed under SCM control. Ideally, this means the components are accessed directly from their primary repositories. Less ideal is to put the delivered components under version control yourself. The first case usually requires some way to replicate or copy the repository and keep the data in the two copies in sync. The second case requires some way to import a set of files and directories and then to import them again when an update or new release of a component is received.

Increasing Number of Platforms to Support

The ability to support more platforms brings with it some unique SCM challenges. As more and more platforms are supported, the load on the test organization increases. Often a separate porting group must be formed to optimize the release of new features on the main platforms while ensuring the system will be available on all of the required platforms.

From a SCM perspective, new platform support usually involves two key concerns. First is access to the software on the new platform. This requires either that the SCM tool be directly supported on that platform or that some way exists to get the software out of the SCM repository and onto the desired platform.

The second concern relates to building the software. Software builds and SCM go hand in hand. If you cannot determine what versions of the files were used in a particular build, reproducing customer-reported problems will be difficult. Further, providing patches to the release will be very difficult. SCM tools and processes must provide this information. This could be more difficult if the platform on which you need to build your system is not also supported by the SCM tool that you are using.

2.1.2   Increasing Project Environment Complexity

A project's development environment grows in complexity for the following reasons:

- An increase in the number of team members
- A need to support parallel development
- The location of development teams at different sites
- An increase in the number and frequency of product releases

Increasing Team Size and Parallel Development Support

The increasing complexity of an evolving software system usually requires changes in the complexity of the project development team. Most often this is seen in an increase in team size and/or the number of teams. With only one developer, communication obviously is fast and efficient. With two, there is 1 line of communication. Four developers communicate in 6 lines, and ten in 45. A team of 100 has 4,950 lines! With this many communication lines, disseminating information becomes more difficult and time consuming. Fast and accurate communication becomes essential to meeting project schedules and developing high-quality software systems.

From an SCM perspective, an increase in team size also increases contention for common software system files and resources. The SCM tool must support locking and concurrent changes to common files. *Concurrent changes* are changes made by two or more developers to the same files at the same time. The SCM tool must also support the merging or integration of the changes to recombine the work that was done in parallel. Concurrent changes made by two or more teams working on the same software system are referred to as *parallel development* (e.g., a maintenance team working on release 1.1 of a software system and a development team working on release 2 of the same system). The issues of managing concurrent change and parallel development are core to SCM and are explored in more detail later in this chapter.

Geographically Distributed Development Teams

Another area of complexity introduced in the project environment is the need to support development teams located at different sites, or geographically distributed development. Geographically distributed development may involve two or more large teams, either at different sites in the same city or in different countries. It may also involve individuals working from home or while traveling.

Geographically distributed development severely increases the complexity of any software development effort primarily because of communication issues. This topic is covered in detail in chapter 10, Geographically Distributed Development.

Increasing Number and Frequency of Product Releases

The number of releases supported in the field and the frequency of product releases can significantly affect the choice of tools and processes used for SCM. The number of releases is the number of different releases of a software system being supported at any given time. For example, a company might release version 1 of a product, followed by version 1.1, and then version 2. When it releases version 3, it must decide whether to continue to support version 1 or to withdraw support for it, thereby forcing its customers to upgrade to a newer version. The more releases supported, the more sophisticated and automated the patch, support, and testing processes must be. Some software systems are custom systems, that is, every system at every customer site has been modified explicitly for that customer. In that case, the number of supported product releases directly relates to the number of customers. Each one of those releases is often called a variant of the software system. For example, there may be a major release, such as release 1, but 10 variants of that release for each of 10 customers.

Customer variants are one of the most complex configurations that a SCM tool must support. If you must work with this constraint, you need to build in process support and automation for moving bug fixes between variants. Otherwise, bug fixes will not be efficiently propagated to other variants and might even be lost or overlooked.[2]

Also contributing to complexity is the frequency of product releases. More frequent releases means more automation to make the release process less error-prone and more efficient.[3]

---

2. New and smaller companies with only one product should be careful not to fall into the trap of developing variants unless this is explicitly part of their business model because this increase in complexity comes at a cost and does not scale well.

3. I have seen anything from releases every two years to daily releases.

2.1.3   Changing Lifecycle Phase

As a project moves through development lifecycle phases, the project's requirements for SCM tools and processes will change. Lifecycle phase changes differ from the previous two change categories, system complexity and project environment complexity, which typically increase over time. Lifecycle phase requirements increase and decrease as the project progresses. This is seen particularly in a project that is practicing an iterative development approach.[4]

Good SCM tools and processes maximize one's ability to make changes while still maintaining effective control over the software. For example, early in the lifecycle, you want to encourage as much change as possible, so you should relax controls. As a software system approaches time to release, you want to make explicit decisions about what changes can and cannot be made, usually based on assessing risk. At this point, you want strict controls and accurate tracking of the changes being made. Therefore, to maximize the rate of change, you must be able to modify the SCM tool controls from lifecycle phase to lifecycle phase.

A process-oriented example of changing project requirements based on lifecycle phase is the level of approval required for accepting changes into the project build. In early phases of development, you might require only a peer-level code review. Late in the development cycle, the approval of a change control board might be required before changes are accepted into the project build.

The balance at each lifecycle phase should be between auditing and enforcement. Auditing is the recording of who made a change, what change was made, when the change was made, and why a change was made. By auditing, you can loosen controls thus allowing changes to be made more rapidly, while ensuring your ability to back out of a change or determine why a change was made. Auditing must be automated and must be as transparent to the end user as possible so as to involve a minimal amount of overhead. That is, as much information as possible should be automatically recorded by the SCM tool.

Enforcement is proactive control that disallows changes unless certain conditions are met. This can hinder the speed at which change occurs, since approvals or additional steps are required before changes can be made. Enforcement is essential, however, when applied at the right time during the development lifecycle.

---

4. See in Kruchten the chapter entitled Dynamic Structure: Iterative Development for more information on the iterative development approach [Kruchten 2000].

2.1.4 Changing Processes and Personnel

The fourth category of change in project requirements results from changes to an organization's processes and/or personnel (particularly management). Of the four categories of change, process and personnel changes are the most unpredictable and often the most severe in their impact. The two changes usually go hand in hand. The most extreme example is an acquisition, in which new management is brought in to run the project using the acquiring company's processes, procedures, and tools.

Process Changes

Process changes usually result from a desire to fix existing problems or perceived problems in the software development process. Often, the project team itself will suggest changes in existing tools and processes. This internal effort is often the most effective. Sometimes process change results from an organizationwide effort to document and improve the organization's processes. The best examples of this are the Software Engineering Institute's Capability Maturity Model (SEI-CMM) assessments and ISO-9000 certifications.[5] Most often, the organization makes these efforts to show customers or prospects that it develops quality software by meeting industry standards on software development.[6]

Process-related efforts often result in changes to the SCM tool, changes to the way the tool is used, or the development of additional automation layers on top of an existing SCM tool. Process change should be made explicitly to fulfill the SCM requirements of a project. There should be an understanding of how the process changes will improve either productivity or quality. Ideally, a means will exist to measure the effect of a process change. Process change simply for the sake of change is not a good idea.

Personnel Changes

Personnel changes are equally hard to predict and plan for. These happen in any number of ways. A common example is a change in project manager. Every project manager brings experience from previous projects that influences man-

---

5. For more information on the SEI-CMM, refer to [Humphrey 1989] and the SEI Web site at *http://www.sei.cmu.edu/*. For more information on ISO standards, see the ISO Web site at *http://www.iso.ch/*.

6. Organizationwide process change can often be ineffective, or even destructive, unless the project teams themselves are engaged and feel some ownership in the process improvement efforts.

agement and development style. Changes to management often cause a change in process and tools, particularly when a project manager is being replaced because of project problems.

Another personnel issue that can affect the SCM tools and process is the mix of experience on a software team over time. A project at its start might have a high degree of experienced personnel who have used SCM tools for many years and understand the product they are developing, as well as all aspects of the system architecture. As the team size increases, not all team members can have a detailed understanding of all areas of the system architecture. Many team members might be fairly new to software development, and some might have limited exposure to SCM and development in a team environment. A project team with less experience might require any or all of the following:

- Additional controls on who can change which pieces of the software system
- Control of SCM functions based on the role of a user
- Improved ease-of-use of the SCM tool
- Additional user training in tools and processes

2.2 Evolution of SCM Tools

Not so many years ago, a software product typically was developed by one person, and there was little need for SCM. As software products grew in size and complexity, their development required more than a single individual. Projects remained relatively easy to manage when project teams consisted of two or three individuals all sitting in close proximity to each other. However, it was not long before project teams grew to tens and even hundreds of developers, who might not be located at the same site.

Early on, SCM processes were developed to manage change. Typically, these processes were performed manually. One or more librarians were tasked with controlling who could access the source code. To modify a file, the developer filled out a form (paper-based) and submitted it to the librarian. This form recorded which files needed to be modified and why. The librarian ensured that none of the files were being modified by someone else at the same time. If the file was free, the librarian gave a copy of it to the developer and recorded when and to whom it was checked out. The developer, when done, provided the modified copy of the file to the librarian, who recorded the new file and placed it in the appropriate archive.

Soon, SCM tools were developed to help automate and assist librarians with their jobs. Usually one tool dominated on any given operating system. The basic version-control features of these tools were as follows:

- To maintain a library or repository of files
- To create and store multiple versions of files
- To provide a mechanism for locking (to enforce serialized change to any given file)
- To identify collections of file versions
- To extract/retrieve versions of files from the repository

Early SCM tools provided these basic version-control capabilities and automated the manual-librarian approach to SCM. A developer could check out a file without the intervention of a librarian. While the file was checked out, others could not modify it. When the developer was done, the file was checked in and a new version of the file was created automatically. Today, the check out/check in model remains fundamentally unchanged.

One widely used SCM tool was the source code control system (SCCS) developed by Bell Laboratories in the early 1970s. An alternative to SCCS was the revision control system (RCS) developed by Walter Tichy at Purdue University. Both RCS and SCCS became the predominant SCM tools on the Unix platform. Most mainframe machines at the time also had their own primary SCM tool. For example, the configuration management system (CMS) was part of the Digital Equipment Corporation (DEC) VAX/VMS operating system.[7]

These early version-control tools usually offered a way to label or mark a particular version of each file for a set of files. This is called a *configuration* and was used to identify a specific version of the overall product (e.g., release 1).

These tools greatly improved efficiency over the manual approach. They offered the classic SCM capabilities of being able to identify pieces of the system, control change to those pieces, and have an audit trail of who modified which files and when.

Software development projects, of course, continued to increase in complexity and size, thereby requiring larger teams and more coordination. The individuals supporting these version-control tools began developing layers of abstraction, using scripts, on top of the underlying functionality to better han-

---

7. In terms of SCM tool evolution, this chapter uses Unix as an example. Similar tool evolution was occuring in the mainframe environment. In fact, there were even some SCM features built into a few punch card systems.

dle the increase in complexity. At most companies, these layers on top of tools like SCCS and RCS took on a life of their own, defining the usage model for how that company applied SCCS/RCS to its projects and providing more functionality than available in the basic tools.

These layers defined the first level of functionality that was to be incorporated into modern SCM tools. Modern tools extended the basic functionality of early tools by supporting improved parallel development, workspace management, and build and release management.

Today, advanced capabilities are being added to many SCM tools. These advanced tools have objects and features that provide SCM support at a level of abstraction closely aligned with other aspects of software engineering such as change request management and project management. These advanced SCM tools support versioning of all project artifacts (not just source code), software projects whose team members might not be located at the same site, component-based development, and activity-based configuration management.

The remainder of this chapter looks at SCM tool evolution by examining the kinds of problems software projects faced and the solutions employed to solve these problems. For smaller project teams, these problems could be solved using no SCM tool or early SCM tools. For larger project teams, old solutions would not adequately scale to solve new or larger problems, so improved processes and SCM tools were required.

2.2.1   Five Project Team Categories

To discuss SCM tool evolution in some meaningful way the wide variety of software project types must be bounded. This section attempts to do this by defining five broad project categories. Some projects will not fit exactly into any one of them, and some might not fit into any at all. These categories are meant to provide a context in which to organize and discuss SCM problems and SCM tool solutions. The five categories are as follows:

- *Individual*—a team of 1 member, working on one product
- *Small*—a team of 2 to 5 members, working on one product
- *Modest*—a team of 6 to 15 members, working on one or more products in a family
- *Major*—one to ten cooperating teams of 2 to 30 members each, with less than 150 total members, working toward a common release of one or more products in a product family

- *Extreme*—a large number of teams of various sizes cooperating on a release of one or more products, where the total number of team members is 150 or greater[8]

Individual Projects

One person working on one software system (application) constitutes an individual project. This individual owns and controls all of the source code for the system. Example systems include tooling/scripting, Web-based personal home pages, small shareware systems, and systems developed for personal use. When only one person is working on one system, the SCM requirements are minimal. In general, the individual does not require an SCM tool to solve his or her problems. However, an SCM tool can offer such benefits as better organization and security, thereby freeing the individual from doing version control via directory and file copies.

Small Project Teams

Small project teams consist of two to five developers working on a single software application. This team owns and controls all of the source code for its application. An organization might have any arbitrary number of these teams, but the teams do not share any source code or have any dependencies on other project teams. Example applications are small IS/IT applications, Visual Basic applications, small C/C++ applications, Web-based information delivery applications, Web-based information gathering applications, and small corporate intranet sites. Early SCM tool capabilities are typically adequate to support small project teams.

Modest Project Teams

A modest team is any number of smaller teams of 6 to 15 members that develop one or more software applications whose source they own and control. Minimal software sharing occurs between teams and is usually limited to a small number of well-defined core components. Few intercomponent dependencies exist. Examples include Java-based applications, complex Visual Basic applications, modest C/C++ applications, mission-critical IS/IT applications, modest Web-based e-commerce sites, and corporate intranet sites. Modest teams usually require the capabilities available in more modern SCM tools.

---

8. The term "extreme" is used here for classification of team size and complexity. It is in no way related to extreme programming that Beck described [Beck 2000].

Major Project Teams

A major team consists of a small number (1 to 10) of cooperating teams of various sizes (2 to 30 members). Some interproduct code sharing as well as some intercomponent dependencies might occur. A major team might have some teams or team members located at different sites. The total number of members of all cooperating teams is less than 150 members. Product releases produced by major teams consist of changes contributed by the multiple teams all collaborating toward the common product release. Example applications include most software products produced by all but the largest ISVs, major mission-critical IS/IT applications, and major e-commerce Web sites. Major project teams almost always require the capabilities of a modern SCM tool. In some cases, they would benefit from some of the more advanced SCM tool capabilities.

Extreme Project Teams

An extreme project team consists of a large number of cooperating teams of various sizes (5 to 50 members) all working toward a common release of one or more products. The total number of members of all cooperating teams is 150 or greater. Significant code sharing and intercomponent dependencies occur. Extreme teams are highly likely to have teams and team members located at different sites. Product releases are usually longer (12 to 24 months). Example applications include large ISV applications, telecom/datacom systems, and military/government applications. Extreme project teams require the most flexible and advanced SCM capabilities they can find.

2.2.2   In the Absence of SCM Tools

Without an SCM tool, developers make different attempts to overcome the problem of managing multiple versions of files that make up an evolving software system. For individuals, this is often done using copies of system files. For smaller teams, an additional copy of the entire system directory structure can be created to store the latest versions of the software. This is called the shared copy approach. This section discusses both approaches to solving SCM problems without an SCM tool.

▶ **Note:** The solutions presented here should be considered workarounds given the availability of low-cost SCM tools. There is almost no reason not to employ some form of SCM tool on all your software development projects.

Using File Copies to Support Early SCM

One of the first SCM-related problems was the storage of different versions of the software, specifically:

- Storing backup versions of the software system
- Storing intermediate working versions, of certain files or of all the files that make up the system, during the development process

Individuals developing their own software systems were the first to face these problems (see the Individual Projects section earlier in this chapter). Let's consider an example. Suppose that you are writing a small personal-use application that reads in some data from an unformatted text file and outputs a formatted HTML file. You have written a lot of Perl and have a personal library of Perl routines that you include in your application. The application consists of two files, genhtml and myfunctions.pl. You developed and tested this application and have been happy with it for a couple of months. Now you want to add some options to your genhtml script regarding how the HTML is formatted.

If you simply begin modifying the Perl script you will lose the previous version of genhtml that worked! You need a way to store a copy of the previous version of your application as a backup before you begin making changes.

Without an SCM tool, the solution to these problems is rather simple and obvious: store a complete backup copy of the entire system by copying the entire directory tree that contains the system, for example:

```
/mysystem_latest_version
/mysystem_release1
/mysystem_workstoday_jun3_1999
```

Make changes to the application under the directory mysystem_latest_version, and when it is stable or ready to be released, make a copy under a directory using a descriptive name such as mysystem_release1.

You can also use copies to store intermediate file versions. For example, you could save versions such as the following:

```
genhtml.bak
genhtml.bak2
genhtml.030699
genhtml.featureA_working
```

This solution works well for individuals; however, it becomes problematic for small projects and does not scale at all for modest- to extreme-sized projects.

The Shared Copy Approach

With multiple uncontrolled copies of the software system residing on each developer's machine, the next SCM problem, which was first encountered by small teams, was keeping track of the location of the "good" software. The initial solution was to create a common system directory in which each team member could copy new versions of the files, a solution similar to that used by the individual. With the *shared copy approach,* each individual in a small team makes one or more copies of the software system in a private directory and works as if following the individual model, as described previously.

Here's an example. Suppose that you are part of a team of three, including Joe and Shirley, working on a small C-language application. The team has created one common system directory in which to store the finished code, so there are at least four copies of the system (see Figure 2-1). A team member who adds a new feature or makes a change copies the changed files into the common system directory (see Figure 2-2).

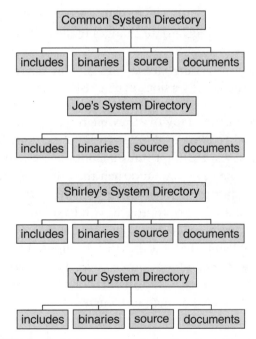

FIGURE 2-1   Copies of the system directory structure

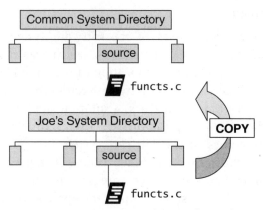

FIGURE 2-2   Using a copy to promote a change from directory to directory

At first, the shared copy approach seems fine. But, in reality, it poses three new problems:

1. The copy-over problem, which causes versions of files to be lost.
2. Recovery from inappropriate changes made to the common code is difficult or impossible.
3. The number of uncontrolled copies of files makes it difficult to determine where the latest version really exists.

The first problem, the copy-over problem, causes working versions to be lost. This happens when two developers work on the same file at the same time. They both take copies of the file from the common system directory and make changes. Then first one developer and then the other copies the new version to the common system directory, thus overwriting one of the new versions (see Figure 2-3). Using the shared copy approach, you have no way to know when parallel changes are occurring or to guard against them.

The second problem is that it is difficult or impossible to recover from inappropriate changes to the common source code. This is because there is no way to see what changes have occurred in the common project area and thus to determine who made those changes and when.

The third problem is that many copies of the applications files are stored in many places under many different names. It quickly becomes difficult to find out where the latest version of a file is located.

As described earlier, the initial solution to the problems introduced by using the shared copy approach was to assign a CM librarian to manage the common

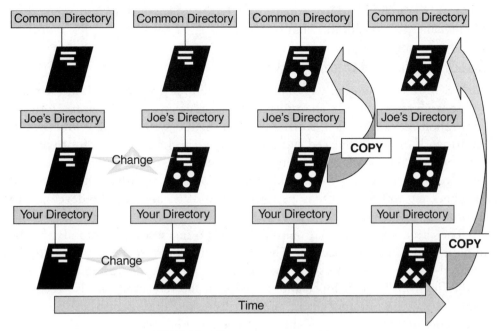

FIGURE 2-3   The copy-over problem

system directory. This manual and error-prone approach to SCM was largely automated by early SCM tools.

2.2.3   Early SCM Tool Support

In order to manage multiple versions of system files, early SCM tools introduced the concept of an SCM repository that stored not only the latest copy of the system (as in the shared copy approach) but all versions of the files. How these tools automated the manual checkout/checkin model is described in the next section. Because every version of every file was being stored, disk space became the next problem these teams encountered. To combat this problem, early SCM tools introduced the notion of storing just the changes made between one file version and the next. This concept, called "delta storage," is discussed in the Delta Storage Mechanism section in this chapter.

However, early SCM tools lacked capabilities required to solve problems being encountered by modest and major project teams. These capabilities were typically implemented as scripts on top of early SCM tools. The problems encountered and the scripting solutions are described in the Early Workspace Management, Early Build Management, and Early Release Management/Product Maintenance sections in this chapter.

The SCM Repository and Checkout/Checkin Model

Early SCM tools, many of which are still in use today, were based on the manual library system model. The tools created a repository in which to store the application files rather than storing them in the file system. A developer wanting to work on a file checked out the file. The checkout operation provided a copy of the file to work on, thereby ensuring that the developer worked on the latest version of the file. The checkout operation also recorded who performed the checkout and when it was performed and often allowed the developer to record why the file was checked out.

The checkout also locked the file so that no one else could modify the file until it was checked back in. The developer would make changes to the checked-out file and then issue a checkin operation. This operation took a copy of the file from the developer and placed it in the repository. It also recorded who did the checkin and when, and usually asked the developer to record a brief description of what was changed. The checkin then released the lock on that file, thereby allowing other developers to make changes (see Figure 2-4).

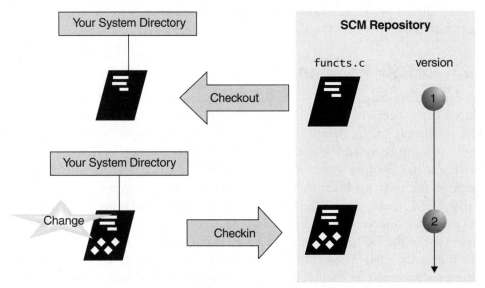

FIGURE 2-4   The checkout and checkin operations

The locking step was designed to avoid the problem encountered when two developers made changes to the same files at the same time (see The Shared Copy Approach section in this chapter). It had the effect of serializing changes to any file in the system. This introduced other problems, which are discussed in the Concurrent Changes to the Same Project Files section in this chapter.

Delta Storage Mechanism

With the introduction of an SCM repository, every version of a file ever produced was stored. This caused a disk space problem at a time when disk space was not cheap. So SCM tools introduced a new technique of storing only what had changed from one version to the next. What has changed is called a *delta*.

The delta storage mechanism conserved disk space at a cost, measured by the time it takes to construct any particular version of a file. Most SCM tools had an additional operation called Get or Fetch that was used to extract a specific version of a file from the repository.

There are three basic approaches taken to delta storage: forward, backward, and in-line. The first, *forward delta* storage, stores the first version of a file in its entirety and then stores incremental deltas. The forward delta mechanism is very space-efficient since it does not require full contents of versions at every leaf node in the version tree. However, the more changes made to a file, the longer the time it takes to construct versions of the file. Consequently, it takes the longest amount of time to construct the most often-needed version, the latest one.

The second approach, called *backward delta* (or reverse delta) storage, is used by RCS. This mechanism stores the latest version of the file in its entirety and keeps deltas of the previous versions. This greatly improves the time that it takes to construct the latest version in comparison with forward delta storage. However, it is less inefficient in constructing earlier versions.

The third mechanism, used by SCCS and ClearCase, is called *in-line delta* storage. With this approach, no whole copy is stored. Rather, the deltas are stored in place in the file, with some special notation. In this way, constructing any version of the file takes a consistent amount of time.

ClearCase takes this approach even further: It caches a full copy of any version that is accessed often. These copies are stored in one or more managed caches called cleartext caches. In this way, all versions of a file that are being accessed on a regular basis are available immediately. A ClearCase utility, called the Scrubber, is used to remove versions from the cache that have not been recently accessed. The Scrubber can be configured to specify how often it runs and how long file versions remain in the cache. This allows the organization to optimize for both access speed and disk space use.

Early Workspace Management

Early SCM tools provided a means of only "getting" specific versions of files out of the repository. To construct a development environment, one needed to create a system directory structure and then populate it with the "right" versions of the "right" files. With many hundreds or thousands of files this became difficult.

A new abstraction, not yet implemented in the early SCM tools, came into being, called the *workspace*. A workspace is a copy of all the "right" versions of all the "right" files in the "right" directories, which can then be used to perform a specific task. The process of creating and maintaining a workspace is called *workspace management*. For example, suppose that you are a developer and you need to fix a defect found in release 1 of your application. You will need a copy of the release 1 version of all the files organized in the release 1 directory structure.

The lack of any workspace management in early SCM tools caused two problems:

1. errors and time lost because of inconsistent workspaces; and
2. longer integration times near the end of the development cycle.

The first problem is caused by constructing a workspace by manually picking the wrong versions from the library. This is inefficient because these versions might not build together. Worse, they might build together, and you end up fixing problems against the wrong source code. For example, suppose that you need to fix a bug in release 1. You erroneously create a workspace using the latest versions of the files, not the release 1 versions. You fix the bug. The integrator then tries to incorporate the files that you changed into the release 1 versions of the files, causing everything to break.

The second problem, long integration times, results from developers' being isolated with their own copies of the system files and having no means to easily update the files they are working on to include other team members' changes. Absent additional tooling, you'll find it difficult and error-prone to update your workspace with changes that other developers are making, so you may continue to make changes against an ever older set of source versions. This situation may not be apparent until later in the development cycle. Essentially, the last period of useful development time is given up to getting everyone's changes to work with everyone else's changes.

To avoid these problems, much scripting work went into providing early workspace management functionality. Scripts were written on top of the Get functionality provided by early SCM tools. These early tools did not do any version control on the product directory structure, so scripts also provided automation that recreated an empty directory tree and populated it with particular versions of the files. Which versions were used was another usage model decision that varied widely by project. Also needed were mechanisms to update these early workspaces with changes made by other project members. Scripting provided these as well.

As projects became more sophisticated and SCM tools caught up, workspace management became a key component of many modern SCM tools.

Early Build Management

Build management is the management of the build process both at the individual developer level and at the project level. This was another area in which SCM automation was required so as to reduce errors and improve efficiency. The build management strategy for SCM should be to minimize build times, to conserve disk space, and to maintain an audit of the build itself. Early build management focused on the first two points. It incorporated aspects of workspace management. A development workspace was not populated with all of the source files and prebuild libraries required to perform a build. Instead, the build tools knew where to find the "right" versions of the files to be built/linked.

Suppose you were going to do a build. In order to find a file to compile or a library to link, the SCM-automated build would look first in your application directory, then in the common application directory, and last in the latest production application directory (see Figure 2-5).[9]

Early build management was established mainly to minimize the number of rebuilds, conserve disk space, and avoid having many uncontrolled copies of the software residing all over the network.

---

9. Many variants of the widely used Unix build tool called "make" refer to this as "viewpathing"—see in Oram Viewpath (VPATH Macro) [Oram 1991].

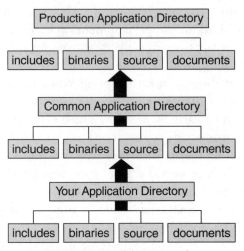

FIGURE 2-5   Build view path

Early Release Management/Product Maintenance

Early release management focused on being able to rebuild a previous release so that it could be maintained (patched). An early solution was generally to copy the entire directory structure and the libraries being used from one major release to the next. This was a low-cost solution and required only more disk space. To fix a bug on release 2, you went to the release 2 area and used the release 2 source libraries.

This worked, but it was an inefficient and error-prone process. Fixes to a release in the field also had to be made to the release being developed. Errors often were discovered when a known bug that had already been fixed re-appeared in the latest release of the software. This was particularly problematic because often the bug would show up at the same customer site where it had originally been reported. That customer may have already been using a fixed version of the software when the new buggy release was installed (see Figure 2-6).

Release management incorporates aspects of workspace management and build management. The idea is that, starting from a clean slate, you create the right directory structure, extract the right files and their correct versions, and rebuild any important release of a software system from source.

The automation and scripting you do to support releasing and rebuilding largely concern how file versions are labeled at release time. This is often trickier than you might expect. Files are in uncontrolled directory space, and a build

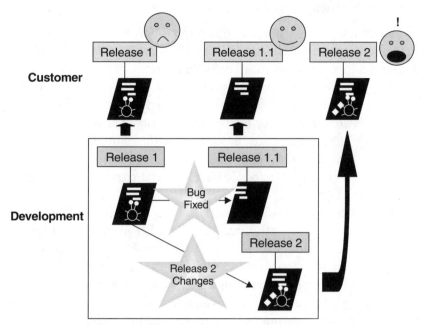

FIGURE 2-6   A bug reintroduced between releases

can span multiple workspaces, so once you have a final build that successfully passes tests, it is crucial that you be able to determine what went into that build. This usually involves either scripting the labeling process with algorithms similar to those used to create the build environment or doing builds in a clean single workspace. The workspace script "extract these things from the library" becomes the script "label these things in the library." The "build the directory structure like this" piece of workspace management becomes the "remember how to build a directory structure like this" piece.

Typical problems at this stage included the following:

- Difficulties in developing the necessary scripting
- Differences in the algorithms used, causing the wrong versions to get labeled
- Failing to store the directory structure
- Failing to capture other aspects of the build environment, such as the version of the compiler that was used

See the Modern Build and Release Management section in this chapter for details on how these problems are solved with modern SCM tools.

2.2.4   Modern SCM Tool Support

The amount of automation needed to support small teams early on was fairly significant. Very few modern day SCM tools were available. Each company tended to build its own SCM tool layers and scripts. Worse, many projects in the same company built their own project-specific scripts. This meant that each project had to solve its own SCM problems and was plagued by issues in the SCM scripts that other projects in the same company had already solved or avoided. In the 1980s, the costs associated with maintaining these internal scripts became such that the build versus buy decision took on a new slant. Modest-sized project teams started looking for third-party solutions rather than trying to build their own.

A number of tools were developed, each approaching SCM from its own perspective. ClearCase was introduced to the market in the early 1990s. It provided out-of-the-box solutions to many of the problems that previously had required scripting. It was based on its own version management technology and improved on a number of shortcomings of the predecessor tools of the time. It did not dictate any particular usage model, which further enhanced its success.

This section discusses some of the advances in modern SCM tools, including support for multiple individuals to modify the same file at the same time, support for multiple teams to modify the same software system at the same time, modern workspace management, and modern build and release management.

Concurrent Changes to the Same Project Files

When a developer checks out a file, typically the file is locked to that developer until he or she is done making changes. Locking via the SCM tool was used to solve the copy-over problem (see The Shared Copy Approach section in this chapter). However, locking also serializes changes to any one file, which can slow down development and in some cases may cause developers to work around the SCM tool by taking a copy of the source without checking out the file. One approach to reducing contention for files is to break up the system into more files. However, this does not adequately solve the problem since no matter how small you break up a system there will always be times when two or more developers need to access the same file. To remove the bottleneck, you need an SCM tool that supports the ability for two or more developers to change the same file at the same time. In addition, it must also support a way to merge those changes at the right time!

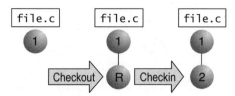

FIGURE 2-7   Normal reserved checkout

ClearCase solves this problem by slightly modifying the checkout/checkin paradigm. Traditionally, once a file is checked out, nobody else can check it out until the original person either checks it in or cancels the checkout. With Clear-Case, anyone can check out a file. Checkins, however, are controlled by using different types of checkouts.

A checkout can be either of two different types: reserved or unreserved. A *reserved checkout* means that the person who has the file checked out is guaranteed to be the person who will check it in first. Thus there may be one and only one reserved checkout for any given file.[10] If a file has a reserved checkout, attempts by other developers to perform a reserved checkout will fail. Once the developer with the reserved checkout, checks in the file, a new version is created for that file as usual. Figure 2-7 illustrates a reserved checkout and subsequent checkin.

An *unreserved checkout* differs from a reserved checkout only in that you cannot guarantee that you will be the next person to check in. There can be any number of unreserved checkouts on the same file. This means that even if a file has a reserved checkout, you can still check out the file using an unreserved checkout.

In general, the first person, say developer A, to check out a file acquires a reserved checkout. The second person, say developer B, to check out the file will receive an error that indicates that the file is already on reserved checkout. Developer B can wait until developer A checks in or go talk to developer A to see what changes are being made (a good idea) and how long they will take or issue an unreserved checkout.

Therefore, the unreserved checkout offers a way for any developer to get access to any file at any time. It avoids the problem of developers working around the SCM tool to gain access to a file that has been exclusively locked.

---

10. For those of you familiar with SCM and ClearCase, you know that really this is one reserved checkout per element per branch; but we aren't there yet, so hang on.

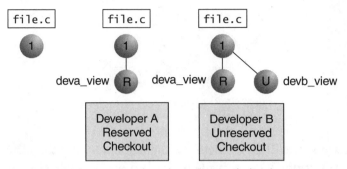

FIGURE 2-8   Reserved and unreserved checkouts

Figure 2-8 illustrates a file named "file.c" that has been checked out using both a reserved checkout made by developer A and an unreserved checkout made by developer B.

What happens during checkin? For developer A, who has a reserved checkout, checkin will proceed as usual. Developer B, who has an unreserved checkout, will receive an error when trying to check in until one of three things occur:

■ *Developer A, with the reserved checkout, checks in the file.*

If developer A checks in the file, developer B, with the unreserved checkout, will not be able to immediately check in. ClearCase requires developer B first to merge B's changes with A's changes. This is done to avoid the copy-over problem described in The Shared Copy Approach section in this chapter. Once this merge has been performed, then developer B can check in the file containing the combined changes. Figure 2-9 illustrates this scenario.

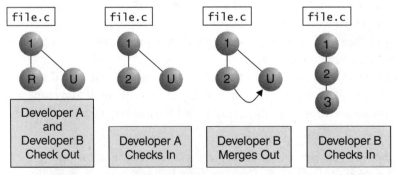

FIGURE 2-9   Reserved/unreserved checkout: normal resolution

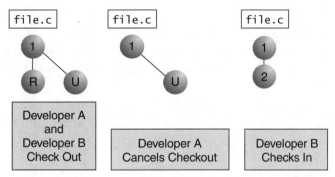

FIGURE 2-10   Reserved/unreserved checkout: resolution through cancellation

■ *Developer A,* with the reserved checkout, cancels the checkout.

Then developer B can check in without performing any merge operation, since there are no changes to merge. Figure 2-10 illustrates this scenario.

■ *Developer A,* with the reserved checkout, changes the type of checkout from reserved to unreserved.

With ClearCase, developer A can change the type of A's checkout from reserved to unreserved. In this case, the file now has multiple unreserved checkouts but no reserved checkouts. Developer B can now check in without performing any merge operation, since there are no changes to merge. When this situation occurs, the first file to be checked in does not require any merge. Note, how-ever, that developer A will now be required to merge developer B's changes before being able to check in, just as in the first case. Figure 2-11 illustrates this scenario.

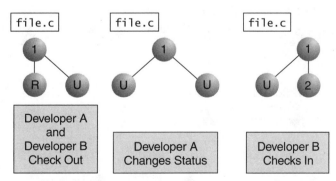

FIGURE 2-11   Reserved/unreserved checkout: resolution through change of reservation status

By modifying the checkout/checkin paradigm using reserved and unreserved checkouts and supporting a tool for merging file changes, ClearCase allows parallel changes to occur to the same files at the same time. Thus you can avoid a common SCM bottleneck, as well as the errors and complexity introduced by the other workarounds.

Not only is it essential to be able to modify the same files at the same time, but you also must be able to work on parallel releases of the entire software system at the same time. This topic is covered next.

Parallel Development Support

Demand for more functionality available sooner in software development continues to increase. This leads to larger development teams and more complex software systems. Reducing time to market requires reducing or eliminating serialized change by supporting parallel development. Parallel development, or two or more individuals or teams making changes to individual files and/or an entire software system at the same time, also includes the ability to merge these changes after they have been made in parallel.

In the past you developed releases serially: release 1, followed by release 2, and then release 3, and so on. Ensuring that defect fixes made during maintenance were also made in later releases was sometimes problematic but manageable. To further reduce time to market, however, you must apply more resources so that you can develop release 2 at the same time as release 1, and sometimes release 3 at the same time as well. This is parallel development occurring on the entire software system. Figure 2-12 illustrates the time savings associated with developing releases in parallel.

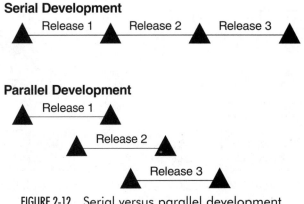

FIGURE 2-12   Serial versus parallel development

The introduction of parallel development not only decreased time to market but also meant that some functionality as well as defect fixes had to get into later releases. At this point, the shared copy approach to parallel releases truly breaks down. It requires too much overhead in merging work and maintenance time and lacks traceability between the various copies of the files or the copies of the source libraries. However, doing parallel development was essential to surviving in the fast-growing, competitive software market. The next section explores the SCM tool approach used to support parallel development, which does not lose traceability between file versions and makes it easier to merge changes between parallel releases.

Branching is used to support parallel development across all files in a software system. A *branch* is a means to organize file versions and show their history. It is called a branch because the version organization looks like a tree. Early SCM tools used a built-in numbering convention that often became difficult to interpret. Modern SCM tools allow you to name branches, as can be seen in Figure 2-13, which has branches named `main`, `fuji_rel1`, `fuji_rel2`, and `fuji_boston_rel2`.

For any given file, a set of versions is produced over time. These are collected for any specific line of development, such as a release. When releases are developed in parallel, you must maintain multiple lines of development simultaneously. This is done by branching. A branch records the version from which it originated. This allows you to maintain parallel lines of development and see this record visually. Branching is similar to the unreserved checkouts used for individual files, except that branches are permanent.

Figure 2-14 shows an initial release 1 that was produced on a branch called `main`. After the release was produced, development of release 1.1 and release 2 was executed in parallel.

Another key aspect to branching is the ability to merge (or integrate) changes from one release to the next. This is similar to the merge that occurs during an unreserved checkin, except that it occurs across the entire source code base. The record of the merge is important as it helps to determine what files require merging in the future. Figure 2-15 shows a merge that has occurred from the final version of release 1.1 into both the main branch and into the release 2 branch. Both mergers are indicated by arrows from a version on one branch to a version on another.

In addition to developing parallel releases, there are other reasons for parallel work and branches, including the following:

- Prototype development
- Customer variants

- Platform variants or ports
- Serialized major releases
- Patches
- Patch bundles/service packs
- Emergency production fixes
- Individual task isolation
- Promotion model support
- Individual workspace isolation

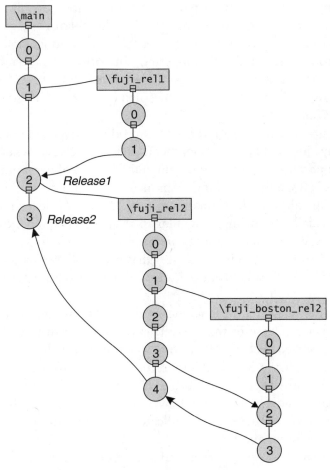

FIGURE 2-13   Version tree

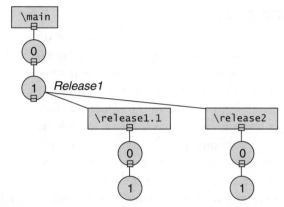

FIGURE 2-14   Version tree: release 1.1 and release 2 branching

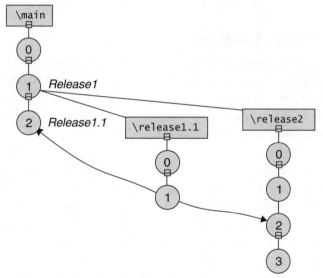

FIGURE 2-15   Version tree: release 1.1 and release 2 merging

Regardless of the reasons, modern SCM tools must provide strong support for branching so as to allow parallel development. They must also provide strong support for merging changes at the appropriate time. Merge support must be for both merging individual files and merging complete lines of development across the entire source code base.

Modern Workspace Management

As discussed in the Early Workspace Management section in this chapter, early tools such as SCCS did not provide any workspace management, only a means of pulling a particular version of a particular file from the library. Therefore, scripting was required. The key operations needing support were recreating the product directory structure, populating the directory structure with the "right" file versions, and later updating a workspace to include newer versions.

The next generation of commercially available SCM tools, therefore, had to support these operations in order to support larger and more complex software development efforts. Support for this in the SCM tools themselves reduced the amount of scripting required by each project team and reduced the number of errors that can result from manually creating/populating/updating workspaces.

ClearCase provides workspace management out of the box. This is discussed in the Workspaces: Snapshot and Dynamic Views section in chapter 4.

Modern Build and Release Management

Major teams usually face more complexity when building their software applications than smaller teams, making it more difficult to reproduce any given build. Modern build and release management techniques are aimed at ensuring that significant builds of the system can be reproduced and maintained. The build and release process involves the following steps:

1. *Identify the versions of the source to be built.* Modern tools provide a mechanism to identify and label specific versions of files. This labeling process identifies a consistent configuration. ClearCase provides both a mechanism to identify specific file versions (labeling) and a means to identify a set of file versions that make up a component. It also provides a means of creating versions of a component, called a *baseline*.

An additional step that is often overlooked and not supported in early SCM tools is version control of the directory structure. Directories are versioned in ClearCase, so a particular version of a directory is identified when determining what sources to build. In this way, if you are building release 1 of a system, you will see the directory structure as it was when release 1 was built. If you are building release 2, the directory structure will reflect the structure as it existed for release 2.

2. *Create or populate a clean workspace that selects those versions (and is locked).* This step is the same as creating a workspace for doing development, except that no source files will be checked out and you want to ensure that versions of the files selected do not change or get updated while the build is in progress. So, there must be a means to lock the versions that are being selected. A clean workspace means that there are no unnecessary files or old build objects left around in the workspace prior to the build being performed.

3. *Perform and audit the build.* Building means turning the source into objects, libraries, and executables or downloadable images. Auditing is keeping track of how each build output file was built. This includes recording who built it, when and on what platform it was built, which versions of any include files were referenced during the build, and which options were sent to the build tools (e.g., compiler, linker). This audit trail can be used later to compare two different builds, assist in reproducing a build, as input to the labeling process, and so on. It is often necessary to be able to completely reproduce the build environment. This may mean storing the versions of the build tools used, the operating system include files, and even the hardware machines used to perform the build.

4. *Stage the files produced by the build and the build audit.* *Staging* is the process of putting the built or derived objects under version control. This is another key step that is often overlooked. In particular, at least the derived object files and other files that are shipped to a customer or put onto the release media should be placed under version control, along with the audit information. This provides a secure copy of released media and supports component-based development, since specific versions of these runtime objects (e.g., libraries) can be used by other teams rather than each team's having to fully build the entire system.

5. *Identify the staged files.* Once the files and their audit history have been placed under version control, the versions should also be identified by attaching a label or creating a new baseline.

6. *Produce the necessary media.* The final step is to produce the necessary media, for example, by burning a CD-ROM, downloading to an embedded processor, or pushing content to a Web site.

Chapter 9, Integration, Build, and Release, discusses how ClearCase supports build management and the release process.

2.2.5   Advanced SCM Tool Support

When projects reach extreme size, their primary difficulties concern communication and complexity. Managing change is imperative. Automation and more advanced administration capabilities are key to success.

Fundamental capabilities needed in an SCM tool for extreme-sized teams include support for geographically distributed development, component-based development, and activity-based configuration management. These are discussed briefly here and in more detail later in the book.

Geographically Distributed Development

Geographically distributed development is the development of a software system by team members and/or teams located in different geographical regions. This could be teams distributed at different sites in the same city or in different cities around the world. Such development is almost unavoidable in extreme-sized projects and is becoming normal today because of the many acquisitions and mergers that are occurring. Chapter 10, Geographically Distributed Development, covers this topic in detail.

Component-based Development

Management of large, complex software systems being developed by extreme teams requires breaking down the software system into smaller building blocks. *Component-based development* is the development of a software system by decomposing it into smaller pieces called components, either during design or while rearchitecting an existing system. Components have well-defined interfaces and can have build-time or runtime dependencies on other components.[11] For configuration management purposes, you need to be able to identify component versions and to assemble a consistent set of component versions so as to create a version of the system as a whole.

The SCM best practice of component management is discussed in the Organizing Artifacts into Versioned Components section in chapter 1. ClearCase UCM support of component-based development is discussed in the ClearCase Components section in chapter 3.

---

11. See the chapter entitled Components in Booch for more general component information [Booch 1999].

Activity-based Configuration Management

Activity-based configuration management is the management of changes to a software system that is based on higher-level activities (e.g., task, defect, enhancement) rather than individual file versions. This requires an SCM tool to track which file versions implement the work required for a specific activity and then to present activities as a key object in the SCM tool. The idea is to simplify complexity and ensure that when the system says a defect is included in a specific build, it has in fact been included.

The best practice behind activity-based configuration management is discussed in the Organize and Integrate Consistent Sets of Versions Using Activities section in chapter 1. ClearCase UCM support for activity-based configuration management is covered throughout the remainder of this book. Particular attention is given to the project manager role in chapter 6, Project Management in ClearCase, and to the developer role in chapter 8, Developing Using the Clear-Case UCM Model.

2.3   Summary

Software configuration management is an essential engineering discipline for the success of your software projects. A project's SCM requirements will change over time because of the increasing complexity of the software system being developed, the increasing complexity of the project environment needed to develop the software system, changing requirements based on the development lifecycle phase, and changes to an organization's management processes and/or personnel.

The SCM tool that you use must be both flexible and scalable so as to meet your changing project requirements. It is up to the project manager to take software configuration management seriously and to strike the right balance between process enforcement and configuration audit. The objective must be to maximize the rate of change (productivity) while still maintaining control in order to produce a high-quality product on time with the required functionality.

ClearCase is a commercially available SCM tool that provides the capabilities described in this chapter. The remainder of this book focuses on how ClearCase supports SCM and the SCM best practices and how it can be applied to a wide variety of software development projects. Much of the discussion is oriented to Rational Software's approach to managing change, called unified change management.

Chapter 3   An Overview of the Unified Change Management Model

This chapter describes *unified change management* (UCM), Rational Software's approach to managing change in software system development from requirements to release.

3.1   What Is UCM?

Unified change management spans the development lifecycle, defining how to manage change to requirements, design models, documentation, components, test cases, and source code.

A key aspect of the UCM model is that it unifies the activities used to plan and track project progress with the artifacts being changed (see Figure 3-1). The UCM model is realized by both process and tools. The Rational products Clear-Case and ClearQuest are the foundations of UCM. ClearCase manages all the artifacts produced by a software project, including system artifacts and project management artifacts. ClearQuest manages the project's tasks, defects, and requests for enhancements (referred to generically as activities) and provides the charting and reporting tools necessary to track project progress.

While all Rational tools support the unified change management model across the development lifecycle, this book focuses on the UCM processes and functionality that are supported by ClearCase. Chapter 11, Changing Request Management and ClearQuest, covers the ClearQuest UCM functionality as it relates to ClearCase.

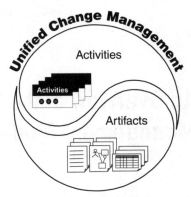

FIGURE 3-1   Unified change management, combining activities and artifacts

3.2   What Is ClearCase?

ClearCase is an SCM tool that provides automation and support for the SCM
best practices (see the SCM Best Practices section in chapter 1). ClearCase provides an open architecture that is used to implement and automate a wide range
of SCM solutions. ClearCase is employed in many different development environments on many types of applications, such as IS/IT systems, embedded systems, telecommunication systems, financial applications, Web site content, and
other commercial and government software systems. Today companies in many
diverse industries are successfully using ClearCase as the cornerstone of their
SCM environments.

ClearCase solves a broad range of SCM-related problems and provides both
general-purpose and specific solutions. The general-purpose solutions make
very few assumptions about how ClearCase will be applied to a development
environment. A certain amount of effort is required to determine how best to
apply the general-purpose solution to specific SCM needs. This general-purpose
SCM functionality is referred to in this book as "base ClearCase." For those
looking to apply SCM in the shortest period of time with the least effort, Clear-
Case also supports UCM's out-of-the-box usage model, which provides a specific solution. You must decide whether to invest in tailoring base ClearCase
(the general solution) to your environment or to begin with the UCM model
(the specific solution) and later extend it for your own requirements.

The ClearCase UCM model reflects Rational Software's 18 years' of experience with providing software development and SCM solutions to a broad range
of customers. Rational studied the companies using the general-purpose Clear-

Case solution and found that many of them followed similar usage model patterns. Rational studied these models and applied their best practices to the ClearCase UCM model, generalizing the implementation for easy configuration in diverse development environments.

ClearCase UCM is based on two key concepts: activity-based SCM and component management. Both of these concepts are evident in the more advanced usage models built on top of ClearCase.

Activity-based SCM is a means of creating and manipulating a consistent change as a single named entity rather than a set of file versions. A set of versions is called a *change set* in ClearCase. The change set is an *attribute* of an activity. An *activity* is a named object that identifies the specific task, defect, feature, or requirement implemented or satisfied by the versions in the activity's change set.

Component management is a method of breaking a software system into smaller manageable pieces. Specifically in ClearCase and SCM, component management is a means of collecting a set of files and directories into a larger entity that can be versioned and managed as a whole.

The UCM model focuses on minimizing the disruption to the software developer while maximizing the benefits gained from following sound SCM best practices. The project manager and integrator are provided with the tools necessary to manage the SCM aspects of the project in an intuitive fashion. Because the UCM model provides higher-level objects and a well-defined process, a significant number of manual steps have been automated. Therefore, for example, a developer does not need to understand the branching structure being used to manage parallel development.

Briefly, ClearCase UCM works as follows:

1. Software files and directories are organized into versioned components (ideally based on your system architecture).
2. Project managers create projects and assign project teams to work on these components.
3. Developers make changes to components, files, and directories based on assigned activities (tasks, defects, change requests).
4. New file and directory versions are collected during development and associated with activities (i.e., change sets).
5. Once complete, activities and their associated change sets are delivered and integrated in a shared project integration area.
6. New component baselines are created, tested, and promoted.

7. Component baselines are assembled into a system.

8. Systems are tested and released.

3.3   ClearCase UCM Process Overview

To provide an overview of the ClearCase UCM process, this section discusses it in terms of five roles and the steps these roles perform. The roles (in order of appearance in the process) are architect, configuration manager, project manager, developer, and integrator.

Your organization may use different names, but each role is key to successful SCM. A single individual may take on more than one role, or multiple individuals may share responsibility for a single role. The role(s) an individual performs usually depends on his or her technical background, the size of the project, and the size of the system being developed. You might want to map the ClearCase UCM roles to the individuals and roles in your own organization as you work through this book.

Figure 3-2, an overview of the UCM process, lists the roles involved and the steps they perform. For example, a developer's first step is to join a project. The main team members are listed followed by the steps they perform. Arrows indicate the typical order of the steps.

3.3.1   The Architect

The architect has a deep understanding of the system architecture. In terms of SCM, the architect is responsible for determining how the system architecture should be physically realized (that is, how to group and map the various design objects to the physical files and directories that will implement the design).

3.3.2   The Configuration Manager

The configuration manager is familiar with an organization's configuration and change management processes and with the SCM tools being used. The configuration manager is responsible for creating and maintaining the physical infrastructure necessary to implement the design. This primarily involves the creation and maintenance of repositories and the importing of existing files and directories.[1]

---

1. In some organizations the configuration manager is also responsible for things such as disk space allocation, network resources, and backup strategies as they relate to SCM data. The process described here allocates these activities to the system administrator.

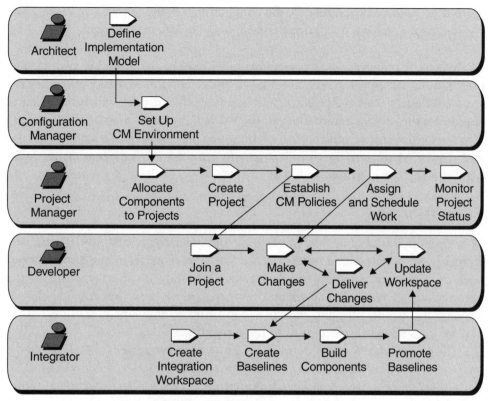

FIGURE 3-2 UCM process overview

Source: This figure is based on the configuration and change management
core workflow of the Rational Unified Process [RUP 5.5 1999].

3.3.3 The Project Manager

The project manager understands an organization's change management processes and project management policies. In terms of SCM, project managers are responsible for assigning and scheduling work activities and scoping components to project teams. Once components are scoped, the project manager for a given project is responsible for creating the physical ClearCase projects and for defining the SCM policies by which the project is governed. Policies are defined both in terms of written policies as well as SCM tool settings that define automation/enforcement policies supported by UCM.

▶ **Note:** In some organizations, the configuration manager may be responsible for carrying out the policy decisions made by the project manager.

In larger organizations, a project manager may be two different people. The traditional division is between a management-oriented role, which allocates the work and establishes the policies, and a technical-lead role, which creates and configures the project and carries out the work.[2] Typically, project managers are also responsible for producing and maintaining a SCM plan. Because ClearCase and the UCM do not provide any specific automation for creating an SCM plan, this topic is not discussed here.[3]

3.3.4   The Developer

The developer is responsible for finding out what activities need to be performed. Developers either receive activity assignments from the project manager or formulate activities on their own depending on the formality of the organization's change management policies. Developers are responsible for making changes to files and directories in order to implement those activities and for delivering those activities to the integrator.

The role of developer is defined here in a very broad sense. A developer is anyone who makes changes to any elements that are under version control. A developer can be a project manager modifying a project plan, a technical writer modifying a user manual, a tester modifying some test scripts, an architect modifying a design model, or a Web author modifying an HTML page.

3.3.5   The Integrator

The integrator is familiar with the build strategy and build tools being used on a project, with the SCM processes of an organization, and with the organization's SCM tools. The integrator accepts activities from developers, creates new component baselines, builds the components of the system (for small systems, this may be one component containing the entire system), ensures that the builds are tested (they may or may not perform the actual testing), and promotes the new

---

2. Other key activities of the project manager are to create, monitor, and maintain a project plan. These are project management tasks and not part of the SCM process. With respect to SCM, the project plan should be placed under version control, and in this capacity the project manager acts as a developer.

3. Refer to IEEE Standard 828-1998, *IEEE Standard for Software Configuration Management Plans,* for details on SCM plans [IEEE 828-1998].

baselines when testing is complete. For large systems that have multiple projects per release producing multiple components, a system integrator is responsible for assembling components, performing system testing, and creating baselines for the entire system.

3.4   The Architect: Defining the Implementation Model

Typically, software development requirements and budgets are established at product inception and evolve during product elaboration and development. The architect uses the requirements to create a software architecture or to modify an existing one. The software architecture serves as a logical framework to satisfy the requirements.

The concept of architecture has many facets, some that are relevant to software configuration management and others that are not. The authors of *The Unified Modeling Language User Guide* [Booch 1999] and *The Rational Unified Process: An Introduction, Second Edition* [Kruchten 2000] define architecture as:

> Software architecture encompasses the following:
> - The significant decisions about the organization of a software system
> - The selection of the structural elements and their interfaces by which the system is composed together with their behavior as specified in the collaboration among those elements
> - The composition of these elements into progressively larger subsystems; the architectural style that guides this organization, these elements, and their interfaces, their collaborations, and their composition
>
> Software architecture is concerned with not only structure and behavior, but also usage, functionality, performance, resilience, reuse, comprehensibility, economic and technologic constraints and trade-offs, and aesthetic issues [Kruchten 2000, p. 277].

In terms of SCM, architecture is concerned with the organization, grouping, and versioning of the physical files and directories of the system, both as they are organized in the development environment and as they are deployed on the target system. Some projects use high-level design documents to describe these aspects of architecture. More recently, models are being employed to visually represent the architecture, providing different architectural views of the system.[4] One of these views, the most important for SCM, is the *implementation view,* which maps logical system design objects (e.g., classes) to the physical files and directories that implement them. These files and directories will be placed under version control. One of the jobs of the architect is to produce this implementation model of the system.

3.4.1   ClearCase Components

Terminology used for the decomposition of a software system varies widely and is not standardized. Humphrey defines five layers: system, subsystems, products, components, and modules [Humphrey 1989]. Whitgift defines three layers: system, subsystem, and elements [Whitgift 1991]. IEEE defines three layers: computer software configuration items (CSCI), computer software components (CSC), and computer software units [IEEE 1042-1987]. The Rational Unified Process defines four layers: system, implementation (or component) subsystems, components, and files [RUP 5.5 1999]. For the purposes of SCM, ClearCase defines a general-purpose set of objects that can be used to represent any of the preceding models. These objects are components and elements. (Details on UCM objects and the object model can be found in chapter 4.)

Elements are the files and directories that are under version control in ClearCase. Components are used to group elements. A ClearCase *component* is a physical object that identifies a root directory, under which exist the elements that comprise the component. ClearCase components are versioned, shared (reused), and released as a unit. A large system will typically consist of many components; a small system may be contained in a single component.

3.4.2   Components in the Unified Modeling Language

The word "component" is one of those overused terms that means different things to different people in different contexts. One of those contexts is the Unified Modeling Language (UML). UML is a language for visualizing, specifying, constructing, and documenting a software system. The UML definition of the term component is relevant to our discussion here. In light of the broad adop-

---

4. The term "view" as used here refers to an abstraction of a system architecture. An abstraction shown from a given perspective omits entities that are not relevant to that perspective. This use of view is not related to the ClearCase view object. Elsewhere in this book, any mention of the term view refers to a ClearCase view (see [Kruchten 1995]).

tion of UML in the market, it is worth a few words to explain how UML components relate to ClearCase components.

The authors of *The Unified Modeling Language User Guide* define a component as "a physical and replaceable part of a system that conforms to and provides the realization of a set of interfaces" [Booch 1999]. They also define three kinds of components: deployment components, work product components, and execution components. Deployment components are elements of the system as deployed on the target machine. Examples are executables, libraries, and other files needed to support a running system. Work product components are the elements that make up the development environment. Examples are source files, headers, and other files used to derive or build the deployment components. Executable components are those produced by the system executing on the target machine.

ClearCase components can be UML deployment components, UML work product components, both, or neither, depending on the elements being managed in the ClearCase component. However, UML components are generally too fine-grained to apply SCM controls (exceptions do exist). For a large system, you may be dealing with hundreds of UML components. While this is certainly better than dealing with thousands of files, there is still significant SCM overhead.

UML also defines two higher levels of abstraction that are better mapped to ClearCase components. These are systems and subsystems. A system, "possibly decomposed into a collection of subsystems, [is] a set of elements organized to accomplish a specific purpose and described by a set of models, possibly from different view points" [Booch 1999]. Systems and subsystems are rendered in UML as stereotypes of a package.

If you are using UML to model your system, ClearCase components should relate, one to one, to the UML concept of systems or subsystems. Figure 3-3 shows the UML representation of systems, subsystems, and components and how they map to ClearCase components and elements Mapping your system architecture to ClearCase components is not a requirement for using ClearCase UCM. However, a strong mapping between the organization of the system (the architecture) and the implementation of the system (the files and directories) reduces integration problems, eases build development (e.g., makefiles), reduces the risk of accidentally violating the architecture, and facilitates integration. (How to map architecture to physical ClearCase components is discussed in more detail in the Defining the Implementation Model section in chapter 5.)

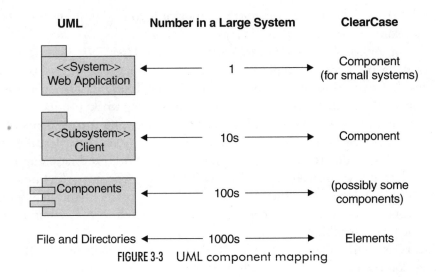

FIGURE 3-3   UML component mapping

Once the architect has completed the implementation model, the configuration manager physically creates the repositories, components, and directory structure where development will take place.

3.5   The Configuration Manager: Setting Up the SCM Environment

Before the first developer can start making changes, the configuration manager must establish the SCM environment. There are two key steps: establishing the hardware environment and establishing the development environment.

To set up the hardware environment, the configuration manager works with the system administrator to assess and allocate machine resources (e.g., designated servers and disk space). To complete the hardware environment, the configuration manager must work with the system administrator to install and configure the necessary software tools on both server and client machines (e.g., ClearCase).

The second step, establishing the development environment, involves the following:

1. The configuration manager works with the architect to finalize the implementation model (the mapping of design objects to logical packages and then to ClearCase components).
2. The configuration manager determines where the components will be stored (which SCM repositories).
3. The configuration manager creates the repositories and the components.
4. The configuration manager creates the product directory structure.
5. The configuration manager imports any existing files and directories into the repositories to create the initial set of versioned elements.
6. The configuration manager establishes an initial baseline for all components. A component baseline records a specific version of every element (files and directories) in a component.

Once the configuration manager establishes the development environment, the project manager can create a new project.

3.6   The Project Manager: Managing a Project

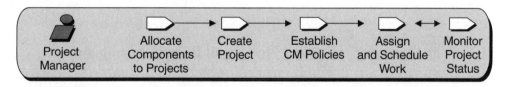

A ClearCase project is created by the project manager and is used by a team to produce new baselines of one or more components. A ClearCase *project* is an object that contains the configuration information needed to manage a significant development effort. Project managers configure the ClearCase project to define the scope of work for the project (the set of components) and to set policies that govern how developers access and update the set of source files. A ClearCase project also defines a shared area where development changes are integrated.

The size of the overall development initiative will influence the number of projects that are created to fulfill it. Small initiatives may have one project that is producing a new release of an entire system. Large initiatives will have multiple projects working together to produce a single release of a system. It is important to distinguish between the product being produced and the project or projects producing the product.

The project manager does the following:

1. Creates the project
2. Identifies the components needed by the project
3. Identifies which components are to be modified (writable) and which components are merely referenced (read-only) by the project
4. Identifies the baseline (version) of each component from which developers will start their work
5. Defines the policies that govern how the usage model is applied to the project

Defining policies for a project means configuring how ClearCase will automate and enforce policies during development on that project and defining other project policies, which may not be automated by ClearCase but must be documented and followed manually.

Once the project manager has created the project, defined the scope of work for the project (indicating which components will be modified or referenced), and established the project's policies, developers can join the project and begin working.

3.7   The Developer: Joining a Project and Doing Development

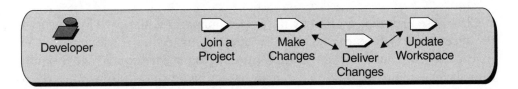

Developers join one or more projects where they perform their work. The process of joining a project creates the developer's *workspace*. In ClearCase, a developer's workspace is comprised of a ClearCase view and a development stream. A ClearCase view provides a window into the files being managed. The stream defines the configuration for the view and determines which versions of the files will be displayed.

Once developers join a project, they can work directly in their view or through any number of integrated development environments (IDEs) (e.g., Microsoft Visual Studio). In views, developers check out, edit, build, unit test, debug, and check in file and directory elements as needed to accomplish their tasks. All modifications are associated with an activity, forming a change set.

Activities represent the tasks that developers work on. Examples include "implement feature A," "fix defect 109," or "redesign the search algorithm for orders." In UCM, the project manager can plan and assign activities if a change request management tool such as ClearQuest is being used (see chapter 11, Change Request Management and ClearQuest). Developers can also define activities when they start doing work if a project is using an informal change management process. The developers need only track the change sets.

When developers complete an activity, they deliver their changes to the project's integration stream, making them available to the integrator for integration and inclusion in the next component baseline(s). Developers must also keep their own development stream current with changes being made by other developers on the project. ClearCase supports an explicit operation called *rebase* (short for "rebaseline"). Rebase takes new baselines created by the integrator and incorporates them into the development stream. After a rebase, developers will see new baselines that include changes other developers have delivered and the integrator has integrated.

After developers have created, tested, and delivered changes, it is time for the integrator to build and test those changes.

3.8 The Integrator: Integration, Build, and Release

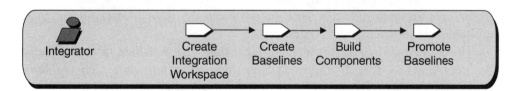

The job of the integrator is to take changes that developers deliver, produce new baselines of components, and promote those baselines for internal project consumption or external use.

Each project has one integration stream into which developers deliver their activities. The integrator uses an integration view attached to the integration stream to create a working environment for performing the first step of the integration: creating a new baseline. The integrator creates an integration view, configured by the integration stream to select the previous project baseline plus all the new versions identified by the delivered (but as yet unincorporated) activities.

The integrator freezes the integration stream to ensure the integration view will select a fixed set of versions and then builds the system. If the build succeeds, the integrator creates new baselines of the components that have changed.

If the system passes a certain level of testing, the integrator can promote the baselines. "Promotion" is a means of marking baselines as either having passed or failed a certain level of testing. For example, a integrator could promote a baseline to "Built," "Tested," or "Rejected." These promotion levels are defined by the project manager as part of defining project policies and are largely used by external consumers of the baseline. By promoting project baselines to a certain level of quality, the integrator implicitly selects the baselines as the project's recommended baselines. The recommended baselines will be the default baselines presented to developers when they rebase (update) their development streams.

3.8.1   Releasing a Component

To release a component, the integrator places all product deliverables, which are artifacts, under version control. The product deliverables may reside in one of the development components or in a separate component reserved for deliverables. "Deliverable components" are components that contain elements that have been built and are shared with other teams. These elements are included in the build process (e.g., statically linked libraries), included in the final system's runtime environment (e.g., executables, dynamically linked libraries), or make up the deliverable (e.g., documentation).

The elements of a deliverable component are also included in a baseline of that component. Other development teams can select and share deliverable or source elements by referring to the appropriate component and its baseline.

3.8.2   System Integration

For large systems, there is likely to be more than one project producing modifications to many components, generating a need for system integration. System integration happens when component baselines are assembled into a final system.

With the UCM, system assembly is done by creating a system project and selecting the component baselines that are being produced by the various sub-projects. In other words, all components for the system project are reference (read-only) components. The complete system can then be built and tested as a whole.

3.8.3   Releasing a System

All of this work leads up to the release of the system. A system integrator places all product deliverables under version control (including any additional deliverables produced during the system build). The final system baseline is promoted to the appropriate level to indicate it has passed all testing operations. The final step is to produce the necessary media or simply deploy the files on the target system (e.g., Web sites or internal production machines).

3.9   The UCM Baseline+Change Model

ClearCase UCM provides support for the SCM best practices of organizing and integrating consistent sets of versions using activities and maintaining stable and consistent workspaces. This is done by implementing an approach to workspace configuration called a "baseline+change model." A configuration consists of an identified set of files and directories in which there is one and only one version of each file and directory. You could define a configuration by specifying a list of files and the exact versions of each of those files, but that would be highly inefficient unless you are dealing with only a handful of files. This approach is also error-prone as you may pick an inconsistent set of file versions. Figure 3-4 shows an example of defining a configuration based on file versions. Each file, a through h, has a number of versions. A configuration picks a subset of the files and identifies one version of each file (e.g., `filea` selects version 1, `fileb` selects version 3, and so on.)

It is far easier to group files into a larger unit if the larger unit is versioned. In ClearCase UCM, that unit is a "component," and a version of a component is a "baseline." So, by picking a set of component baselines, ClearCase can automatically pick the right versions of the all files. In this way, you are more likely to get a consistent set of file versions. The set of component baselines defines the "foundation" for the stream's configuration. Since baselines cannot change content (they are immutable), you know that you have a stable point from which to begin your work. Figure 3-5 shows an example of picking.

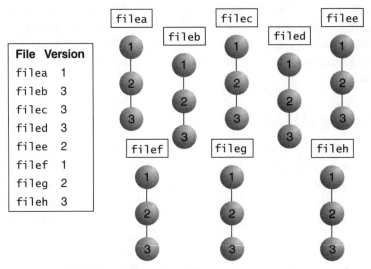

File	Version
filea	1
fileb	3
filec	3
filed	3
filee	2
filef	1
fileg	2
fileh	3

FIGURE 3-4   Example of file/version selection

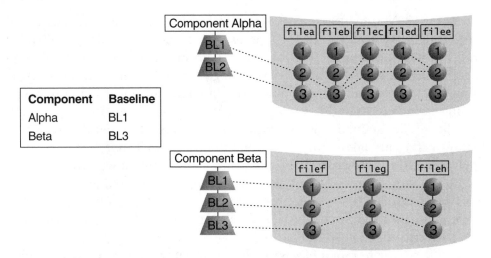

Component	Baseline
Alpha	BL1
Beta	BL3

FIGURE 3-5   Example of component baseline selection

component baselines. This is the "baseline" piece of the baseline+change model. Illustrated are two components: Alpha and Beta. Component Alpha contains five files, a through e, and has two baselines, BL1 and BL2, which select a particular version of each of the elements. Component Beta contains three files, f through h, and has three baselines, BL1, BL2, and BL3.

Once you begin working in your development stream, you make changes to individual files and create new versions of files. You could list all the file versions you have created and select the component baselines and the file versions for your stream configuration. But this is an inefficient and error-prone approach since you may forget you changed some files or list the wrong versions. It is easier to indicate which component baselines and activities you want to have in your stream and let ClearCase figure out the right files and versions to select. (The activities represent the "change" piece of the baseline+change model.)

In summary, you can determine any stream configuration in UCM by looking at its foundation baselines plus the activities that are being worked on or have been worked on in the stream. Figure 3-6 illustrates a development stream configuration based on component baselines and activities.

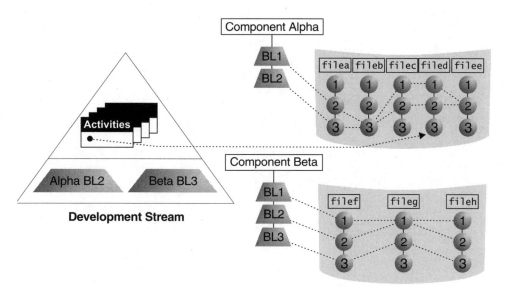

FIGURE 3-6   Baseline+change view/stream configuration

Chapter 4   A Functional Overview
   of ClearCase Objects

This chapter provides an overview of ClearCase objects and concepts. It serves as a bridge between general SCM terminology and ClearCase-specific terminology.

4.1   The Repository: Versioned Object Base

At the heart of any SCM system is the object repository. ClearCase repositories are called *versioned object bases,* or VOBs. The ClearCase on-line help reads, "A VOB is the permanent data repository in which you store files, directories, and metadata." Anything that can be represented as a file or directory can be managed in a ClearCase VOB.

ClearCase VOBs support all of the characteristics listed in the first SCM best practice—the SCM repository must be scalable, fault tolerant, distributable, and replicable. (see chapter 1):

- *Scalable*
ClearCase VOBs can grow from hundreds of files and directories to many thousands of files and directories. Files and directories in a ClearCase VOB can be moved between VOBs if a VOB becomes too large. VOBs can be split and joined.

- *Fault Tolerant*
ClearCase VOBs have an internal database that does not require additional database management. The VOB database and ClearCase architecture ensure

that transactions such as checkout on a file are atomic and so ensure that the permanent datastore does not get corrupted.

■ *Distributable*

ClearCase VOBs can be distributed across different servers in the network transparently to the end user. Since VOBs can be moved, you can distribute the load as needed to meet project demands.

■ *Replicatable*

ClearCase VOBs can be replicated in two or more sites. Replication means full copies are made and kept up to date (in sync) with each other at different geographic sites. This is critical for geographically distributed development, where the network between sites is often not as reliable or often does not have as high a bandwidth as the local area network.

ClearCase VOB technology has an interesting twist not found in traditional SCM systems. In systems such as the revision control system (RCS), the repository and the file system are two separate entities. With ClearCase, you can combine the two.

Rather than being a black-box repository from which things need to be inserted and extracted, the ClearCase repository displays its contents as files in a file system, which can be operated on in the same way as you would files in the native file system. In the same way you add disks to a file system, you can create as many ClearCase VOBs as required. The VOBs can be distributed across many machines but referenced as if they were one single repository. Figure 4-1 shows two servers and three VOBs and how the VOBs plug into the native file system. A scalable solution such as this one is particularly critical for large organizations.

ClearCase VOBs store files and directories. In ClearCase terminology, these versioned objects are called *elements*. Figure 4-2 shows the relationships between VOBs and elements in UML format.

Along with elements, VOBs also store metadata associated with the version control environment, as well as user-defined metadata. *Metadata* is data associated with an object. It supplements the object's file system data. Metadata can be used to implement, enforce, or automate certain aspects of the development process.

ClearCase has two primary types of VOBs. The first is the standard VOB as described earlier. The second type is called a *project VOB*, or PVOB. PVOBs hold objects associated with the project environment such as projects, components, activities, and baselines, all described later in this chapter. The PVOB is

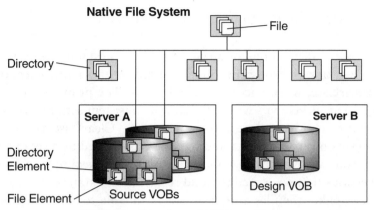

FIGURE 4-1   Distributed VOB architecture

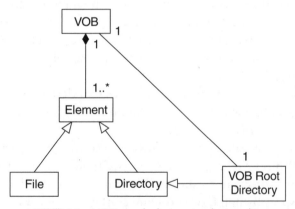

FIGURE 4-2   VOB and element relationships

Note: See UML Diagram Format in the Conventions Used section in the preface
if you are unfamiliar with UML format. See Booch for more complete information
on UML [Booch 1999].

basically the central point of administration for a set of projects working on a
set of components. For example, in the development of the ClearCase product
itself, there is one PVOB, which contains all the projects working on the forty-
odd components that comprise the ClearCase product family source base. In
short, VOBs store and organize the objects that make up the system being
developed, while PVOBs store the objects used to organize and manage the
projects doing the development. For information on a range of topics related to
VOBs, see chapter 5, Establishing the Initial SCM Environment.

4.2 Workspaces: Snapshot and Dynamic Views

One of the essential functions of an SCM tool is to establish and manage the developer's working environment, often referred to as a *workspace,* or "sandbox." In ClearCase, workspaces are called *views.* The primary purpose of the view is to provide developers with a stable and consistent set of software, where they can make changes and perform unit testing. ClearCase views select the appropriate versions of the files and directories, as defined by a set of configuration rules, from all available versions in a VOB. For example, a view might select all versions that were used to build release 2 of a system.

The view makes the files and directories available for browsing, modification, and building. The versions selected in a view should be stable (the versions of the files and directories you are working on should not change without warning) and consistent (the versions of multiple elements selected should be complementary). For example, if you are fixing a bug in release 1, you don't want to select some element versions from release 1, some from release 2, and some of the latest element versions. Rather, you want all the release 1 element versions plus your own modifications.

Every ClearCase view contains a set of rules that define the configuration for that view (that is, define which versions should be seen). These rules are called a *configuration specification,* or "config spec." For projects using the UCM model, ClearCase automatically generates these config specs (for a discussion of streams see the Project Management: Projects, Streams, and Activities section in this chapter). For projects not using UCM, you can use the default config spec, generate config specs by hand, or automate config spec generation using scripts.

ClearCase provides two types of views, *snapshot* and *dynamic.* Each type has its own advantages, and you should expect to use both types to maximize the benefits of ClearCase. Snapshot views have copies of the files loaded into them from the VOB. While they take longer to set up and require more disk space than dynamic views, build performance is better since there is no dependency on the network to access the files. Dynamic views reference files directly out of the VOB. No copies are made, so setting up a dynamic view is fast and takes very little disk space. The following sections go into more detail on each type of view.

4.2.1 Snapshot Views

Snapshot views are similar in approach to traditional development sandboxes (i.e., uncontrolled copies of a software system's files and directories). When you create a snapshot view, you specify a local directory into which the files and directories you want to work on are copied. This is referred to as a Get operation or a Read-only Checkout by some SCM tools. ClearCase refers to this as loading a snapshot view.

The use of ClearCase snapshot views differs from the traditional approach of local file copies in a number of ways. Snapshot views have a database that keeps track of what versions have been loaded into the working directory. Snapshot views mirror the directory structure as part of a load/update operation. They keep track of when a developer changes the read-only bit on a file and modifies it without issuing a checkout command, called "hijacking" the file. During update operations, hijacked files are not overwritten and can be turned into checkouts.

Another difference from traditional sandboxes is that snapshot views can be "updated" in a single operation. Rather then performing Gets on individual files or directories, a snapshot view user performs a single Update operation. The Update does the following: checks for hijacked files, asks the user if he or she wants to check out these files, and compares the versions of the files in the snapshot view's local directory to the versions that are selected in the VOB based on the views config spec. If these are different, it will copy only those files that have changed into the snapshot view. This Update operation is crucial for maintaining consistency in the developer's working environment.

Generally, you may not want to make a copy of all the files that make up the system (unless in fact you need the entire system to do your work). For example, you may want to copy only the files associated with the component you are working on. This is done by specifying a set of load rules in the configuration specification, which define what pieces of the system are interesting. This information is used to limit the set of elements copied from the VOB to the snapshot view. A GUI interface can also be used to specify what pieces of the system get loaded into the snapshot view.

Another aspect of keeping the development environment consistent is ensuring that the right elements get loaded. This may change over time based on the activities the developer is performing. The snapshot view Update operation not only downloads new element versions, but also "unloads" files that have been removed from the view's load rules or files that have been renamed, deleted, or moved from one directory to another.

For example, I'm working on component A fixing a bug, so I load component A into my snapshot view and do my work. When I'm done, I'm now assigned to fix a bug in component B. I change my load rules to select component B and deselect component A. Component A will be unloaded at the same time component B is loaded. This frees up disk space and ensures that I do not introduce any unknown dependencies between components A and B.

4.2.2   Dynamic Views

Like snapshot views, dynamic views establish a developer's workspace by providing a set of element versions based on the config spec rules. Unlike snapshot views, dynamic views do not copy elements to a local storage directory. They provide access to element versions by using a virtual file system that refers to elements directly from the VOB (see The Repository: Versioned Object Base section in this chapter). The virtual file system mechanism provides transparent version control. Existing tools can open files without creating separate copies or ever removing the files from the repository. The dynamic view approach to development workspaces is unique to ClearCase.

How does this work? Dynamic views deal directly with the operating system and the file system. The implementation supports the operating system's file system interface and user environment. Because of this, dynamic views are presented differently depending on your development platform (e.g., Unix and/or Windows).

When full ClearCase is installed, a file system called the *multiversioned file system* (MVFS) is installed as well (see The Multiversion File System in chapter 5). The MVFS uses standard operating system protocols to add a new file system type. Multiple file system types are common: Windows NT has FAT and NTFS; Unix has NFS and DFS. When you are in the MVFS file system space and you access a file using a tool such as an editor, the MVFS intercepts the file Open call, determines what view the user is working in, determines the right version of the file to select, and opens that version of the file.

Unix Example

Here is a Unix example. Let's say we have a software system under version control. Using the "hello world" project example, here is the project directory structure:

```
/vobs/hw
/vobs/hw/Makefile
/vobs/hw/src/hello.c
/vobs/hw/inc/hello.h
```

Let's say we have two developers, Ann and Jim. They each have their own dynamic view: `ann_view` and `jim_view`. Ann is working on fixing a bug in release 1. Jim is working on release 2.

Ann performs the following commands:[1]

```
noview>    cleartool setview ann_view
ann_view>  cd /vobs/hw/src
ann_view>  cat hello.c
main {
    printf("hello world\n");
}
```

Jim performs the following commands:

```
noview>    cleartool setview jim_view
jim_view>  cd /vobs/hw/src
jim_view>  cat hello.c
main {
    printf("You are now running with \n");
    printf("the power of version 2\n");
    printf("hello world\n");
}
```

Ann's view and Jim's view see different output from the cat command even though they are in the same directory: This is because they are using different configuration specifications and, in the case of `hello.c`, they are selecting different versions of the file. This is what is meant by "transparency with dynamic views." Tools can work with the files in place, and Makefiles do not have to be tailored to support search paths and other user-specific settings.

The result of using dynamic views is that Ann and Jim can work in isolation without impacting each other. There are many benefits gained by using dynamic views. First, the software is not being copied to various places in the network. Multiple software copies consume disk space and cause confusion. Second, there is no need to specify which pieces of the software need to be copied or loaded. With dynamic views you have access to all the software all of the time. Third, build problems that result from builds being performed in different environments/directory trees are avoided. Finally, dynamic views provide unique build support, such as audited builds and derived object sharing. These

---

1. "setview," as seen in this code, establishes the view context for the shell session in which the setview command is issued. You can also do things like 'cleartool setview -exec <application>' to start an application in the context of a view. For Unix gurus, setview is performing a "chroot" operation to a directory structure maintained by ClearCase that mimics the entire Unix directory tree. This directory is located under /view on Unix and under a specific drive letter (usually configured to M: or V:) on Windows.

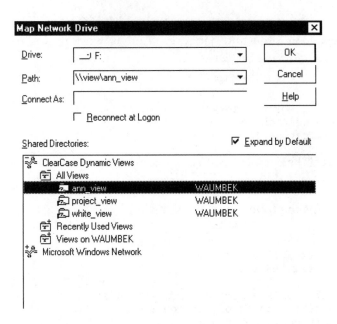

FIGURE 4-3   Mapping a dynamic view to a network drive

features are covered in the Building: Clearmake, Derived Objects, Configuration Records section later in this chapter.

Windows Example

On Windows, dynamic views are presented consistently with the Windows NT file system (and are therefore presented differently from how they are presented on Unix). In the example, Ann runs the Windows Explorer and performs the menu command File->Map Network Drive. As seen in Figure 4-3, she selects her dynamic view and a network drive to which it will be mapped.

Ann can now access her project through the Windows Explorer on drive F. She could also use any other interface, such as Microsoft Visual Studio. Using our hello world example, Figure 4-4 shows Ann's view accessing the hello world VOBs from within the Explorer.

4.2.3   Differences between Snapshot and Dynamic Views

Dynamic views provide a global view on the source base without the need to have a full copy of the entire source tree. This means they can be created very quickly. Updates occur automatically and do not require the copy time associated with

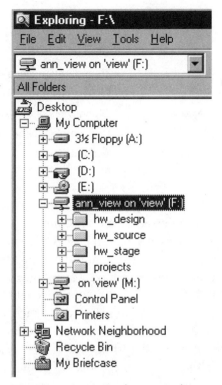

FIGURE 4-4   Ann's Explorer window

ClearCase Pro Tip

For a more detailed explanation of how dynamic views work and the benefits of transparent file access, refer to a paper by the creator of ClearCase, David Leblang, entitled "The CM Challenge: Configuration Management That Works" [Leblang 1994]. It is part of the book *Configuration Management*, edited by Walter Tichy [Tichy 1994]. This paper is particularly useful for Unix-based teams evaluating ClearCase as a potential SCM tool.

snapshot views. Dynamic views provide significant build capabilities such as derived object sharing and build audits. Snapshot views cannot.

Snapshot views provide two key benefits over dynamic views. Because files are copied to the local disk, the build performance is faster than in dynamic

TABLE 4-1   Differences Between Snapshot and Dynamic Views

Snapshot Views	Dynamic Views
Copies loaded from VOB	Transparent access to VOB
Periodic updates	Fast creation and immediate updates
Ability to load a subset of the code	Global view of code base
Fast local build speed	Derived object sharing
Ability to work off-line, disconnected use	Audited Builds

views. Also, because of the local copies, it is possible to work off-line with snap-shot views. This is usually referred to as "disconnected use." It is particularly important for people using laptops at home or while traveling. Table 4-1 sum-marizes the differences between snapshot and dynamic views.

Snapshot and dynamic views each have advantages and disadvantages. You should expect to use both types to maximize the benefits from ClearCase. Use dynamic views when you need to conserve disk space, require all the source code, desire frequent and automatic updates, or want to take advantage of ClearCase's build facilities. Use snapshot views when you want to work off-line, only require a small subset of the code, or want to maximize your build performance.

4.3   Project Management: Projects, Streams, and Activities

Because of the complexity and size of software development efforts, project managers need automation and tools to help organize and manage large soft-ware projects. ClearCase UCM has objects and automation that assist in the management and organization of software projects: projects, streams, and activities (see Figure 4-5).

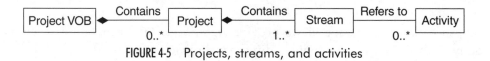

FIGURE 4-5   Projects, streams, and activities

4.3.1 Projects

The Project Management Institute defines a project as follows:

> Projects are performed by people, constrained by limited resources, and planned, executed and controlled. A project is a temporary endeavor undertaken to create a unique product or service. Temporary means that every project has a definite beginning and a definite end. Unique means that the product or service is different in some distinguishing way from all similar products and services. Projects are undertaken at all levels of the organization. They may involve a single person or many thousands. They may require less than 100 hours to complete or over 10,000,000. Projects may involve a single unit of one organization or may cross organizational boundaries as in joint ventures and partnering. Projects are often critical components of the performing organization's business strategy [PMI 1996, p. 4].

A ClearCase *project* directly maps to this definition in the context of how it relates to the SCM. A ClearCase UCM project represents a group of individuals collaborating to produce new baselines of one or more components of a system (or perhaps the entire system). A ClearCase project is an object whose attributes define the scope of work for that project (i.e., which components are being worked on), the policies that govern the work for that project, the workspaces (streams and views) used on that project, and which activities are being worked on by the team members.

Project objects are created in PVOBs and can be organized into folders. A Project Creation Wizard is used to create a new project, and a Project Explorer is used to browse and modify projects.

4.3.2 Streams

A workspace is a logical concept in ClearCase UCM that is implemented with two objects: a *stream* and a view. A stream defines the working configuration for the view (or views) associated with it. It contains the information needed to automatically generate a configuration specification for the view. Unlike base ClearCase users, ClearCase UCM users do not have to create or modify the config specs. Streams logically define configurations in terms of baselines and activities.

Figure 4-6 illustrates how this works. The VOB shown on the left contains many elements and many versions. In the middle, the triangle represents a stream. The base of the triangle lists one or more foundation baselines for the stream. The upper portion of the triangle lists a set of activities (along with their change sets). The view (shown on the right) uses the stream's activities and baselines to display particular versions of elements stored in the VOB.

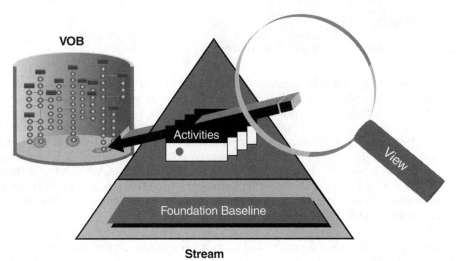

FIGURE 4-6   Stream/view relationship

Streams serve two purposes: development and integration. A stream that refers to the activities being worked on by a developer is called a *development stream*. A stream that contains the combined activities of all developers for a given project is called an *integration stream*. Each project has one integration stream and multiple development streams (see Figure 4-7).

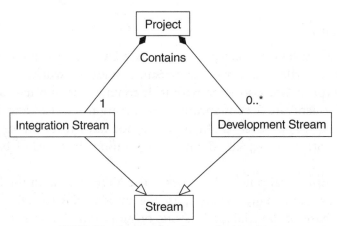

FIGURE 4-7   Stream/project relationships

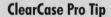

ClearCase Pro Tip

In some cases, it is necessary to have more than one view sharing the same configuration (stream), for example, with multiple development views attached to the project's integration stream. This allows developers to deliver their changes in parallel.*

Two cases that require multiple views attached to a single development stream are cross-platform builds and small team collaboration. For cross-platform builds, you may need to build your system on both Windows NT and Unix. To do this, you need to have a Unix view and an NT view, but both must select the same versions of the files (at least if you are writing portable code). This is accomplished by having two views attached to the same development stream.

For small team collaboration you may have two or more developers cooperating closely. Since the activity is part of the stream configuration, both developers can associate their own view with the same development stream and work semi-isolated from one another, recording changes against their activities. The checkin operation, in this case, makes changes visible to those members who are sharing the development stream. Before delivering, it is important for the collaborating members to check in all changes and test them in a single view.

---

*True, this may lead to element contention, but allowing parallel deliveries was felt to be a better option then disallowing them just to avoid contention. The deliver operation ensures that all necessary files are checked out before proceeding so no deadlock situations will be encountered.

Streams serve two primary purposes:

1. *They configure the views attached to them.* That is, they configure the view to select the right versions of the files for doing work on that project in that stream (see Figure 4-8). ClearCase users will understand that the stream supplies the appropriate configuration specification to its attached views.

FIGURE 4-8   Stream / View Relationship

2. *They physically store the activities that developers have worked on in their view.* When a developer checks in a new version, it is recorded in the stream in the activity they are working on. In this way, streams behave like ClearCase branches.[2]

Stream objects are created and stored as child objects to the project object. Integration streams are automatically created as part of project creation when the Project Creation Wizard is used (see Creating a ClearCase Project in chapter 6). Development streams are created when developers join a project (see Joining a Project in chapter 8).

4.3.3   Activities

The Conceptual UCM Activity

The concept of "activity" in the UCM model differs depending on the project context. In the development of the UCM model, one of the key ideas was that the model itself could scale without changing the way a developer interacted with the system. For example, the UCM model is designed to scale around the importance of the activity object.

In general, there are three components to the initiation of work in a project: an issue, a response, and a result. An issue forms the stimulus for work. For example, an issue could be the discovery of a defect or a request for enhancement from a customer. Second, there is a response to the stimulus. This takes the form of a task or action on the part of someone. For example, a developer is assigned to fix the defect. Finally, the work response culminates in some result, for example, new element versions that fix the defect (e.g., the change set). Depending on the complexity of your environment and the tools you employ there are often different physical objects that represent these concepts, and in many cases they overlap (see Figure 4-9).

In a very complex development environment, each one of these objects (issue, response, and result) is physically recorded and tracked independently. For example, a defect record is filed when the defect is found. Once the organization decides to work on the defect, a task record is created in a project manage-

---

2. In fact, the implementation of a stream in ClearCase 4.0 includes a branch type per stream. View profile users could think of streams in terms of a view profile combined with a "private branch." Branches are described in the Versioned Objects: Elements, Branches, and Versions section in this chapter.

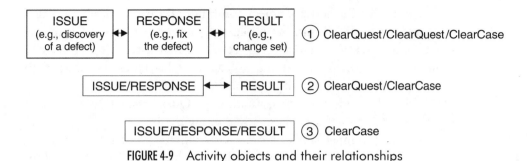

FIGURE 4-9   Activity objects and their relationships

ment or workflow product to track the assigned work. This task is associated with the defect record in the defect-tracking system. Finally, a change set is created in the SCM system that is linked to the workflow/project management task object.

In less complex environments, the issue and response are often combined into one object that reflects both the defect data and the task progress data. For example, a defect is recorded in a defect-tracking system. The defect record is then assigned to a given user and goes through a set of states to indicate work progress on fixing the defect. In these cases, the defect record is tracking both the "issue" and the "response." Often, the change set information is also recorded in the defect record.

In SCM-centric environments, where there is no defect-tracking system or a highly disconnected approach to defect tracking, a change set object is created to track the change set for SCM purposes only. The relationship between the change set object and any issue or task may be recorded loosely in a textual description.

Based on the complexity of your software development environment any of these approaches can be effective and efficient. Designers of the UCM model needed to take into account all three approaches and allow for increased activity information as a project grows in size and complexity. In UCM, a developer is always working with an "activity." That activity could be a simple change set, or it could be a more complex object that represents a defect or task.

ClearCase Activity Objects

An *activity* tracks the work required to complete a development task. It includes a text headline, which describes the task, and a change set, which identifies all versions that you create or modify while working on the activity. Activity objects are created in a PVOB in the stream in which they will be used.

In ClearCase UCM, the activity object combines all three concepts just discussed: issue, response, and result. However, the primary job of the ClearCase activity object is to track the change set or result. If defect-tracking or activity management software (such as Rational Software's ClearQuest) is used, then the change set portion of the activity lives in the PVOB, but all other activity data resides in the ClearQuest database. With ClearQuest, the UCM model can then support the other two approaches shown in Figure 4-6.

In any case, the developer simply works with activities. For information on activity-based SCM, see The Developer: Joining a Project and Doing Development in chapter 3. For information on how activities are exposed to the developer, see Making Changes in chapter 8. For information on how ClearQuest extends the UCM model, see chapter 11, Change Request Management and ClearQuest.

4.4   Versioned Objects: Elements, Branches, and Versions

The atomic object put under version control in ClearCase is referred to as an *element*. Elements are file system objects: files and directories. Every element records versions of the file or directory it represents. So, when a user checks in a file, a new version is created for that element. These element versions are organized into branches. A *branch* is an object that specifies a linear sequence of element versions. They are used for many purposes such as parallel development and maintaining variants of the system.

Each element starts life with a main branch and a null zero version that does not have any content. This is represented in ClearCase as `/main/0`. The first new version checked in creates version 1 on the main branch or `/main/1`. The organization of versions into branches provides a time-ordered representation of each element's history. The relationship between the repository (VOB), the elements it contains, and each element's branches and versions can be seen in UML notation in Figure 4-10.

ClearCase provides both a command line and graphical way to view an element's branches and versions, both called a *version tree*. A graphical example of

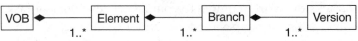

FIGURE 4-10   VOB, element, branch, and version relationships

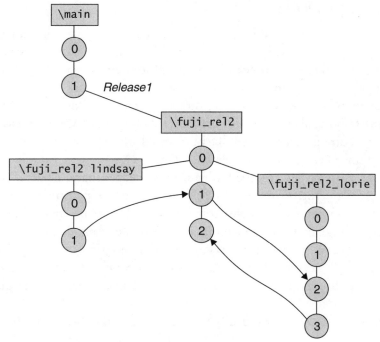

FIGURE 4-11   Graphical version tree

a version tree display is shown in Figure 4-11. Boxes indicate the branches. Circles indicate time-ordered versions as they are checked in. The arrows indicate merges of changes from one branch to another. The text next to a version indicates a label that has been applied to that version.

The following is the same version tree as shown in Figure 4-11 displayed from the text-based command line:

```
prompt> ncleartool lsvtree example.c
example.c@@/main
example.c@@/main/0
example.c@@/main/1 (RELEASE1)
example.c@@/main/fuji_rel2
example.c@@/main/fuji_rel2/0
example.c@@/main/fuji_rel2/fuji_rel2_lorie
example.c@@/main/fuji_rel2/fuji_rel2_lorie/0
example.c@@/main/fuji_rel2/fuji_rel2_lorie/1
example.c@@/main/fuji_rel2/fuji_rel2_lorie/2
example.c@@/main/fuji_rel2/fuji_rel2_lorie/3
example.c@@/main/fuji_rel2/fuji_rel2_lindsay
example.c@@/main/fuji_rel2/fuji_rel2_lindsay/0
example.c@@/main/fuji_rel2/fuji_rel2_lindsay/1
example.c@@/main/fuji_rel2/1
example.c@@/main/fuji_rel2/2
```

4.4.1   Directory Versioning

Directories are also versioned in ClearCase primarily to allow rebuilding of previous versions of a software system. Directories define the name space for files. This allows files to refer to other files either absolutely or relatively. Being able to rebuild previous versions of a software system is typically necessary to fix a bug in a previous release. Often if the directory structure has changed between releases, the build tools (e.g., make or clearmake) may not work unless the old directory structure is restored. Similarly, internal file references may be broken if files have since been renamed, deleted, or moved.

Like files, directories are checked out and checked back in whenever they are modified. Directories are modified during the following operations: renaming an element, moving an element from one directory to another, adding a new element, removing an element, or removing the name of an element.[3]

Typically, on Windows, the process is automated through the GUI. For example, if you select a file and say, "Add to Source Control," ClearCase checks out the directory, creates the new element, and checks in the directory, all in one operation.

On Unix, this is done specifically by checking out the directory itself, as follows:

```
prompt> cleartool checkout -c "adding new.c" sources
prompt> cd sources
prompt> cleartool mkelem -c "first version" new.c
prompt> cleartool checkin -nc .
```

In the last line, -nc stands for "no comment." ClearCase automatically comments all directory operations for you since it knows what you are doing. The period is Unix shorthand for the current directory.

4.4.2   Element Types

In ClearCase, each element placed into a VOB is of a specific element type. Element types can be used for a number of purposes, for example:

- to define what storage/delta mechanism is used for the element

---

3. Removing an element's name (rmname) is a ClearCase-specific operation because of the support for directory versioning. The command rmname removes the element from the current version of the directory, but not from the VOB itself (as does rmelem). In this way, earlier versions of the directory will have the element and later versions will not. You almost always want to do an rmname rather than an rmelem.

- to scope which versions are selected in a configuration (for example, "show me release 1 of all the design documents")
- to scope policy rules (see the Process: Labels, Attributes, Hyperlinks, Triggers section later in this chapter)
- to define the mechanism used for comparison and merging

ClearCase has predefined element types, which are primarily used to determine the storage, or delta, mechanism that should be used for the type. The predefined elements types are as follows:

- *File (file)*

Each new version of file elements will be stored as a complete copy. No delta computation is used for disk space savings.

- *Text file (text_file)*

This element type identifies the file as a text file and uses in-line delta storage[4] to store only the changes made between one version and the next. This is the primary type used for most text files.

- *Compressed text file (compressed_text_file)*

The compressed text file element type uses the same delta storage mechanism as the text file, but additionally compresses the delta file after changes are added. This element type is used to maximize disk space conservation.

- *Compressed file (compressed_file)*

The compressed file element type is used for files to which you do not want to have any delta mechanism applied but you want to conserve some disk space. Elements of this type are identical to type file, in that they are stored as a complete copy of each version. They differ in that each complete copy version is compressed.

- *Binary delta file (binary_delta_file)*

The binary delta file element type uses a delta mechanism that efficiently computes and stores only the differences between one version of a binary file

---

4. This differs from the forward delta or reverse delta storage mechanisms and is felt to be the more efficient mechanism for significant development efforts (see Delta Storage Mechanism in chapter 2).

and another. This type manager can significantly reduce disk space consumption if large binary files are being versioned regularly.

■ *Directory (directory)*

New versions of directory elements are stored directly in the VOB database, using an internal format. This element type is used to identify and manage directories.

Element types can have supertypes. For example, you could define an element type of c_source that identifies C files. This element type might have a supertype of text_file. In this way, the element type c_source inherits the storage characteristics of the text_file element type. The purpose of defining your own element types is for use in queries, configuration specification rules, and triggers.

There are some additional predefined types that build on the basic element types and have their own specialized compare/merge capabilities. These are as follows:

■ *Hypertext markup language (html)*

This element type is used to identify and manage HTML-formatted files. The supertype of an html element is text_file, so it also uses in-line delta storage.

■ *Microsoft Word (ms_word)*

This element type is used to identify and manage Microsoft Word documents. The type manager uses Microsoft Word's compare/merge tools. The supertype of an ms_word element is file, so the whole copy is stored.

■ *Rose Models (rose)*

This element type is used to identify and manage Rational Rose diagrams. The type manager uses the Rose model integrator to perform compare/merge operations. The supertype of a rose element is text_file, so storage is via in-line deltas.

■ *eXtensible Markup Language (xml)*

This element type is used to identify and manage XML files. The type manager uses new XML compare/merge tools to support parallel development of XML files. The supertype of an xml element is text_file, so storage is via in-line deltas.

If you are an advanced ClearCase user, you may also want to take advantage of the ability to define your own type manager for files that have specific compression/delta mechanisms that are proprietary to your company. Type managers also define how to handle comparing two (or more) versions and how to merge two (or more) versions.

4.5   Component Management: Components and Baselines

A ClearCase *component* groups files and directories that should be developed, integrated, baselined, and released together. The files and directories grouped into a ClearCase component usually implement a reusable piece of the system architecture (although this is not enforced).

Components are defined by identifying a root directory. That directory and all files and subdirectories are considered to be part of that component.[5] For more details, see The Architect: Defining the Implementation Model in chapter 3.

A version of a component is a *baseline*. A component baseline identifies zero or one version of each element that is contained in that component. Component baselines are used to configure a stream and ultimately to provide the right information to the view to determine what versions of the files and directories should be displayed.

▶ **Note:** Components have baselines the way elements have versions. When you change an element, you create a new version of that element. When you change elements in a component, you create a new baseline of that component. A stream groups together a set of component baselines. However, the concept of a projectwide baseline does not exist. Rather, when you perform a baseline operation on the project's integration stream, you are creating a new set of component baselines, one for each component that has been modified.

Each baseline has a user-defined quality or promotion level. That is, with ClearCase a company can define different levels of testing and can mark baselines indicating the level of testing that each has passed. This makes it easier to perform reuse since other project teams can determine what level of quality any given component baseline has reached.

---

5. In ClearCase 4.0, component root directories are limited to VOB root directories, so components are fairly large-grained pieces of a system corresponding to subsystem objects.

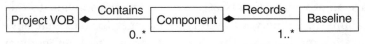

FIGURE 4-12   Project VOB, component, and baseline relationships

Figure 4-12 shows the relationship between the project VOB, components, and baselines.

4.6   Process: Labels, Attributes, Hyperlinks, Triggers

ClearCase provides a number of additional objects that are useful for a wide variety of purposes. In many cases, these are used by ClearCase itself to implement specific functionality, but they are also available to you when you want to automate or enforce project processes and/or record additional data and relationships between objects in the system. The major objects, which are often referred to as *metadata,* are labels, attributes, hyperlinks, and triggers. These objects have been used to implement specific project policies as part of UCM.

4.6.1   Labels

A *label* is an instance of a label type and is attached to a version of an element. A *label type* is a named tag that can be used to identify a consistent set of element versions. For example, you could create a label type called RELEASE1 and attach a label of that type to all the versions of the elements that make up release 1. Labels do not in and of themselves represent any semantics between elements other than those your organization defines.

In general, UCM users will be using components and baselines and should not need to create and manipulate labels themselves (this is handled by UCM automation). However, if a project using UCM needs to share code and interact with a project using base ClearCase, labels would be used. The UCM project would identify the label associated with a given component baseline for sharing outside that project. For sharing internally, a ClearCase label can be imported as a UCM baseline. Figure 4-11 shows how labels are displayed in the Windows version tree browser.

4.6.2   Attributes

Attribute types form a name/value data set that can have *attribute* instances attached to almost any ClearCase object. For example, you might create an attribute type called review_status, which has one of the values of passed, failed, pending. An instance of this type can be attached to each version of an element, indicating the code review status of that version.

Basically, attributes can be used to associate arbitrary data with objects in the system. Attributes can be attached to elements, baselines, branches, versions, hyperlinks, projects, components, and activities.

Attributes are defined to contain one of these data types:

- Integer—integer values
- Real—floating point values
- Time—date/time values
- String—character string values
- Opaque—arbitrary byte sequence values

Any of these can also have an enumerated list to restrict the legal values. For example, a string attribute type named priority could be defined as string, enumerated type HIGH, MEDIUM, and LOW.

4.6.3 Hyperlinks

Hyperlinks define relationships between objects. For example, a predefined hyperlink type "Change" links versions to activities, as part of the change set implementation.[6] Another predefined hyperlink type "Merge" defines merge relationships between versions on different branches.

You can define hyperlinks and use them to establish relationships between objects in your system. For example, if you store your detailed design documents in ClearCase, you could link these documents to the source code that implements the design or to the component containing the source code.

4.6.4 Triggers

Triggers are user-defined events that fire when ClearCase operations occur. Coupled with attributes and hyperlinks (as just described), triggers allow you to automate the creation of interobject relationships, attach data, and enforce policies based on ClearCase events.

---

6. When writing custom automation tools, you should not use this internal implementation for getting the change set. Use 'cleartool lsactivity' or the ClearCase Automation Library.

Triggers are of two different types: pre-event and post-event. Pre-event triggers fire before a ClearCase event occurs and can cancel the triggering event. They are typically used to enforce policies. For example, a pre-event trigger could disallow a checkin if the review_status attribute on that version was not set to "passed." Post-event triggers are typically used for notification. For example, after an event has occurred, e-mail could be sent notifying a project team that a key system header file was modified.

4.6.5   Creating and Managing Types

Use of any of the metadata types is a two-step process. The first is defining the type. The second is creating instances of the type. Element types and branch types also behave similarly. So, for example, you have to create an element type before you can create an element instance of that type.

ClearCase provides both GUI and command line access to creation and management of types. With Unix, administrators usually use the command line interface. The key command line operations are as follows:

- List type:
  ```
  cleartool lstype -<XX>type
  ```
- Make type:
  ```
  cleartool mk<XX>type
  ```
- Make instance of a type:
  ```
  cleartool mk<kind>
  ```

Where <XX> is as follows:

- el—element type
- br—branch type
- lb—label type
- at—attribute type
- hl—hyperlink type
- tr—trigger type

Where <kind> is as follows:

- element—element instance
- branch—branch instance

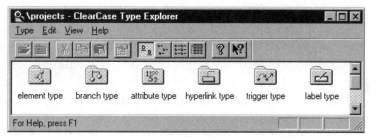

FIGURE 4-13   ClearCase Type Explorer

- label—label instance
- attr—attribute instance
- hlink—hyperlink instance
- trigger—trigger instance

On Windows, the Type Explorer application is generally used for managing types (see Figure 4-13).

4.7   Building: Clearmake, Derived Objects, Configuration Records

One aspect of configuration management that is often overlooked is build management. ClearCase provides significant functionality aimed at supporting reproducible builds, object sharing between developers, parallel builds, and distributed builds. ClearCase supports these best when you are using 'make' technology as your build engine. The key build features are described in the following subsection.

4.7.1   Build Audit

Typically, when a software system is built, many object files, libraries, and executables are produced. ClearCase calls these *derived objects*. Often, the traceability between the derived objects and the versions of the source used to produce them is lost, making it impossible to reproduce builds. This can lead to an inability to maintain, debug, and patch releases being used by your customers.

ClearCase provides a make-compatible build tool called *clearmake*. When clearmake is used to build derived objects, a record is kept of who built each derived object, when it was built, on what platform it was built, and, most important, what files and what versions of those files were referenced during the build. This information is called a *configuration record*. All the configuration records for all derived objects that are part of a build make up the *build audit*. ClearCase provides the ability to generate a bill of materials for any build (that is, what versions of what files were referenced for the entire build).

The build audit can be used to compare builds, allowing you to see what versions of what files are different between two builds or even what compiler options may have changed. A frequent problem in debugging is having an error show up in code that everyone is convinced was not changed. One of the big advantages of being able to compare two builds is the ability to quickly determine if something did change or if it was something in the build process itself.

4.7.2   Object Sharing

By keeping a configuration record for each derived object, it becomes possible to automate sharing of derived objects. This means that instead of rebuilding the same object, library, or executable over and over, it can be shared between developers. This happens automatically when using clearmake because clearmake can determine that the derived object you are about to build uses the same versions, same compiler, same compiler switches, and so on, as one that already exists. This derived object sharing can significantly reduce both the development build times and the amount of disk space required for each developer's workspace.

4.7.3   Parallel and Distributed Builds

Clearmake supports parallel and distributed builds on Unix platforms. Parallel building is the ability to run multiple compiles simultaneously by understanding the build order dependency graph described in the make file (i.e., the order in which files must be built, based on their dependencies). (See Oram for more information on using make to build your software projects [Oram 1993].) Distributed builds allow you to use multiple machines to perform build steps. This is often advantageous for performing nightly builds, as there are usually quite a few idle CPUs after normal working hours. For each machine that might be used in a distributed build, you can specify at what hours and what load limits that machine should be used. Clearmake uses this information to determine if/when it can use any given machine.

4.7.4   Clearmake versus Classic Make

Typically, 'make' build environments use a 'make depends' step, which stands for "make dependencies." This step parses the source files looking for language-specific constructs (e.g., 'include file.h') that indicate dependencies. These dependencies are used to construct the appropriate dependency rules in the makefile. When using clearmake and dynamic views in ClearCase, this is not necessary as ClearCase records these dependencies in the configuration record. This eliminates an extra build step (which is sometimes forgotten) and is more accurate since it is based on the files that are actually opened during the build instead of a parse scanning for language-specific include constructs.

Another advantage of clearmake over classic make is that clearmake uses the version information of the files to determine when a rebuild needs to take place. Make uses the date/time to determine whether a rebuild is required. So, for example, if you decide to reconfigure your view to see an older version of a file, clearmake will rebuild, but make will incorrectly conclude that a rebuild is not necessary.

Chapter 5 Establishing the Initial SCM Environment

The quickest way to get started using ClearCase is by creating one project VOB (PVOB), one source VOB, and importing your existing source code. However, this is only effective for small projects and small systems. For most projects, some advanced planning is advised. This chapter covers the information you need to know to do this planning and the steps you must take to set up the initial SCM environment. We will cover the basics of ClearCase architecture, discuss the hardware resource requirements for ClearCase, suggest some guidelines for taking a system from its logical design to its physical implementation, cover the creation of ClearCase VOBs, and discuss setting up component baseline promotion levels.

ClearCase installation and other administrative details are not covered in this book. It is expected that you will consult the ClearCase documentation set for installation and administration.

5.1   ClearCase Architecture Basics

The first step in creating any SCM environment is to obtain or allocate the necessary hardware and install and configure the SCM tool. This section gives you a high-level overview of the ClearCase architecture and makes some hardware configuration recommendations. Admittedly, the information provided here is a simplified view of the actual ClearCase architecture.[1] However, you should find it sufficient for basic planning purposes.

---

1. The ClearCase administration manual provides much greater detail.

ClearCase is a multiserver, distributed SCM tool that allows for a great deal of flexibility and scalability in hardware configuration. To understand the hardware resource requirements for ClearCase, you should start with a basic understanding of the ClearCase architecture. ClearCase is specifically designed to spread the workload across multiple machines. During evaluations, it is certainly possible to install and configure one machine to use ClearCase, but typically a ClearCase environment will consist of at least one server and several clients.

When determining your hardware environment for ClearCase, you must find a home for six types of processes and the multiversion file system (MVFS). The processes are as follows:

- License server
- Registry server
- VOB server[2]
- View server
- ALBD server
- Client processes (e.g., cleartool)

The multiversion file system is a client-side requirement and is used on platforms that support dynamic views.

5.1.1   The License Server and Registry Server

The two administrative processes are the *license server* and the *registry server.* The purpose of the license server is to manage license keys and ensure that the licensing constraints are not violated.[3] The purpose of the registry server is to maintain the directory and machine locations on which all view and VOB data is being stored. In this way, any ClearCase client can locate any ClearCase data regardless of where in the network this data is stored. The license server and registry server require very little in the way of server resources. The primary

---

2. In fact, there are three types of servers associated with a VOB. The actual number of server processes running depends on the load being placed on the VOB. ClearCase automatically starts additional server processes when needed and stops these processes when demand drops.

3. ClearCase includes its own license manager. ClearCase licensing is truly per user. A single user can be using ClearCase at his or her desk on a Windows machine and in a test lab on two Unix machines and only consume one ClearCase license. ClearCase licenses are floating and have a default time-out period of one hour.

consideration is that the machine on which these servers reside should be very reliable. Often, the license and registry servers are placed on the same machine as the primary VOB server processes.

5.1.2   The VOB Server and View Server

ClearCase VOBs store all the files and directories being managed by ClearCase. As such they are a global resource that most clients will need to access. Each VOB has a set of VOB server processes associated with it that handle read and write traffic to the VOB. For small projects at small companies, you may start with only one VOB. Large numbers of projects at large companies may have hundreds of VOBs. A single VOB can contain from zero to tens of thousands of elements (files and directories). The number of elements you place into any given VOB depends largely on three factors: how many people will be accessing the data concurrently, whether or not you take advantage of ClearCase's build capabilities, and the size of the machine on which the VOB server will be running.

ClearCase views provide a working set of files for a developer. ClearCase views have a small database associated with them, the view database, which keeps track of what files are being changed and what files should be visible to the user. ClearCase views tend to be used by a single individual. The number of ClearCase views you need depends on how many users and how many projects are underway at any given time.

The storage location for VOB or view data determines where ClearCase VOB and view servers will be running. Both the VOB server and view server processes run on the same machine that physically contains the VOB and view databases.

There are three basic configurations for VOB and view storage:[4]

- VOBs and views on the same server machine
- VOBs and views on different server machines
- VOBs on a server machine and views on client machines

These configurations are discussed in the Example Hardware Configurations section later in this chapter.

---

4. ClearCase offers additional options, such as splitting source code, build objects, and caches into multiple pools, that can be distributed across multiple disks or put onto high-end machines optimized for file services. These more complex scenarios are covered in the Clear-Case administration manual.

VOBs and Views on the Same Server Machine

It is possible to store both VOBs and views on the same server machine (see Figure 5-3 on page 104). This is usually done for demonstrations and evaluations of ClearCase. It may also be done for smaller teams that have limited client-side computing power. In this configuration, one server holds both the VOBs and views, and the client machine runs the ClearCase client processes. In general, this configuration is not recommended for a production environment.

The primary reason not to store views and VOBs on the same machine is that both VOB and view servers cache data and will compete for memory resources. ClearCase is designed as a distributed system, and one of the assumptions is that the VOB and view servers will be running on different machines. With the VOB and view servers on the same machine, both processes will compete for memory, I/O, and CPU resources. The problem you may encounter if you choose this configuration is slow performance. Typically, increasing machine memory or I/O capacity will alleviate the issue. However, ideally, the VOBs and views should be on different machines.

VOBs and Views on Different Server Machines

In this configuration, the VOBs live on one or more dedicated VOB server machines, and the views live on one or more dedicated view server machines (see Figure 5-6 on page 106). Users interact with ClearCase running client processes on their desktops. This configuration is primarily used by larger development organizations. It is appealing to organizations that prefer common central servers with lightweight desktop machines. This approach allows ClearCase server capacity to be easily increased. As more users come on board, you simply add more view server machines. As more source code is managed, you simply add more VOB server machines.

This configuration also has the advantage of making it easier for the administrator to back up view storage directories since these reside on a central server rather than on multiple desktop machines. This approach has two drawbacks. The first is the cost of purchasing one or more additional server machines. In the long run, this cost is small compared with the improved development productivity and reduced administration costs. Second, when an organization is using dynamic views, you may experience performance problems on the view server machine due to the MVFS, particularly on Windows NT. This configuration is recommended when using snapshot views in the split mode, where the view's database lives on the view server machine and the storage directory for the files resides on the client.

VOBs on a Server Machine and Views on Client Machines

In this configuration, the VOBs live on one or more dedicated VOB server machines, and the views live on the client machines. This configuration was the basis for the original ClearCase design and remains the preferred configuration for ClearCase (see Figure 5-5 on page 105).

In this configuration, views live on the desktop machine and communicate directly with the client-side processes. The benefits of this configuration are that you do not need to maintain another server machine and you reduce the amount of network traffic ClearCase generates. This may result in a performance improvement if you have a heavily loaded network. Another benefit is that users are generally better at managing their own disk space if the view storage resides on their desktop machine. The disadvantage to this approach is that it is much harder to back up view storage. As long as users check in their changes frequently, this is usually not a problem. However, if users rarely check in changes, the need to back up view storage becomes more critical.[5]

In short, a single server is recommended for the evaluation process; VOB and view servers are recommended for large organizations that have dedicated IS/IT groups using snapshot views; and VOB servers with views on the client for small- to medium-sized projects who maintain their own servers and large organizations that primarily use dynamic views.

Of course, mixed configurations are possible. For example, you could store user views on desktop machines while storing project build views on the VOB server machine.

5.1.3   The ALBD Server and Client Processes

The client machine is the primary machine for the ClearCase user. It offers a variety of end-user client processes, ranging from the 'cleartool' command line interface to many GUI interfaces such as the ClearCase Project Explorer or graphical merge tool. These client processes communicate with the license, registry, view, and VOB servers to perform their functions and provide the information a ClearCase user requires.

The ClearCase ALBD[6] server is a broker between ClearCase processes and data. It provides other ClearCase processes with the information needed to

---

5. It should be said that the practice of not checking in changes regularly should be discouraged. Key to this is ensuring that checkin is not also used as a means to promote the change to group visibility.

6. ALBD stands for the Atria Location Broker Daemon. "Atria" was the name of the company that originally designed and developed ClearCase.

locate and communicate with other ClearCase processes regardless of where in the network the processes exist. Typically, the ALBD server is set up as part of every ClearCase installation.[7]

5.1.4   The Multiversion File System

As discussed earlier, ClearCase supports two types of views: snapshot and dynamic (see Workspaces: Snapshot and Dynamic Views in chapter 4). Dynamic views do not have copies of the shared read-only files but rather provide them to the user directly from the ClearCase VOB. The mechanism used to deliver the files is the multiversioned file system. The MVFS is unique in the industry to ClearCase.

Most operating systems provide a file system interface that allows you to plug in different types of file systems (see Figure 5-1). For example, NFS is the network file system that can be plugged into a Unix or Windows system. NFS is dominant on Unix. On Windows, the NTFS and FAT file systems plug into the Windows NT file system interface. ClearCase uses this file system interface to plug the MVFS into the operating system. That is, the MVFS supports the operating system's file system interface, as does NFS, NTFS, SMB, and FAT. The result is that the MVFS appears similar to the predominant file system on both the Unix and Windows operating systems.

The key difference between the native OS file system and the MVFS is that the MVFS understands versioning. When a user opens a file, the MVFS uses the

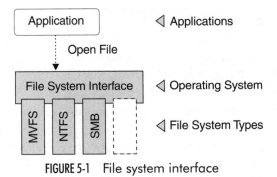

FIGURE 5-1   File system interface

---

7. The exception is a client-only install on the Windows platform. This installation favors snapshot views, where the snapshot view server is *not* running on the client. In this mode, there are no servers running on the client and so no need for the ALBD server.

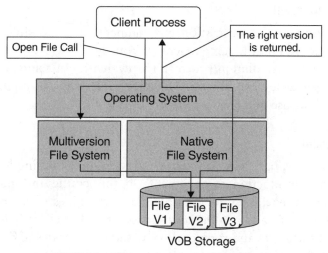

FIGURE 5-2   The multiversion file system

rules in the user's view to determine which version of the file to open. Because the processing is done at the OS file system level, any application such as Emacs, Vi, Notepad, or Word can seamlessly retrieve the right version of the file. In marketing speak, this is called "transparency." In other words, the version control and version selection are done in a way that is transparent to the end user and to any application accessing the data (see Figure 5-2).

The MVFS and dynamic views offer significant advantages, the first of which is transparency. Others are the time saved in updating or creating a workspace (since files are not copied) and the capability of build auditing (during the build process it is possible to accurately track what files are opened and read for any step in the build).

From an architectural basics standpoint, the key thing to note is that the MVFS is a client-side piece of ClearCase that does its thing on the client machine. To be clear, if you never create or use a ClearCase view on a VOB server machine, you will never need the MVFS on the VOB server.

5.1.5   Example Hardware Configurations

This section examines the hardware configurations of four common distributions of the processes just discussed.

Evaluation Environment

In an evaluation or demonstration environment, it is possible to install all ClearCase processes on the same machine. You should select a "server" configuration during the installation process. The evaluation machine and the Clear-Case server processes are shown in Figure 5-3. This configuration is not recommended for use in a production environment.

Basic Environment

For a smaller site, a basic environment configuration is the simplest when using ClearCase in a production environment. In this configuration, there is one ClearCase server machine and multiple client machines. The server machine holds all of the VOBs and administrative processes. The client machine has disk space to hold the views and runs both view server processes and ClearCase client processes. This basic environment is shown in Figure 5-4.

Modest Environment

The modest environment is easily scalable to larger project teams. You can add multiple ClearCase servers and distribute the VOBs across these servers. In this configuration, the clients still run the ClearCase client processes and the view servers for the views stored and used on the client machine. A modest environment is shown in Figure 5-5. The modest environment is also recommended for large teams who are primarily using dynamic views.

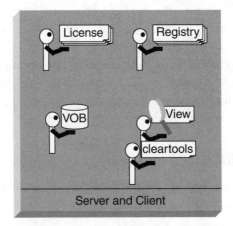

FIGURE 5-3   Evaluation environment

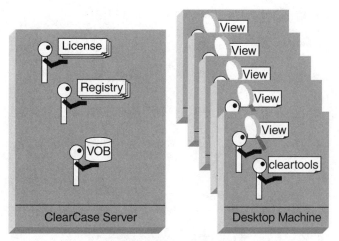

FIGURE 5-4   Basic environment

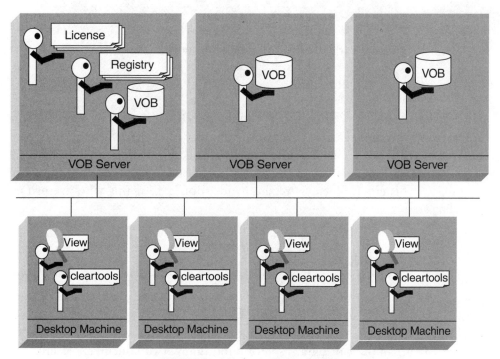

FIGURE 5-5   Modest environment

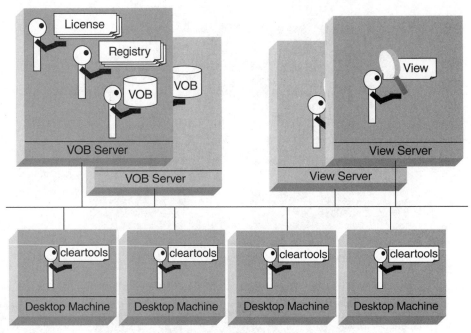

FIGURE 5-6   Complex environment

Complex Environment

For very large sites, it is often useful to introduce dedicated view servers. This makes administration easier as view servers are centralized. Larger environments may also have dedicated build machines used for project-level building. A more complex ClearCase environment, with dedicated view servers is shown in Figure 5-6. This environment is recommended for large teams who are primarily using snapshot views.

5.2   ClearCase Hardware Resource Requirements

One of the questions most often asked is what kind/size/make/model/type of machine should you use for a VOB server. The answer invariably is "it depends." Many factors contribute to what type of machine will be best for your company (e.g., amount of data, type of data, number of concurrent users, and build strategy). The information in this section and the following section on the client should be viewed as a starting point in your quest for the perfect environment.

The key to a well-performing ClearCase environment is a well-performing server machine. How do you ensure your server machine (or machines) performs well? Easy, buy the most loaded and most powerful machine you can because sooner or later you will grow into (or out of) it and you never know if your budget will get cut next year. However, if your company is like most, hardware resources are not always easy to acquire, and you may need to start off with what you already have. So, it is useful to understand where to apply your dollars with respect to ClearCase.

Typically, the VOB server machine is the most resource-intensive and the most critical. A VOB server machine is a machine that is dedicated to running VOB server processes. There may be more than one VOB on a single VOB server machine, and there may be more than one VOB server machine in the network. The key resources to consider when sizing a VOB server are memory, disk I/O, network bandwidth, and CPU. These are listed in order of priority to ClearCase performance with memory being the most important and CPU being the least.

5.2.1 Memory Requirements

VOB server processes, view server processes, and the MVFS do a lot of caching and background data writing. The best thing you can do to make sure you have a well-tuned ClearCase environment is to ensure that your server and client machines have enough main memory. Once a machine starts paging ClearCase data to disk, you can guarantee that performance will suffer. Memory is the cheapest way to improve ClearCase performance. Lack of sufficient memory is the most common cause of poor ClearCase performance.

VOB server machines should have a minimum of 512MB.[8] The rule of thumb is that you add up all of the database space consumed by VOBs stored on a machine and divide by two. This is the minimum amount of main memory you should have on a dedicated VOB server machine (see the Other Recommendations section later in this chapter for more on what dedicated means). You can use cleartool space or the ClearCase administration console to determine this amount. So, in short, for every 2MB of database space you have, you should have 1MB of main memory. The assumption here is that one-half of the data in a ClearCase VOB will be actively accessed at any given time. A more conservative approach, and one recommended if you have the resources, is to have 1MB of memory for every 1MB of VOB database size. This allows the

---

8. As of this writing, this pertains to ClearCase 4.0.

entire set of the VOB data to be available in memory at any given time. Since VOBs will continue to grow over time, it is also good practice to have extra memory on a VOB server machine.

For client machines, a minimum of 128MB of main memory is recommended. Many may feel this is too high, but this recommendation covers a minimum amount of memory for a software developer's client machine rather than specifically for ClearCase. There is clearly a trend toward Windows machines on the desktop, and often developers need many applications running at the same time. For example, a developer may have a defect-tracking tool such as ClearQuest, a design tool such as Rose, and an IDE such as Microsoft Visual Studio all open at the same time. If you add one or two ClearCase views and some ClearCase client processes such as the difference tool or version tree browser, the memory requirements quickly add up. To keep ClearCase views from paging their caches to disk, you need to ensure that sufficient main memory is available on the client machine.

In summary, memory is the cheapest and easiest way to boost ClearCase performance, particularly on the ClearCase VOB server machine. Check the size of your VOB databases periodically, and make sure you have a minimum of one-half of this available in memory for the VOBs.

▶ **Note:** For ClearCase 4.0, Rational Software documents a minimum configuration of 128MB on the server and 64MB on the client. Smaller sites (with a small number of VOBs and a small number of users) can experience acceptable performance with this minimal configuration, but because of the low cost of memory, I recommend starting with more.

5.2.2   Disk I/O Requirements

The second possible performance bottleneck in a ClearCase environment is the speed at which data can be written to disk. The key is to ensure that you have sufficient I/O resources on your VOB server machines. This is critical if you have a large number of VOBs on a single machine actively being written to. VOBs that are predominantly being referenced will not contribute to the need for fast disk I/O (unless you do not have enough main memory, and then I/O speed will influence the disk caching). Writing to the VOB takes place when you are using ClearCase's build facilities (e.g., clearmake) and during operations such as checkin, deliver, and baseline creation.

The following two recommendations will help you reduce I/O performance issues.

■ *Do not place busy VOBs on the same disk partition.*

Use multiple disks to balance the load. Technically, there is no reason why you cannot place multiple VOBs on the same disk. However, it is better to plan ahead and distribute the most often accessed VOBs on multiple disks.

■ *Make sure you have sufficient controllers to service busy disks.*

For busy read/write VOBs, there should be one controller per disk. Disk striping, disk arrays, and RAID systems can also improve performance. Having many disks "daisy-chained" to one channel is not recommended as data can be transferred to only one disk at a time. It is better to have controllers that support multiple channels if your controller is servicing more than one disk. Optimal performance results from having one dedicated controller and channel per disk.

5.2.3   Network Bandwidth and Reliability

Since ClearCase is a distributed application, adequate network capacity and reliability are required for good performance. Some pieces of ClearCase are more dependent on the network then others. For example, in order to use ClearCase, you need access to the license server; when you use dynamic views, files are accessed directly over the network from the VOB; and clearmake makes extensive use of the network to reduce build times by sharing binary files that have already been built in other views. Using snapshot views can reduce the reliance on the network—at the cost of not using other ClearCase functionality.

If you find that limited capacity and/or reliability of your network is causing your ClearCase environment to be suboptimal, there are a few recommendations to solve this. Machines hosting views and VOBs should be on the same subnet (i.e., there should be no router hops to get from one machine to another). If the local area network (LAN) is too saturated (i.e., you are seeing RPC time-out and NFS server not responding messages), you may need to add a subnet for Clear-Case machines or increase network capacity. In general, collisions greater than 10 percent are a problem in a ClearCase network. In short, you need to have a reliable network with sufficient capacity when using ClearCase.

5.2.4   CPU

In general, ClearCase is not a CPU-intensive application. Before you increase your CPU capacity, make sure you are really having a CPU problem on a server machine. (This is fairly easy to determine by looking at CPU loading and which processes are consuming CPU.) UCM use tends to utilize more CPU resources compared to base ClearCase. However, the most likely scenario you will encounter with ClearCase is that many active VOB server processes running on the same machine or that the VOB server machine is being used as a build machine. In the first case, you can try adding processors to the machine if it supports this. The most likely solution, however, is to move some VOBs to another server machine. In the second case, simply stop using the VOB server machine as a build machine.

ClearCase is a multiprocess application and as such can take advantage of multiple processors on a machine. However, you are not likely to experience improved performance past four processors.

5.2.5   Other Recommendations

Dedicated ClearCase Servers

VOB server machines should be dedicated to ClearCase.[9] Dedication means:

- No compiles, builds, or testing are performed on the VOB server.
- No ClearCase views are stored or used on the VOB server.
- No third-party tools, other than ClearCase, (e.g., Oracle or Sybase) are used.
- The VOB server does not act as a file server (e.g., no user home directories).
- The VOB server does not act as a mail server.
- The VOB server does not act as an NIS master or DNS service.
- The VOB server does not act as a Web server (e.g., HTTPD or IIS).
- There are no direct user logons.

The VOB server machine may act as a license server or registry server without any significant impact. In fact, for sites with one VOB server machine, it makes sense to have the single VOB server act as the ClearCase registry and license server to reduce the points of failure.

VOB Disk Space

When determining VOB storage location, allow room for disk space growth. New VOBs should have at least 50 percent free space on their disk partitions.

---

9. To be clear, there is no technical reason why you cannot run other processes on a VOB server machine.

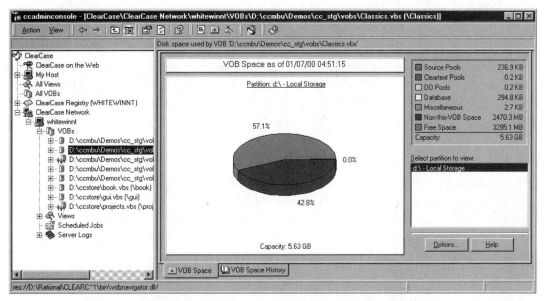

FIGURE 5-7   ClearCase administration console—VOB space example

The rule of thumb is to allocate 2GB of disk space per VOB. VOB growth occurs across four areas: database, source pool, cleartext pool, and derived object pool. The size of the database and VOB pools can be found using cleartool space or the ClearCase administration console (see Figure 5-7).

The four areas of VOB growth are:

1. *Database storage.* Every VOB has a database, which grows slowly over time. The size of a VOB database depends on a number of factors such as the type and amount of metadata used, event record history, number of directory element versions, and clearmake usage.

2. *Source pools.* Every VOB has one or more source pools, which contain all the versions for the files stored in ClearCase. The size of the source pool depends on the number of elements stored and the number of element versions. The amount of new data stored for each version depends on the size of the change itself and the type manager being used. For example, a whole_copy type manager will store an entire copy of an element for each new version, whereas a text_file type manager will store only the delta between the new version and the previous version.

3. *Cleartext pools.* Every VOB has one or more cleartext pools, which are file caches that store the most recently accessed versions of elements (this is called the "working set"). The size of the cleartext pool depends on how many versions of how many elements are being accessed over a period of time. This cache is predominantly used to support dynamic views. A ClearCase scrubber process is configured to control the size of this pool by determining how long unreferenced element versions remain in the cache.

4. *Derived object pools.* Every VOB has one or more derived object pools, in which ClearCase stores shared built objects, referred to as derived objects (e.g., libraries or executables). The size of this pool depends on the size of the system being built and the number of derived objects being shared between views. A ClearCase scrubber process is used to control the size of this pool.

5.2.6   User, VOB, and View Limits

The ClearCase architecture allows for a high degree of scalability since it can take advantage of additional hardware resources as the size of the system and the team grow. There are very few physical limits in the ClearCase application itself. For example, there are no technical limits on the number of users, VOBs, views, or elements. The maximum number of concurrent users any given VOB can support is highly dependent on many variables, such as the type of data in the VOB, how it is accessed, what the working set is (what elements are being access concurrently), what users are doing with the data, how/if clearmake is being used, the ratio of elements to derived objects, the amount of metadata in the VOB, and, of course, size of memory, disk I/O, network bandwidth, and CPU. There is a certain amount of system and administrative overhead associated with each VOB, so typically you should try to minimize the number of VOBs you use.

Ultimately, good performance is relative, subjective, and highly dependent on your own configuration and usage patterns.

5.2.7   VOB Sizing Considerations

The number of VOBs you need depends on the number of files and directories that make up the system you are managing, the number of concurrent users accessing those VOBs, whether users are using clearmake, what hardware server resources are available, what type of data is stored in the VOB, and the number of components in your system. The number of variables involved makes it very difficult to provide any general-purpose recommendations.[10] However, in this section we will look at some suggestions that should help you get started.

If you have fewer than 3,000 files and directories in your software system and fewer than 20 developers, then you can skip this section! Almost any machine being sold today will be a good-enough VOB server machine for small numbers of files and developers, and you should be able to put all your files into one VOB, as a bonus! However, if your project doesn't fall within these parameters, read on.

The type of data in a VOB affects concurrent usage patterns and, ultimately, performance. When looking at the type of data, explore two extremes: a VOB containing source code and a VOB containing documentation. In the case of source code, these files are changing and being built daily by some number of concurrent users. In the case of documents, these are files primarily being referenced and changed only occasionally. (Note: I would place HTML files that are changing frequently in the source code category.) In short, an active read/write source code VOB can accommodate fewer elements than a documentation VOB with no build traffic and fewer writes.

For example, if your VOB is holding source code and your team is doing software development using clearmake, then the rule of thumb is approximately 3,000 elements per VOB. Clearmake makes use of a lot of VOB server resources in order to provide derived object sharing and the build audit configuration records. If your team is not using clearmake, you can store more elements in that particular VOB—say, approximately 5,000 elements. If you are storing HTML pages or Word documents and these are primarily being referenced (i.e., the majority of the work being done by the VOB server is servicing read requests, not checkout/checkin requests), then a VOB can easily support 10,000[+] elements. I've seen VOBs whose primary purpose was to store design and process documents hold upward of 40,000 elements with no performance issues.

▶ **Note:** The number of lines of code and the size of the source code files do not have a significant effect on ClearCase performance. Rather, it is the number of elements (files and directories) that makes the biggest difference.

The number of anticipated concurrent users can also affect performance, but that number is largely related to hardware resources. That is, the more

---

10. By the time this book is published, Rational Software should already have some example hardware configurations for a UCM environment. Take these and extrapolate when establishing your own ClearCase environment.

concurrent users you have, the more hardware you may need. Also, when you have a few VOBs being accessed by a large number of users, it is often necessary to place them on different servers or at least make sure that they are on separate disks with multiple I/O controllers.

Here is one data point: During my first ClearCase installation, years ago, we used a SUN Sparc 20 as a dedicated VOB server, with 128MB of memory, two disk controllers, and 2GB disks. This supported four VOBs with approximately 1,500 elements for 20 developers using clearmake. This group grew to 40 over an 18-month period. The configuration provided adequate performance through this stretch of time.

5.3   Defining the Implementation Model

Defining the implementation model involves going from the logical design to the physical implementation of the system. Logical design elements, such as classes, are grouped into physical files and organized into physical directories. The Rational Unified Process calls this structuring the implementation model, whose purpose is the following [RUP 5.5 1999]:

- To establish the structure in which the implementation will reside
- To assign responsibilities for implementation subsystems[11] and their contents.

Moving from logical design to physical implementation is a very important step and if done incorrectly can cause problems. In *Large-Scale C++ Software Design*, John Lakos discusses this issue in a section entitled "Physical Design Concepts."

> Developing a large-scale software system in C++ requires more than just a sound understanding of logical design issues. Logical entities, such as classes and functions, are like the flesh and skin of a system. The logical entities that make up large C++ systems are distributed across many physical entities, such as files and directories. The physical architecture is the skeleton of the system—if it is malformed, there is no cosmetic remedy for alleviating its unpleasant symptoms. [Lakos 1996, p. 97]

---

11. The Rational Unified Process defines implementation subsystem as a collection of components and other implementation subsystems and is used to structure the implementation model by dividing it into smaller parts [RUP 5.5 1999].

This instruction applies to any large-scale software system, not just one implemented using C++. When defining the implementation model, it is important to take SCM into account. This is done by having a clear mapping between the high-level design entities and the high-level SCM entities used to manage groups of files.

When using ClearCase, you must establish a mapping between the architecture and ClearCase components. In UML terms, this means establishing a mapping between the logical design packages (implementation subsystems) and the ClearCase components that contain the files that will implement those packages.[12] The mapping should be at a high level in the architecture, usually the subsystem level. For small systems, there may be only one ClearCase component and no further decomposition. Systems with hundreds of components should not be mapped directly, one-to-one, to ClearCase components. Rather, you should identify a higher level in the architecture by grouping the hundreds of components into a smaller set of subsystems (see Figure 3-3 on page 60).

For both SCM purposes and good architecture, there must be a high degree of cohesion between internal elements of a ClearCase component and a low degree of coupling between ClearCase components. This is key for successfully mapping architecture to versioned components. David Whitgift explains, "Each item within the hierarchy should be cohesive: it should possess a single defining characteristic that relates its [elements]. The coupling between items in different parts of the hierarchy should be weak; in CM terms, this means that dependencies should be minimized" [Whitgift 1991]. Dependencies here refer primarily to build-time dependencies.

The implementation subsystems, managed in ClearCase components, should have clearly defined interfaces with other parts of the system and be independently buildable and testable, which allows for independent and parallel development of major parts of the software system by independent teams. This can significantly speed up development, as well as improve reuse and ease of system maintenance.

5.4 Creating the VOBs

Once you have determined how many ClearCase components you will need, you are ready to actually create the project VOB, source VOBs, and the

---

12. The Rational Unified Process defines this as the "implementation view" of the architecture. See [Kruchten 2000].

components. This section provides an overview of creating ClearCase VOBs and the use of administration VOBs. It is not a replacement for the ClearCase administration manuals. When actually creating VOBs, refer to these manuals for more detailed information. The purpose of including this information here is to give you a better idea of how ClearCase really works, which will aid in understanding later chapters.

As discussed in The Repository: Versioned Object Base section in chapter 4, there are two types of VOBs: standard and project. Any VOB can also act as an administration VOB, which store metadata (e.g., branch types or label types) that is shared among a set of linked VOBs. This section provides an overview of how VOBs are created on different platforms and discusses the use of administration VOBs.

5.4.1   Creating the PVOB Using the Command Line Interface

In this example, we will create a PVOB using the command line interface. This example uses Unix syntax, but the command line interface is also available on the Windows platform. The first step in creating a PVOB is determining where it will be stored. This means both which machine the PVOB server will run on and which disk partition it will physically be stored in. Second, you must determine where in the Unix file system the VOBs mount point will be created. Unlike, Windows, the mount point for a VOB on Unix can be anywhere in the file system. Typically, VOBs are mounted under a common mount point such as /vobs.

For an example, let's say we will create a PVOB mounted under /vobs with the name "projects." The PVOB storage will be on a machine called ccserver1 in a directory that has been exported as /ccserver1_store1.

To create the project VOB, you would log onto the machine ccserver1 and issue the following command (all on one line):

```
prompt> cleartool mkvob
        -tag /vobs/projects
        -ucmproject
        -c "My New PVOB"
        -public /ccserver1_store1/projects.pvb
```

Let's break this down:

- `cleartool mkvob` is the ClearCase command.
- `-tag /vobs/projects` is the flag that determines the mount point for the PVOB. That is the point in the Unix directory structure that end users will go to to access the data in the PVOB.

- -ucmproject is the switch that indicates that this VOB should be a UCM project VOB rather than a regular VOB that contains only file and directory elements.

- -c "My New PVOB" is the comment you enter that will be stored and displayed as the description for this PVOB.

- -public is the flag that indicates this PVOB will be used by a group of users on many machines. When using this flag, you will be required to enter the public VOB password set by the administrator when ClearCase was installed. This allows the VOB to be mounted on multiple machines automatically.

- /ccserver1_store1/projects.pvb is the storage directory for the PVOB data. The storage location must be a directory that is globally available from all client machines. If the local directory on the server machine (ccserver1) is different from the global mount point for the storage directory, then you can use specific options to the mkvob command to indicate this.

5.4.2   Creating the PVOB Using the Graphical User Interface

In this example, we will create a PVOB using the Windows graphical user interface. You can also create PVOBs graphically on Unix with a similar Motif-based interface. To begin, from the ClearCase home base you go to the VOBs tab and select "Create VOB" as shown in Figure 5-8. This starts the VOB Creation Wizard (used for creating any type of VOB), the first step of which is illustrated in Figure 5-9. In this illustration, we have called the PVOB "projects," filled in a comment field describing the PVOB, and checked the box that says this VOB will contain project data, thus identifying this VOB as a PVOB. In this example, the PVOB will store all the ClearCase projects for a fictitious company called Classics Inc.

5.4.3   Using Administration VOBs

ClearCase supports the ability to manage common metadata by using a single administration VOB. The ClearCase on-line help defines an administration VOB as "a VOB containing global type objects which are copied to client VOBs on an as needed basis when users wish to create instances of the type objects in the client VOBs" (see Creating and Managing Types in chapter 4 for more details on types and type instances). In short, an administration VOB is where common data for a set of VOBs can be stored and ClearCase will manage

FIGURE 5-8   ClearCase Home Base—VOBs tab

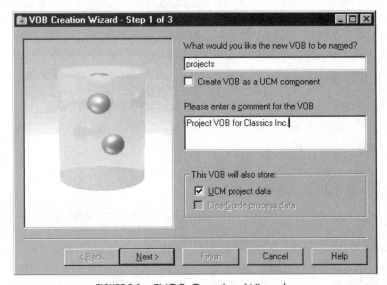

FIGURE 5-9   PVOB Creation Wizard

getting these common (or global) definitions of data types into each of the respective VOBs.

For a UCM environment, the PVOB serves as the administrative VOB for common metadata shared between the other VOBs containing component elements. See Figure 5-10 for an illustration of this.

If you are an existing ClearCase user and have already established an administration VOB for your site, the PVOB and VOBs containing component data may use the existing administration VOB (see Figure 5-11).

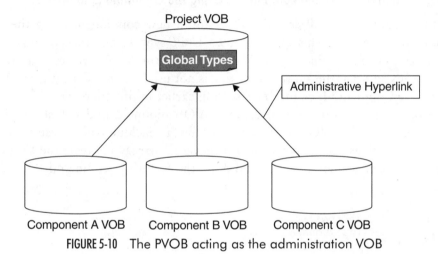

FIGURE 5-10   The PVOB acting as the administration VOB

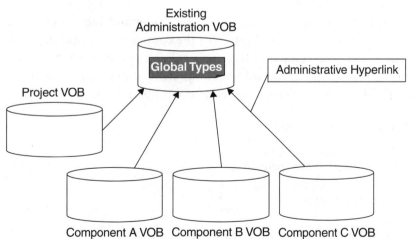

FIGURE 5-11   Using an existing administration VOB with a UCM PVOB

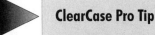

ClearCase Pro Tip

The relationship between an administration VOB and a client VOB is established by creating a special hyperlink between the VOBs. This is done automatically on Windows when using the VOB Creation Wizard. From the command line, it must be done separately from the VOB creation action.

5.4.4   Creating VOBs and Components Using the Command Line Interface

In this example, we will create a VOB and a new component using the command line interface. This example uses Unix syntax, but the command line interface is also available on the Windows platform. VOBs are created just like PVOBs, except that the -ucmproject flag is not used (see the Creating the PVOB Using the Command Line Interface section earlier in this chapter).

For example, you want to create a VOB mounted under /vobs with the name gui_comp. The VOB storage will be on a machine called ccserver1 in a directory that has been exported as /ccserver1_store1. To create the VOB, you log onto the machine ccserver1 and issue the following command (all on one line):

```
prompt> cleartool mkvob
        -tag /vobs/gui_comp
        -c "My GUI Component VOB"
        -public /ccserver1_store1/gui_comp.vbs
```

(Refer to the Creating the PVOB Using the Command Line Interface section in this chapter for a detailed description of the command line options shown here.)

When using the command line, you create the component object independently from the VOB. To create the component object that points to the newly created VOB /vobs/gui_comp, you issue the following command:

```
prompt> cleartool mkcomp
        -c "GUI Component"
        -root /vobs/gui_comp
        gui@/vobs/projects
```

Let's break this down:

- cleartool mkcomp is the ClearCase command.
- -c "GUI Component" is the comment for the component creation.

- -root /vobs/gui_comp is the root directory of the component. Remember that this must be the root directory of a VOB.

- gui@/vobs/projects indicates the name of the component is gui and the project VOB in which the new component object should be stored is /vobs/projects.

5.4.5 Creating VOBs and Components Using the Graphical User Interface

In this section, we pick up from our previous example, where we had created the PVOB called "projects." Our fictitious company, Classics, Inc., has a system that contains three components: database, core, and gui. The database component has all the code needed to isolate the database technology from the application. The core component has all the business logic and isolates the user interface from the key application algorithms. The gui component contains the graphical user interfaces. So, in this case, you need to create three VOBs to support these three components. Let's work through the creation of the gui component. From the ClearCase home base, you go to the VOB tab and select "Create VOB," as shown in Figure 5-8.

Unlike the command line, the VOB Creation Wizard can automatically create the component object when you create the VOB. In this case (see Figure 5-12), leave the box "Create VOB as a UCM component" checked. Name the VOB "gui." This will be used both as the VOB tag and the name of the component. Add a comment such as "Graphical User Interface software for Classics Inc." Since this VOB will not contain project data, do not check the UCM project box. Click "Next."

The next step (see Figure 5-13) is determining where the VOB data will be stored. The decision does not involve a user-visible storage location, but rather on which server and on which disk the VOB data will be maintained. VOBs must be backed up regularly. It will be this storage directory that needs to be backed up. On Windows, ClearCase maintains a registry for VOB storage locations. You will be asked to pick one when creating the new VOB. If you do not see a suitable directory, you can create a new global storage location or just use the Browse button to locate the correct directory. In our example, the storage directory is \\whitewinnt\ccstore. ClearCase VOB storage must be in a shared directory so that it can be accessed from the client machines.

In the final step (see Figure 5-14), you specify the administration VOB. Note that the VOB Creation Wizard offers you the project VOB as the recommended administration VOB. Take this as the default for the purposes of this example. Refer to the Using Administration VOBs section earlier in this chapter

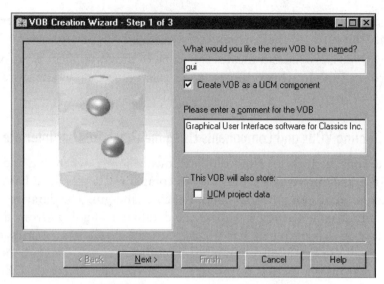

FIGURE 5-12   Step 1—Creating a VOB

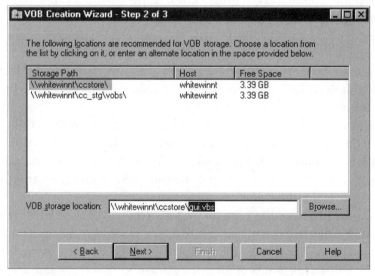

FIGURE 5-13   Step 2—Specify a VOB storage directory

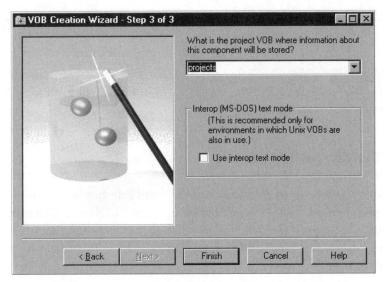

FIGURE 5-14   Step 3—Specifying the administration VOB

for more information on other configuration options. Click on the Finish button, and you have created your first VOB and component all at once.

5.4.6   Importing Existing Source Code

Usually, new software projects are not at the beginning stage when you introduce a new tool such as ClearCase. Often, projects are underway, using no version control or an inadequate version control tool. ClearCase provides support for importing data both from the file system and from other tools.[13]

Importing data is a two-step process. First, an export tool called `clearexport_X` is run, where X is the type of export you are doing. For example, if you have your software set up in a preexisting directory structure not under version control, you would use the flat file export tool `clearexport_ffile`, which produces a data file that is then used by the import tool `clearimport`.

The second step is to run `clearimport`, which creates new elements in the specified VOB and duplicates the directory structure and file elements that match the flat file directory structure. The import automation from existing

---

13. As of this writing, ClearCase 4.0 supports conversion from nonversioned operating system files and directories and these other SCM tools: SCCS, RCS, PVCS, and Visual Source Safe.

tools such as SCCS or PVCS is more intelligent and attempts to retain as much of these tools' metadata as possible.

If you use the export/import procedure multiple times, ClearCase knows how to create new versions for any pre-imported elements. This multiple import approach is the one used when managing third-party software components in ClearCase.

5.5   Baseline Promotion Levels

When using ClearCase UCM, you must perform one final administrative setup task: defining the promotion levels for component baselines. A baseline is a single version of a component. The quality or status of that baseline is indicated by a baseline promotion level. All components stored in a project VOB share a common set of legal promotion levels. This is to ensure a consistent definition of promotion level across multiple projects.

▶ **Note:** If different projects cannot agree on a set of promotion levels, they must be stored in separate project VOBs. However, this is not recommended practice if these projects will be sharing components. A common understanding of baseline promotion levels is key to effective project communication.

ClearCase UCM predefines a set of component baseline promotion levels, illustrated in Figure 5-15. Baseline promotion levels are linear. You can move a

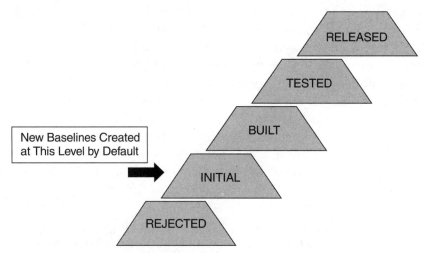

FIGURE 5-15   Predefined baseline promotion levels

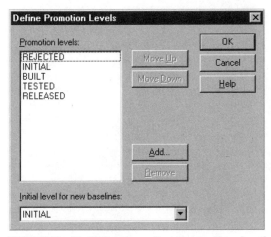

FIGURE 5-16   Defining baseline Promotion levels

baseline upward or downward. You must define at which promotion level a new baseline will begin its life. Within the out-of-the-box promotion levels, this is named "INITIAL."

From the command line, you redefine the promotion levels using the command `cleartool setplevel`. See the command line reference page in the Clear-Case manual for details, including the steps on how to rename an existing promotion level.

From the ClearCase Project Explorer, you can redefine the promotion levels by selecting the project VOB top-level folder and issuing the command "Define Promotion Levels" as shown in Figure 5-16. Once you have established your promotion levels, you have finished setting up the initial SCM environment. Now a project can be created, and development can begin.

Chapter 6 Project Management in ClearCase

This chapter discusses creating, configuring, and managing a ClearCase project and how the SCM project relates to an overall project for teams of various sizes. The ClearCase project policies are also discussed, including when and why to use each of them.

6.1 What Is a ClearCase Project?

Every organization has its own definition of a project. So, what is a ClearCase project conceptually? A ClearCase project consists of one or more people who are working together on activities to produce one or more artifacts. Typically, a ClearCase project represents a large development effort such as a major release or major iteration of a set of components or of an entire software system.

A ClearCase project defines the following:

- Who is making changes
- What is being changed
- How changes are made
- How changes flow from a developer's workspace into a release

6.1.1 Who Is Making Changes?

A ClearCase project organizes a set of people who are collaborating to produce new software component baselines. Depending on the size of the overall development effort, there may be one or more ClearCase projects.

ClearCase project use can be discussed using the five project categories defined earlier (see Five Project Team Categories in chapter 2):

■ *Individual*

An individual is not likely to use a ClearCase UCM project to manage his or her work since a lot of UCM features are designed to improve team productivity and communication. Typically, an individual would use base ClearCase functionality when doing mainline development.

■ *Small*

A small project team would have one ClearCase UCM project created for each major release of the product it is producing. For teams like this, it is important not to confuse "project" and "product." For example, a project may be "Release 3" of "Product X." In ClearCase, the project "Release 3" identifies a group of individuals working together to produce this major release. The team is working on "Product X," which is physically realized in one or more components.

■ *Modest*

Like small teams, modest teams would have one project created for each major release of the product or products on which they are working.

■ *Major*

Major projects consist of multiple teams collaborating toward a release of one or more products. In this case, each team would have its own ClearCase project. There would then be one central project, which would be used to collect the changes from each individual project. So, for example, if there were three components of the system—the database component, the core component, and the GUI component—there would be four projects defined for each major release. These projects might be called "Release 4 GUI" project, "Release 4 Database" project, "Release 4 Core" project, and "Release 4 Integration" project.

■ *Extreme*

Like major projects, extreme projects would have multiple teams defined for each release, but they would have even more projects per release than major projects. Extreme project teams may even have some projects that do not live for the life of an entire release, but rather only for the life of an intermediate iteration.

6.1.2   What Is Being Changed?

ClearCase projects define the scope of the work in terms of what part of the product a certain project team will be modifying. A project manager declares which components will be available for the project members to modify and which components will be available only as reference. This is covered in more detail in the Identifying Your Components and Baselines section in this chapter.

6.1.3   How Are Changes Being Made?

ClearCase projects also define how work will be performed on the project and what project defaults ClearCase should assume. Project policies are designed to provide a nonscripting, intuitive way for the project manager to determine how UCM will behave for his or her project. An example of a project policy is determining what type of ClearCase view should be the default for new developers joining the project. Project policies are covered in more detail in the Determining Your Project's Policies section in this chapter.

6.1.4   How Do Changes Flow and Get Integrated?

ClearCase projects define a fixed flow of change within the project. Each project has one integration stream where all the work for that project is collected. Each developer who joins that project will have a development stream and development view where he or she does his or her work. When developers are done, they deliver their work to the common project integration stream. This movement from development stream to integration stream defines the flow of change within the project.

In terms of configuration management, each project is insulated from changes going on in other projects. That is, each integration stream is isolated from other project integration streams (just like project integration streams do not see changes made in development streams until they are delivered). One project will not see changes from another project until you explicitly update it to a new component baseline or specifically merge changes from the other project. See chapter 8, Development Using the ClearCase UCM Model, and chapter 9, Integration, Build, and Release, for more details.

When defining your own ClearCase projects, keep these points in mind:

- For each project, you should define a project manager (or technical leader) who has ownership of the project.

- Be clear about the project/product distinction.
- Create only the number of projects you need to manage your development.

6.2   Creating a ClearCase Project

A Project Creation Wizard will walk you through the creation of a new Clear-Case project. This is shown in an example in the Creating Your Project section later in this chapter. However, before you run the Wizard, you should understand the decisions you will be asked to make when setting up a new project. The steps you will take are as follows:

1. Identify the project manager for the project.
2. Identify the components and baselines that form your project's foundation.
3. Determine the policies that govern your project's work.
4. Determine where the physical project object will be located.
5. Create your project.

6.2.1   Identifying Your Project Manager

Someone must create the project and be responsible for it. (The role of the project manager is described in The Project Manager: Managing a Project in chapter 3.) For ClearCase projects, the project manager should be a technical individual who understands SCM and the UCM model. Some organizations may refer to this person as a technical lead, project integrator, or configuration manager.

In any case, you must identify the person who is responsible for creating and maintaining the project. It is this person who will make decisions about how the project will be run and what parts of the system will be worked on. It is also this person who will actually create the ClearCase project.[1]

---

1. It is possible to have an administrator or tools engineer create the project for another individual. However, after project creation, a number of ClearCase objects must have their ownership changed. It is, therefore, more straightforward for project managers to create projects themselves.

6.2.2 Identifying Your Components and Baselines

One of the challenges of managing software projects is ensuring that team members are working on the "right" things—what pieces of the software system should be modified and what version of those pieces should be used as the starting point for those modifications. As has been discussed in chapter 3, An Overview of the Unified Change Management Model, one of the key benefits of UCM is that it uses a baseline+change model. This model provides a framework that ensures that only consistent changes move through the system.

When you start a new ClearCase project, you must decide which components will be needed to perform the activities planned for the project and which versions of those components will be used as the starting point (see Component Management: Components and Baselines in chapter 4 for more information on components).

The components and component baselines define the scope of work for your project, or what components that project must reference and modify. The baselines of the components you select are referred to as the foundation baselines for your project. Specifically, the *foundation baselines* define the initial configuration for your project's integration stream.

You define components either one component at a time or by specifying an existing project and inheriting that project's component list (for an example, see the Creating Your Project section in this chapter). You can also modify the component list or which baselines are being used by going to the Project Explorer, bringing up the property sheet on the project's integration stream, and then going to the configuration tab as shown in Figure 6-1.

Another aspect of defining the working configuration is deciding whether a component is read-only or modifiable. This is done as part of defining a project's policies and is covered in the next section.

6.2.3 Determining Your Project's Policies

One of the aims of the UCM design is to make it easy for a project manager to determine how UCM works. That is, you should be able to configure the UCM model without a lot of script writing. The means to do this in UCM is by determining project policies. UCM defines a set of policies that can be configured for each project by the project manager. Any person working on that project is then governed by those policies.

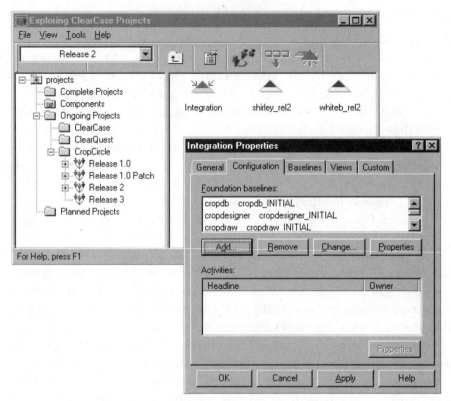

FIGURE 6-1   Project Explorer—Modifying the component list

The list of project policies will grow from release to release of ClearCase, but at the time of writing these are the project policies available:

- View type defaults
- Read-only components
- Recommended baseline promotion level
- Rebase to recommended required
- Deliver with outstanding checkouts allowed
- ClearQuest used/not used
- Predeliver validation (ClearQuest only)
- Prework on validation (ClearQuest only)
- Postdeliver notification (ClearQuest only)

You must decide if and how your project will use each of these policies. The remainder of this section describes each policy and the considerations to think about when choosing which ones to use.

View Type Defaults

Two of the essential functions of ClearCase are establishing and managing the developer's workspace. As discussed earlier, workspaces are called *views* in ClearCase, and two types of views are offered: snapshot and dynamic. Each type has specific characteristics that make it the best choice for different situations (see Workspaces: Snapshot and Dynamic Views in chapter 4 for details).

The view type default policy sets the default type of view presented when a developer first joins the project. The purpose of this policy is to allow you to optimize the choice of view type for both development and integration views on either Unix or Windows platforms. This allows new developers to get started using ClearCase without having to understand snapshot and dynamic views and to decide between them themselves.

If you do not set this policy, UCM will use its own internal default settings. These are dynamic views for both development and integration views on Unix platforms. On Windows platforms, they are snapshot views for development views and dynamic views for integration views.

Read-only Components

A project defines which components developers will have access to. One of the project policy settings is whether each individual component is read-only or modifiable. If a component is modifiable, developers are able to check out and make changes to files in that component. If a component is read-only, developers will not be able to change files in the component but will be able to refer to them.

Read-only components are typically used during runtime testing, during the build process of the components being changed, or for sharing between projects in a producer/consumer model (i.e., one project produces or creates a component while another consumes or utilizes the component). Figure 6-2 shows the project policy tab and how to mark some components as modifiable and some as read-only.

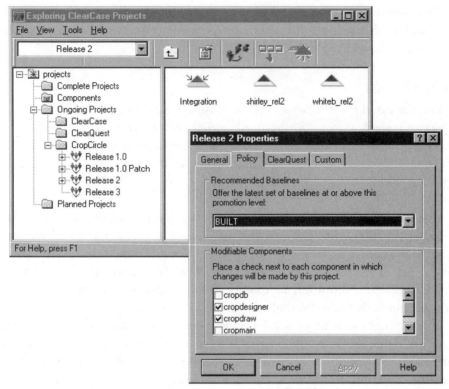

FIGURE 6-2   Project Explorer—Modifying project policies

Recommended Baseline Promotion Level

Each component baseline has a defined promotion level, which typically labels its quality characteristics.[2] For example, the UCM default promotion levels are "Rejected," "Initial," "Built," "Tested," and "Released." An initial baseline promotion level is assigned for all new baselines. For the UCM default, the level of "Initial" is assigned to newly created baselines.

The recommended baseline policy is used to define new baselines that are ready for use by developers on the project. That is, when developers go to update their development streams using the rebase operation, the recommended baselines become the default baselines.

---

2. These levels are defined by the configuration manager so as to ensure consistency across projects in a project VOB (see Baseline Promotion Levels in chapter 5).

You define a recommended baseline by choosing the promotion level at which a baseline may be used by developers. The latest baseline promoted to the level you chose becomes the recommended baseline for any given component and is offered as the default for rebase operations. Your choice of promotion levels depends on your own definition of them and how you perform building and baselining (see Staging and Release in chapter 9). Here are two typical examples:

- You lock the integration stream at some point at night and then run a system build and smoke test automatically. If the smoke test passes, your scripts create a new baseline and then unlock the integration stream. You ask your developers to perform a rebase every morning because you want everyone to keep up to date with each other's changes. In this case you want the latest baselines to be recommended as soon as they are created. To do this, you would select the "Initial" level in the default UCM promotion model.

- Let's say your build/test cycle is less automatic. You create a new baseline before you build. Your nightly build process and test scripts cannot automatically determine whether it was successful or not. Rather, a tester is responsible for verifying the quality of the built baseline before it becomes recommended. In the UCM default model, you would select the "Tested" promotion level as the one to make recommended. In this way, baselines could be created, yet would not be offered during rebase operations until after someone had verified the build and promoted the baselines to the "Tested" state.

The Recommended Baseline Promotion Level policy setting also determines the promotion level to which to promote the latest component baselines when the "Promote Baselines" operation is selected from the Project Explorer. Promotion levels can also be used for reporting purposes and to indicate the latest baselines that are in production in internally managed systems or Web sites.

Rebase to Recommended Required

The purpose of this policy is to allow the project manager to tune how often developers are required to incorporate updates from other developers into their own private development streams. This policy basically says that in order for developers to deliver changes to the project's integration stream, they must have their foundation baselines set to the project's recommended baselines or more recent baselines.

This policy in combination with the frequency at which you promote new baselines will enable you to tune the UCM model during the development cycle, allowing more or less isolation for individual developers. The choice of isolation and how often to force integration is covered in Isolation and Integration with ClearCase in chapter 9.

When you set this policy, developers must rebase to the recommended baselines prior to performing a deliver. In effect, you are saying integrate others' changes into your development stream and make sure they work with your changes before delivering your changes. This policy reduces the amount of build and integration problems that are discovered in the integration stream. It also assists in a more stable and buildable integration stream.

When this policy is not set, developers do not ever need to rebase. This works well if you are trying to develop as quickly as possible and project builds are not yet being performed. Usually, this occurs early in the development cycle. However, the longer this situation persists, the further and further apart each developer will get from working against the same code base and the more difficult integration will become.

I recommend that you always have this policy set, and you should use baseline promotion to control the amount of rebasing on your project.

Deliver with Outstanding Checkouts Allowed

This policy controls whether a developer can deliver a change while files in an activity's change set are still checked out. Only the checked-in changes get delivered, so this means the change set that is being delivered may not have been tested. This is called "delivering a partial change." This policy relaxes the consistency checking that is performed in the UCM model.

Here is one use case where it would be useful to allow partial delivery of changes: A developer is implementing a new feature, and she gets it partially implemented and working. She checks in all the files to save this intermediate working version. She continues working by checking out the files again. The next day the project integrator asks if the feature is ready. The developer says it is partially complete and is good enough for others to use. In this case, the developer would deliver the change (essentially delivering her own checkpoint versions) without delivering the changes she currently has checked out. Once she completes her changes, she simply redelivers the activity.

If you have less experienced developers, allowing this to happen may cause problems. For example, if a developer left a file checked out when he was done with a change and ignored the warning that Deliver provides, a partial and potentially problematic change could be delivered.

This, like all policies, is left to a project manager's discretion. I recommend you do not allow this flexibility unless you find your project team needs to use this feature. If you do allow it, make sure people are trained as to when it is appropriate to perform partial deliveries.

ClearQuest Used/Not Used

This policy simply indicates whether the project will be using ClearQuest, a software product that focuses on activity management, defect tracking, and request management. When this policy is enabled, your project will be using ClearCase and ClearQuest together. This policy also enables additional UCM features, which are described in chapter 11, Change Request Management and ClearQuest. ClearQuest offers your project more rigorous change management processes and additional policies.

It is possible to enable and disable this policy while a project is underway. For example, you could enable ClearQuest when your project is close to release and a more rigorous defect-tracking process is desired.

Predeliver Validation (ClearQuest only)

The purpose of this policy is to allow you to implement an approval process in ClearQuest that is validated by ClearCase before allowing a delivery to proceed. This policy enables a ClearQuest global hook script that is executed prior to a ClearCase delivery. This policy is available only when you are using both ClearCase and ClearQuest. The default behavior for this policy is to allow all deliveries.

For example, you might implement a global hook script that checked to see if the code review field had been filled in for any activity being delivered. The script would only allow deliveries of activities that had been code-reviewed. If the code review field was not filled in, then the script would abort the delivery.

Prework on Validation (ClearQuest only)

The purpose of this policy is to allow you to define what criteria must be satisfied before an activity can be worked on. This policy activates a global hook script that is executed prior to someone initiating work on an activity, whether it be setting work on the activity from ClearCase, checking out a file against the activity from anywhere, or performing a "Work On" action from

ClearQuest. This policy is available only when you are using both ClearCase and ClearQuest.

In default mode, this policy is not enabled. When it is enabled but no parameters are specified, then the policy defaults to requiring that the user assigned to the activity be the same as the one starting to work. If the activity is unassigned, this policy will automatically assign the user starting the work.

You can customize the behavior of this policy by modifying the ClearQuest global hook script. For example, you could specify that the script check to see whether the activity had been approved by a change control board.

Postdeliver Notification (ClearQuest only)

The purpose of this policy is to allow you to change the state of a delivered activity or to send e-mail notification that the delivery occurred. This policy enables a global hook script that is executed after a delivery has been completed. It is available only when you are using both ClearCase and ClearQuest.

The default behavior of this policy when it is enabled is to run the activities' default action. Typically, this is a state transition from an active state to a complete state. By default this policy is not enabled.

You can customize the behavior of this policy by modifying the ClearQuest global hook script. For example, you could have e-mail sent to the project integrator when an activity gets delivered.

6.2.4   Choosing the Location for Your Project

The ClearCase project explorer organizes projects into a hierarchy using folders. Before you run the Project Creation Wizard, you must determine where in the hierarchy you will create the project or whether you need to create a new folder in which to place the new project.

▶ **Note:** For organizational purposes, it can be useful to create three high-level folders in the project VOB that organize the projects into on-going, cancelled, and completed projects. This keeps on-going work easy to access.

Once you have created or located the correct folder for your new project, simply select it and use "File->New->Project" to begin the process of creating the new project.

6.2.5 Creating Your Project

ClearCase UCM provides a Project Creation Wizard to assist you in creating a new project. This graphical wizard is available on both Windows and Unix platforms. This section walks you through the Project Creation Wizard to give you a feel for what it takes to create a ClearCase project. For detailed information and instructions on creating a project, refer to the ClearCase documentation.

To start the Project Explorer from the command line, issue the command:

```
prompt> clearprojexp
```

Alternatively, you can access the Project Explorer from the ClearCase Home Base on Windows platforms and from the xclearcase GUI on Unix platforms. Then perform the following steps:

1. From the ClearCase Project Explorer, select a folder or the top-level project VOB in which you want to create a new project. Then select "File-> New->Project" from the pull-down menu. In this example, the "CropCircle" folder is selected (see Figure 6-3).

2. In the first step of project creation, you are asked for the title of your project and to write a brief description. The title you select is used throughout the GUI interfaces. In this example, we are creating a project titled "Release 3" (see Figure 6-4).

3. After naming and describing your project, you define your project's scope of work or start configuration. On this page of the Project Creation Wizard, you decide whether you would like to pick each component and component baseline by hand or whether you would like to inherit the component and baseline definitions from an existing project. If you pick an existing project (as shown in Figure 6-5), you will inherit that project's components and pick up the latest recommended baselines of those components. In our example, we have selected the "Release 2" project under the "CropCircle" folder as the basis for our project's release 3 configuration.

4. In the next step, you define the set of components your project will use and which baselines your project will start from. If you decided to inherit baselines from an existing project, this dialog will already contain a set of components and component baselines. If you did not inherit from an existing project, it will be blank.

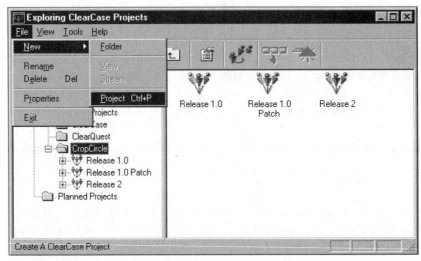

FIGURE 6-3   Creating a new project in the ClearCase Project Explorer

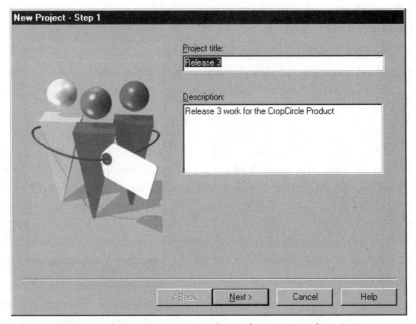

FIGURE 6-4   Selecting a project title and writing a description

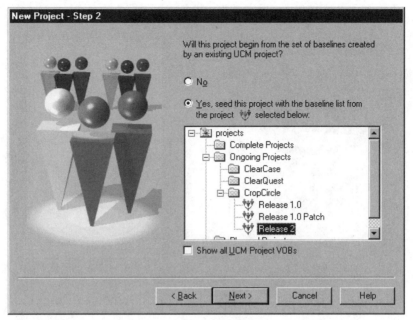

FIGURE 6-5   Opting to inherit component and baseline
definitions from an existing project

ClearCase Pro Tip

Most ClearCase UCM objects have both a title and a name. The title is used by the GUI interfaces when presenting the object. The name is typically used when referring to the object from the command line. ClearCase project names are automatically generated by the ClearCase Project Creation Wizard. If you are a heavy command line interface user, you may want to give the project object a more descriptive name. This is done by using the command `cleartool rename`.

At this point, you can add components, remove components, or change the baseline of any component by selecting a component and using the buttons at the bottom of the dialog (see Figure 6-6).

5. In the next dialog, you set the project policies that govern the work for your project. The component list can be modified later while the project is underway. In the example in Figure 6-7, you set the promotion level for baselines

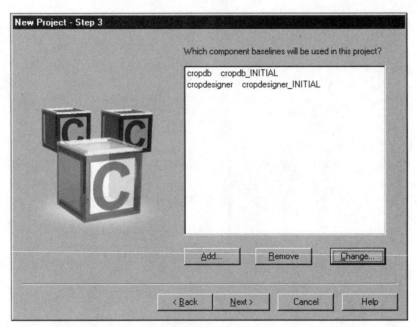

FIGURE 6-6   Modifying the component or baseline list

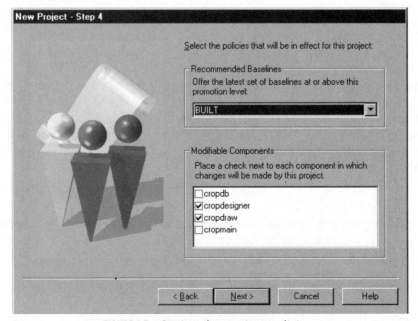

FIGURE 6-7   Setting the project policies

to become recommended and decide which components your project can modify. In our example, we pick the "Built" promotion level and make the cropdesigner and cropdraw components modifiable.

6. In the final step, you decide whether your project uses ClearQuest or not (see Figure 6–8). With the click of the Finish button, you have created your first project.

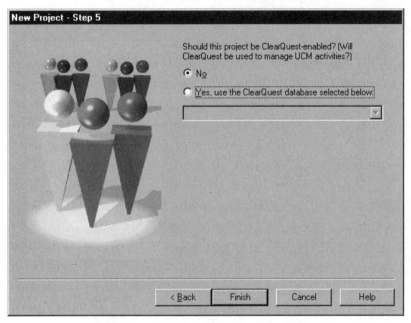

FIGURE 6-8   Opting not to use ClearQuest

Chapter 7   Coordinating Multiple Project Teams and Other Scenarios

This chapter builds on the previous chapter by discussing large, multiproject development scenarios and other interesting project situations including IS/IT application development, documentation-oriented project teams, small project teams, and support for teams who choose not to take an activity-based approach to SCM.

7.1   Organizing Large Multiproject Development Efforts

In large development efforts (major and extreme), there will be multiple projects working together toward one single release of a software system. In very broad terms, there are two approaches to organizing your project teams: by architecture and by feature. The approach you take impacts how you do SCM on your project. Generally, over the life of a software system, a hybrid approach is employed.

▶ **Note:** The differences, as related to SCM, between architecture-oriented and feature-oriented project teams are significant **only** when a change affects multiple components.

7.1.1   Architecture-oriented Project Teams

Architecture-oriented teams are organized along the same lines as the system architecture. So, in our simple example in chapter 6, we have one component each for the database, the core, and the GUIs. For a large system, we would assign one team to work on the database component, another to work on the core component, and a third to work on the GUI component. The relationship between components and projects is not always one to one. In more complex systems, a single team may be responsible for more than one component. For example, each GUI interface in an application may be stored in its own component, but a single GUI team may be responsible for changes to any of the GUI components.

Architecture-oriented teams have the following characteristics and effects on SCM processes.

- The teams generally remain the same from release to release (barring major architectural changes).
- Team member knowledge becomes specialized the longer they work in their product area.
- The integrity of the architecture is easier to maintain than with feature-oriented teams.
- The definitions and stability of component interfaces becomes very important to interteam coordination.
- Iteration planning is more complex since each iteration usually must demonstrate some feature. To demonstrate a feature that spans components, teams must produce baselines that implement pieces of the feature in their components. These components, when integrated, must implement an overall system-level feature.
- Integration is simplified as it involves assembling various component baselines rather than merging changes to common/shared code.
- Component sharing and reuse is much easier to accomplish because component interfaces must be clearly defined.
- Testing of a feature is delayed until all changes required have been performed in all components.

Organizations who wish to follow component-based development practices should organize their teams architecturally. The architecture approach requires more rigorous communication, planning, and coordination. If this is not feasible given organizational constraints, then a feature-based approach is probably preferable.

7.1.2 Feature-oriented Project Teams

Feature-oriented teams are organized based on major pieces of functionality to be implemented in a system. For example, if you had three major features, A, B, and C, planned for the next major release of your product, you would have three project teams, A, B, and C.

Feature-oriented teams have the following characteristics and effects on SCM processes.

- The teams and team members change from release to release based on what needs to be implemented.
- Team member knowledge becomes broader the longer they work on the product.
- The integrity of the architecture is more difficult to maintain than with architecture-oriented teams. This is due to the fact that team members are working across the entire system. They may know of functions they wrote or used in one component that would help them in work on another component. By making a function call in the code between components, they introduce a dependency between these components that may not already exist and may not be architecturally sound.
- Iteration planning is simpler since iteration planning is usually feature-oriented and a single team is involved for each feature.
- Integration is more complex. Since all the source code could potentially be modified by any feature team, integration often involves merging changes made to shared source files. Integration should be planned and performed as early as possible.
- Component sharing and reuse are very difficult without employing a hybrid approach in which key individuals or teams are assigned to specific components.
- Features can be more easily deferred (i.e., left unmerged), which is advantageous for risky features.

Feature-oriented teams are efficient for products that are in maintenance mode (i.e., only undergoing defect fixes or minor enhancements). Feature-oriented teams are often the best approach for legacy systems with monolithic architectures when rearchitecting is not a viable option. The feature-based approach is also useful for IS/IT projects because it minimizes the planning and coordination required.

7.2   Coordinating Cooperating Projects: Independent Components

In many circumstances you may have more than one project team cooperating on producing a final product release. For project teams that are organized architecturally (see the Architecture-oriented Project Teams section earlier in this chapter), it is easy to define producer/consumer component relationships between projects because only one project team is making changes to any given component for any given release.

7.2.1   Project Creation

Here is an example. Let's say you have a product with a core component and a GUI component. You are working on producing release 2 of this product. You have organized your teams architecturally so that you have a core team and a GUI team. For the core team, create a project that will modify the core component. Choose a baseline of the core component you want that project to work on, for example, baseline 4. Allow the core component to be modified. For the GUI team, create another project and include two components: the GUI component and the core component. Pick the same baseline (baseline 4) for the core component and a baseline for the GUI component. Mark the core component as read-only. You now have two projects whose component lists are illustrated in Figure 7-1.

7.2.2   Iteration Planning

The Rational Unified Process defines an *iteration* as "a distinct set of activities with a baselined plan and valuation criteria resulting in a release (internal or external)" [RUP 5.5 1999]. From an SCM standpoint, iteration planning is important because iterations usually mark key integration points.[1]

Let's look at iteration planning. As part of the work on release 2 in our example, you must define internal iterations. Let's say the application is a drawing application, and you would like to demonstrate to a customer a new feature to make sure it meets the customer's needs as early as possible, so you plan it for the first iteration (see Figure 7-2). This new feature is a drop-down dialog that

---

1. For more information on iterative development, refer to the chapter in Kruchten entitled Dynamic Structure: Iterative Development [Kruchten 2000]. For more details on the typical project management aspects of iteration planning, refer to the chapter in Royce entitled Iterative Process Planning [Royce 1998].

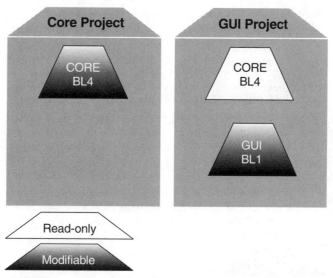

FIGURE 7-1 Initial GUI and core project component lists

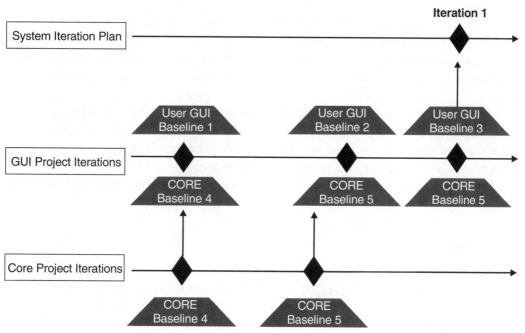

FIGURE 7-2 Iteration planning with multiple projects

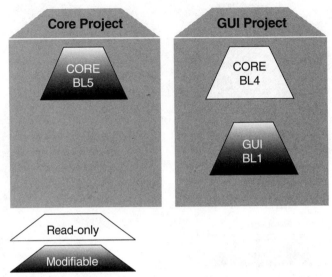

FIGURE 7-3   Project component lists (Core team makes changes.)

displays all the colors used so far in the drawing. Your architect determines that this feature will require the core team to implement a function that retrieves the colors in the drawing and returns the color list. The GUI team will then use this function and, based on the returned data, draw the colors in a drop-down menu.

So, the core team implements a dummy function with the agreed-on interface and creates their first baseline (baseline 5). They test this dummy function, and it successfully returns a fixed set of colors. The core team's project manager contacts the GUI team's project manager and indicates that a new core component baseline is ready for their use. The project's component list at this point is shown in Figure 7-3.

7.2.3   Integration

The GUI team needs to see the new function in the new core component baseline. To do this, the project leader for the GUI team modifies the component list for the GUI project, selecting baseline 5 of the core component. The GUI team rebases and finishes the implementation and testing of the drop-down dialog. Then, they create a new baseline of the GUI component, and iteration 1 is complete and can be demonstrated to the customer (see Figure7-4).

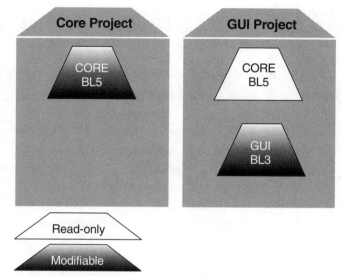

FIGURE 7-4   Project component lists (GUI integrates core changes.)

In iteration 2, the core team could continue and actually implement the code to determine the right set of colors, while the GUI team made any changes the customer requested. In this way, two architecture-oriented project teams could coordinate their work toward producing a final release of the drawing product.

7.3   Coordinating Cooperating Projects: Shared Components

In many circumstances you may have more than one project team cooperating on producing a final product release. Project teams that are organized around major features (see the Feature-oriented Project Teams section earlier in this chapter) will often share components with the result that they may be modifying the same components in parallel. Creating these projects is easy, but integrating changes is more complicated than in the producer/consumer case discussed in the previous section, Coordinating Cooperating Projects: Independent Components.

7.3.1   Project Creation

We'll use the same example as we did in the previous section. Let's say you have a product with a core component and a GUI component. You are working on

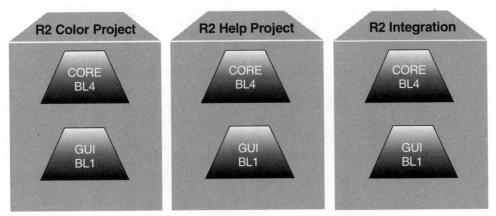

FIGURE 7-5   Feature-oriented project component lists

producing release 2 of a drawing application. There are two major features to be implemented for release 2: new color manipulation routines and interfaces; and an on-line help system.

You decide to organize your teams around features, so you create two projects: "Release 2 Color" and "Release 2 Help." You also create a third project, "Release 2 Integration," where changes will be integrated. You now have three projects whose component lists are shown in Figure 7-5.

7.3.2   Iteration Planning

Let's look at iteration planning. As part of the work on release 2 in our example, you must define internal iterations or milestones. You would like to demonstrate to a customer a new subfeature of the color manipulation routines and a piece of the new help system to make sure both meet the customer's needs. You plan this for the first iteration.

So the color team and the help team implement their pieces and both produce new baselines. Notice that in this case both teams produce new baselines for both components. They test their changes independently and decide they are ready for the first iteration. The three project component lists are shown in Figure 7-6.

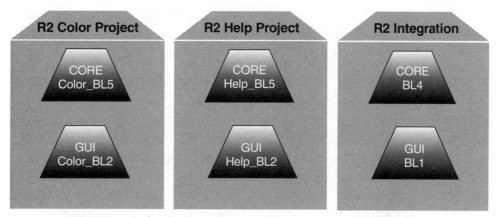

FIGURE 7-6   Color, help, and integration project component lists

7.3.3 Integration

The integrator for the overall "Release 2 Integration" project must now merge the changes from the Color and Help projects to create new system integration project baselines. This is done using the steps defined under Moving Changes between Projects in chapter 9. ClearCase merges any nonconflicting changes automatically. Conflicting changes require manual intervention. Any changes made to the same files by both teams are merged at this point, and the combined system can be built, tested, and demonstrated to the customer. The component baseline graph for the core component (see Figure 7-7) illustrates this integration work.

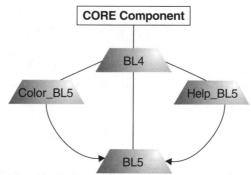

FIGURE 7-7   Core component baseline graph

For iteration 2, both teams would continue working on the full implementation of their features. Using this approach, two feature-oriented project teams coordinate their work toward producing a final release of the drawing product.

7.4   Coordinating Multiple Parallel Releases

As discussed in Parallel Development Support in chapter 2, it is not often that you have the luxury of finishing one release before you begin the next. A project that starts from an existing on-going project is called a *follow-on project*. Follow-on projects are supported in ClearCase UCM by the creation of a new project based on an existing one and the rebasing or merging of the final changes from one project to the next. When you have multiple releases, and therefore multiple projects, underway at the same time, it is good practice to establish a mainline project that is used to synchronize the source code. A *mainline project* is a project that serves as an integration and release point for multiple subprojects. Let's take a look at these types of projects.

7.4.1   The Follow-on Project

This section presents an example of the creation of a follow-on project, from an initial project to the completion of the initial project and through the merging of changes from the initial project with the follow-on project.

Your development team is working on the "Release 1.1" project. Release 1.1 is nearing completion, and it is time to stabilize the release and exert more control over what gets in and what doesn't. At the same time, you would like to get some of the development team members started on release 2.

From the Project Explorer, you would create a new project called "Release 2." When asked in the Project Creation Wizard, you would say yes to basing the new project on an existing project. By selecting "Release 1.1," you copy the release 1.1 component/baseline configuration to the release 2 project. The baselines of the selected components are the recommended baselines from the release 1.1 project. Work can now proceed on the release 2 project (see Figure 7-8).

When the release 1.1 project is complete or possibly at some intermediate interval, you will want to take changes from the release 1.1 project and incorporate them into the release 2 project. This process is known as performing an interproject Rebase.

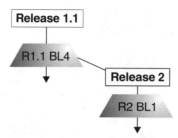

FIGURE 7-8   Follow-on project initial component baseline graph

To finish the release 1.1 project, you should do the following:

1. Lock the integration stream.
2. Ensure that there is no undelivered work.
3. Create a final baseline that incorporates all remaining deliveries.
4. Record the baseline that you created.
5. Lock the project and all the streams.

Once the release 1.1 project is finished, you need to Rebase the release 1.1 changes made since you started release 2 to the release 2 project. To Rebase the final baseline into the release 2 project do the following:

1. Navigate to a view attached to the release 2 integration stream.
2. For each new component baseline you recorded, run the Rebase command (e.g., `cleartool rebase -baseline X -gmerge`)
3. Resolve any conflicts.
4. Build and test the results of the Rebase.
5. Complete the Rebase (e.g., `cleartool rebase -resume -complete`)
6. Create a new baseline that includes the merged changes and promote them to the recommended status.
7. Unlock the integration stream.

Figure 7-9 shows the final baseline graph after the release 1.1 project changes have been merged into the release 2 project changes. This approach works well for a few releases. However, if you are developing many releases over many years, it can cause problems. These problems and how they are addressed are the topics of the next section.

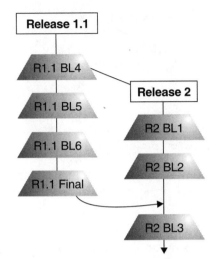

FIGURE 7-9   Final component baseline graph

7.4.2   The Mainline Project

This section discusses the problems with the follow-on approach and how the use of a mainline project solves these problems by providing an integration and release point for multiple subprojects. The primary problems with exclusively using the follow-on approach are losing changes, permanent divergence, and SCM tool failures due to infinite cascading branches. When you are managing many parallel releases, patch releases, and many operating system variants of a software system, it can be easy to lose changes or to allow parts of your system to permanently diverge. Most SCM tools use a mechanism to represent the structure of element versions. If you continue to branch off of other branches, you set up an infinite cascading scenario. Most SCM tools other than ClearCase will reach some limit in branch naming as branches continue to cascade.

The use of a mainline project avoids these problems by providing an approach to SCM that is well organized and includes points of convergence for the entire source code base. The approach is fairly simple: major release projects converge at the mainline project, from which follow-on projects are started. Typically, mainline projects are not used for doing development. If changes are made in a mainline project, they are typically changes used to stabilize a software system that is nearing the point of release.

Let's examine how the follow-on project scenario works when a mainline project is being used. The circumstances are the same as in our previous example. When release 1.1 is nearing completion and it is time to stabilize the release

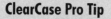

ClearCase Pro Tip

If ClearCase is used without UCM, the mainline project is usually managed on the /main branch. However, UCM does not use the /main branch in order to allow UCM and non-UCM projects to share the same VOBs. So, in the case of UCM, although you still create a mainline project, the actual branch being used will not be /main.

and exert more control over what gets in and what doesn't and when, at the same time, you would like to get some of the development team members started on release 2, you use the following procedure.

The first step is merging changes from the release 1.1 project to the mainline project, as illustrated in Figure 7-10. (Note: release 1.1 started from the mainline project baseline named "R1.0 Final.") The stabilization work for release 1.1 now shifts from the release 1.1 project to the mainline project. (Note: controls on who can make changes on the mainline project may be more strict since the release is approaching completion.)

You are now ready to create the follow-on project called "Release 2." When asked in the Project Creation Wizard, you would base the release 2 project on the mainline project instead of release 1.1. Work can now proceed in parallel on release 2 (see Figure 7-11).

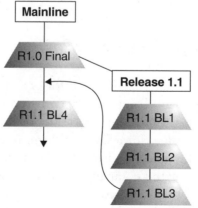

FIGURE 7-10 Moving release 1.1 changes to the mainline project

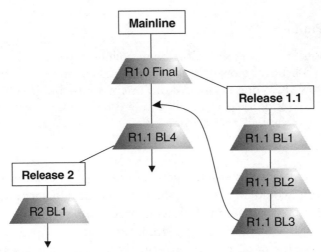

FIGURE 7-11   Follow-on project with mainline project

When release 1.1 is complete, you can incorporate any changes into the release 2 project exactly as described in The Follow-on Project section earlier in this chapter. Alternatively, you can wait until release 2 is ready for stabilization, at which point its changes will be incorporated into the mainline project. The prior approach is recommended because it results in earlier detection of any conflicting changes. Figure 7-12 shows the final baseline graph.

For comparisons' sake, Figure 7-13 illustrates the final baseline graph that would result if a mainline project was not used.

7.5   Coordinating IS/IT Development Projects

ClearCase UCM is particularly well geared for typical IS/IT development projects, which are often projects being developed by an internal group, where the system being developed is deployed for in-house or internal use. A good example would be a trading system for a financial firm. Because the software system is mission-critical for the financial firm, it is developed in-house. It provides a competitive advantage for the company's traders. It is not sold or shipped to other customers. The fact that the system is not sold and that it is deployed to a single internal customer distinguishes these projects from commercial systems. Web sites can also be good examples.

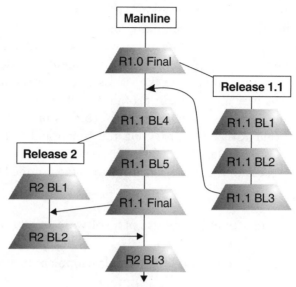

FIGURE 7-12   Final component baseline graph with mainline project

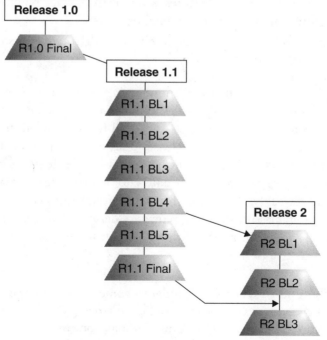

FIGURE 7-13   Final component baseline graph with no mainline project

The second thing that is unique about IS/IT projects is that the development group is controlled by the same company that controls the "customer" group. That means that the customer demands have a stronger influence on the development of the software system than with a commercial system. Commercial systems take in customer input from thousands of customers and must develop products in such as way as to remain profitable. Often, in-house systems have only one customer, and the internal software group is not held responsible for making a profit, but rather for providing the functionality the customer demands as quickly as possible.

The distinctiveness of these projects leads to some unique SCM characteristics, as follows:

- Typically, there is only one release of a software system in use at any given time.
- Major release planning and long-term development projects occur with less frequency.
- A procedure for performing emergency fixes is usually employed rather than rolling back to a previous working version.
- An approval process for features is very critical since planning is handled differently from that of commercial projects.
- A feature-oriented rather than architecture-oriented approach is common.

The single release installed and running at any given time is often referred to as the "production" release. The commercial requirement of maintaining parallel releases in the field is not an issue at all for these projects.

Parallel development of major releases does not occur as frequently in IS/IT projects. Rather, parallel development occurs on smaller features being added to the production system. There is usually no major release planning, rather releases occur biweekly, weekly, or for some organizations daily. Rather than planning the contents of a release, managers define what goes into the release by what is ready when the release occurs. If a feature misses a release, it just gets put into the next release.

▶ **Note:** These IS/IT systems will undergo some major change at some point, such as a change to a new version of the underlying database, an alteration to the platform the production system is running on, or a major re-architecting effort. While these major changes occur, parallel development of a planned release is taking place with changes to the current "production" system. Once the new system is ready, a switch-over plan is executed. The new production system is brought on-line, and the old production system is decommissioned. This is often a major effort for the IS/IT organization, as it can involve retraining of internal personnel and a Big Bang–style shift. This type of development is the same as that covered in the Coordinating Multiple Parallel Releases section earlier in this chapter.

In order to support critical bug fixes to the production system in between releases, there is often an emergency bug fix procedure that allows the production software to be quickly patched. How an organization performs this procedure is often overlooked, introducing many of the same problems described in chapter 2, Growing into Your SCM Solution. When designing an SCM solution, it is important to include this procedure if your projects and systems fall into the IS/IT category.

Finally, the planning of new functionality is usually done differently from that of commercial systems. Planning for each release's content is not usually carried out in as much detail. Rather, releases are performed on a periodic basis, and changes completed at the time of release are approved for that release. Changes are considered complete after defects and requests for enhancement have been collected and reviewed, any changes have been approved (allowing work to commence on that change), and developers have declared that in some way they are done. This declaration prompts an integrator or project manager to approve the change for inclusion in the release. The change then gets incorporated into the project's build and, once successfully tested, will be deployed along with others in the production environment.

Let's look at how to apply ClearCase UCM to this type of project development. First, you create a new project. Rather than naming the project "Product X Release Y," you may name the project by referring to the product being developed (e.g., "Product X").

> **WARNING:** Naming a new project after the product being developed is specific to the IS/IT type of project environment. It works only for smaller development efforts where a single project team is working on the entire product.

Once the project is created, development members can join the project as usual and work in their stable, consistent, and isolated development streams on their activities.

7.5.1   Choosing Which Features to Work On

Developers work on activities in their ClearCase view. These activities track the versions of the files they change and allow subsequent operations on those versions to be performed at the activity level (see The Developer: Joining a Project and Doing Development in chapter 3 and Making Changes in chapter 8). UCM offers two approaches to managing these activities.

The first approach requires only ClearCase. In this approach, developer's receive work assignments through whatever mechanism is available. This could be verbally, by e-mail, or by using their own defect-tracking tool. Once a work assignment has been approved, a developer would go to ClearCase and create a new activity in his or her development stream that represents that work assignment.

The second approach requires ClearCase and ClearQuest. In this approach, activities are planned and created in the system before being worked on. These activities can take the form of defects, requests for enhancement, or any other entity your organization tracks. These predefined activities are then assigned to particular projects and particular people. In this approach, developers do not create the activities themselves. Rather, they pick the activity from their to-do list. This approach is covered in chapter 11, Change Request Management and ClearQuest. With either approach, developers work on a particular activity in their development stream. Once they have completed their work, they can deliver it to the project's integration stream.

7.5.2   Implementing an Approval Process

If you are interested in implementing an approval process, the best approach is to use full UCM, which requires both ClearCase and ClearQuest (see chapter 11, Change Request Management and ClearQuest). However, if you are using just ClearCase, you can do one of two things. First, you can lock the integration stream and unlock it only for particular users. In effect, this approach says, "I will grant Joe the ability to deliver any activity." Second, you can use selective baseline creation to include only the activities that have been approved.

Once the activities are in the integration stream, you can lock the integration stream, build, test, and baseline the system as described in chapter 9, Integration, Build, and Release. Once satisfied with the resulting system, you can install/deploy it to the production machine and promote the baseline(s) to the appropriate level. If you have not defined your own baseline promotion levels, then you would use the default baseline promotion level of "Released."

7.5.3　Performing Emergency Bug Fixes

For emergency bug fixes to the production system, you should create a new development stream that will be used only for that purpose. The stream and view should be identified appropriately. When a new release goes into production, the integrator should update (i.e., "rebase") the emergency bug fix development stream to the latest production baselines of the system. After the update, the development stream will select the versions of the source code that, if built, would produce the current production system.

When an emergency change is needed, you go to the emergency bug fix stream/view and create an activity that represents the fix. The fix is then developed, built, and tested, in the emergency bug fix stream. You should then provide a procedure that enables the developer to create/install/deploy the system, built in the emergency bug fix stream, into the production environment. This is likely to be a set of manual steps or an automated script. Making sure the fix gets into the product and, more immediately, into the next "official" release is simply a matter of delivering it to the integration stream just as with any other change.

7.5.4　Planning for a Major Release

If you do need to run another major release in parallel, simply create a new ClearCase project based on your previous one and start work. This is described in Coordinating Multiple Parallel Releases earlier in this chapter.

7.6　Coordinating Documentation Projects or Small Teams

In some cases, the more advanced capabilities in the UCM model are not required. Two examples are projects that are doing documentation and projects that are very small. Projects with two to five developers working on one single software system are considered small (see Small Project Teams in chapter 2 for more details).

This section discusses applying the UCM model to these types of projects. It covers how you use UCM differently and what you give up by using this approach. Managers of these types of projects should also explore using base ClearCase functionality and just doing branch/LATEST development.

First, make sure your project actually falls into this category. The following are the consequences of giving up the UCM features not included in the approach discussed in this section.

■ *Developers cannot checkpoint their work.*

Checkpointing is the ability of developers to check in an intermediate version of a file they have been working on without the changes being made visible to other team members. In the approach described here, the Checkin operation makes the change available to other project members. If this presents a problem for your developers, then this approach is not for you.

■ *Development workspaces are not fully isolated.*

In this approach, if developers are using dynamic views, they will see changes made by other developers when those developers check in changes (not when they deliver). This can be desirable for very small teams (fewer than five members), as it encourages early integration. If your developers are using snapshot views, they will still be isolated until they perform a Snapshot View Update operation. If you want your developers to fully control when they see changes, you should not use the approach described here.

■ *Development workspaces may become inconsistent.*

UCM ensures that changes are moved around and made visible as a whole. That is, all changes made for a given activity become visible at the same time. The approach described here does not maintain this feature. Therefore, if multiple people are working on the same file or files, version skew can occur, creating an inconsistent development workspace. If your development team members frequently work on the same sets of files at the same time, then the approach described here is not for you.

■ *Deliver and Rebase operations are not performed.*

The approach described here involves everyone working in the integration stream. Since there are no development streams in use, Deliver and Rebase operations are not performed. This is a side effect of the lack of developer isolation, as just described.

■ *The entire system should be contained in one VOB.*

If you are considering this approach and you are managing a system that cannot be contained in one single VOB, you should consider using full UCM. However, if you have a system that can be contained in one VOB component, this approach can reduce some overhead (but at a cost as described in the previous points).

ClearCase Pro Tip

The approach described here explains how to use the UCM model to develop on a single branch using the base ClearCase branch/LATEST approach. This allows you to gain some of the advantages of UCM, such as change sets, without using all UCM's capabilities. In a way, this is similar to using view profiles without using the private branch functionality.

The basic idea behind using just the integration stream is that small teams or teams working serially on documentation require less isolation and so do not need the additional isolation characteristics of development streams and deliver/rebase operations. Simply put, everyone on these projects works in his or her own integration view attached to the common project integration stream. The following sections cover how this approach works.

7.6.1 Project Creation

The project leader creates the project as usual. He or she selects the single component that contains all the files needed for the software system being developed or all the documentation needed by a documentation group. Think of this as the system component or the documentation component.

7.6.2 Joining a Project

Developers or writers do not use the ClearCase Join Project Wizard. Rather they go to the Project Explorer, where they select the integration stream for their project and, using the right mouse context menu, perform a Create View operation. The View Creation Wizard will run with the appropriate settings.

Developers and writers can now work in their own integration views. They must still create and work on activities even though these activities are not delivered. This allows baselines to be created and ensures that operations such as comparisons between two baselines will report correctly which activities were implemented between baselines (see the Using UCM without Activity-based SCM section later in the chapter if you would rather not track activities).

7.6.3 Delivering Changes

One of the differences in this approach from using the full UCM capabilities is that activities are not delivered. Developers and writers make changes visible to other team members simply by checking in their changes. No Delivery operation is performed. Developers and writers must ensure that they check in all changes they have made at the same time to avoid introducing inconsistency. This is facilitated from the command line by using the following:

```
prompt> cleartool checkin -cact
```

7.6.4   Updating the Workspace

Developers or writers using this approach will see each other's changes differently from within the standard UCM model. With standard UCM use, developers use the Rebase operation to see changes made by other team members. Since development streams are not used in the approach discussed here, there is no reason for a Rebase operation. Rather, standard ClearCase mechanisms are used to make changes visible. The choice of dynamic or snapshot views is therefore more significant. In dynamic views, you will see other team members' changes the moment they check them in. With snapshot views, you will see other team members' changes only when you perform a snapshot view Update operation.[2] See Workspaces: Snapshot and Dynamic Views in chapter 4 for more information on how these views work and why you may choose one or the other.

7.6.5   Creating Baselines

The integrator may still create baselines to identify key versions of the source code or documents for use by other groups or just for historical purposes.

7.7   Using UCM without Activity-based SCM

If you are interested in using ClearCase and UCM but are not interested in activity-based SCM, there is a way to work around the system. Let's refer to this approach as the "kitchen sink" approach. This idea is simple: All changes made by a developer go into only one activity.

After joining a project, a developer creates a single activity. For example, if Joe is working on release 1, this activity could be called "Joe's Development

---

2. The snapshot view "update" operation is included as a part of the UCM rebase operation for snapshot views.

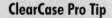

> **ClearCase Pro Tip**
>
> The primary reason you may want to use this approach is if you are an existing ClearCase user and want to gain the advantages of automatic configuration specification generation and baselining on a per-VOB basis, but do not want to introduce activity management to your development team. The advantages of automatic config spec generation should be obvious. If you perform labeling at the VOB level, then component baselining has many advantages, the primary one being the speed of incremental baselines over fully labeled VOBs.

Work for Release 1." Joe can associate the first checkout he makes with the kitchen sink activity. Subsequent checkouts will display this activity as the default, and Joe can simply use it. When Joe wants to make his changes available for the project, he uses the Deliver operation and simply picks the only activity that has undelivered work. Any existing checkouts are ignored by the Deliver operation. Subsequent checkins or additional checkouts can still be associated with the same kitchen sink activity, since UCM sees these as a reopening of an activity that was previously delivered.

The advantage to this approach is that activity-based SCM is ignored. The disadvantage is the same. For example, doing a comparison between two baselines will simply show one activity per developer and not really provide information as to what changes were made between those baselines.

The approach discussed in this section is not recommended in general because you lose the benefits of the SCM best practice described in Organize and Integrate Consistent Sets of Versions Using Activites in chapter 1.

Chapter 8   Development Using the ClearCase UCM Model

This chapter introduces ClearCase unified change management (UCM) for the developer. After reading this chapter, you should be able to find and join an existing project, make changes to files to accomplish an activity, deliver the changes associated with the activity, and rebase your development stream in order to see in your development view changes made by other developers on your project.

8.1   A Developer's Perspective of UCM

As a developer using ClearCase UCM, you must understand what project or projects you are working on, where your ClearCase views are located, and what activity or activities you are performing. Figure 8-1 shows the developer's workflow (see ClearCase UCM Process Overview in chapter 3 for more details).

The first step is to establish your working environment. ClearCase does this automatically when you join a project. The second step is to make changes to accomplish a specific activity (or task). This is done by checking out elements, making changes (editing files), and checking the elements back in. As elements

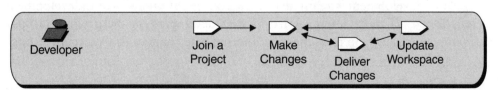

FIGURE 8-1   Developer process flow

are checked out and in, new versions are created in the VOB and associated with the activity you are working on. These versions are referred to as an activity's change set.

Once you have finished making changes and testing those changes, you deliver your changes to your project's integrator. This is done by performing a Deliver operation and specifying the activity or activities you wish to deliver. The versions that get delivered are dictated by the activity or activities you select using the activity's change set. On a periodic basis, you update your workspace (i.e., your development stream and development view) with changes that have been made by other developers on the same project.

The following sections describe these steps in more detail.

8.2   Joining a Project

ClearCase UCM organizes development teams into projects. For example, a project may be created to develop release 2 of a software system. You join a project in order to participate in that project. Joining a project results in the creation of two logical workspaces: one for doing development and one for integrating your changes with other developers' changes. As you read in chapter 4, A Functional Overview of ClearCase Objects, a logical workspace is implemented with two ClearCase objects—a view and a stream.

ClearCase UCM provides a Join Project Wizard to walk you through getting started. This GUI wizard is available on both Windows and Unix platforms.[1] The Join Project Wizard is available in the Project Explorer and the Project Tab on the ClearCase Home Base, shown in Figure 8-2.

When you join a project, ClearCase creates three new objects: a development stream, a view associated with your development stream (development view), and a view associated with the project's integration stream (integration view). You use your development view for doing development and your integration view for delivering and integrating your changes. Figure 8-3 shows the Join Project Wizard during the view creation step.

Your development stream defines a configuration for your development view, which isolates your work from other developers on the project. In your development view, you may check in intermediate changes to the secure storage

---

1. It is also possible to completely script this step by using the command line interface and by making all setup decisions.

FIGURE 8-2   ClearCase Home Base—Projects

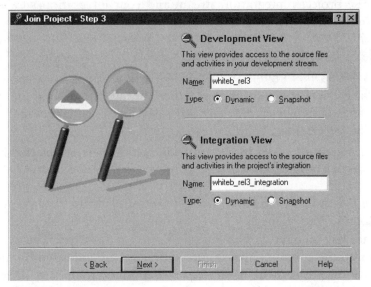

FIGURE 8-3   Creating your development and integration views

of the VOB without making them visible to other team members. The development stream's configuration also isolates you from other developers' changes. You can make changes to a stable baseline of the software without being disrupted by changes going on elsewhere in the project. You are in control of when changes are made visible (by performing a Deliver operation) and when you see other developer's changes (by performing a Rebase operation).

Your development stream/view selects element versions in this order:

- The version of an element you have checked out and are currently modifying
- If the element is not checked out, then the latest version of that element you have checked in
- If you have not modified the element, then the version from the baseline in the development stream (This baseline came from your last Rebase operation.)

The integration view you create is associated with the project's integration stream and may select different versions of the files than your development view. This view is used during Deliver operations, and its primary purpose is to allow you to build and test your delivered changes against the latest project sources. The project's integration stream and your integration view select element versions in this order:

- The version of an element you have checked out (typically this is checked out during an on-going Deliver operation)
- If the element is not checked out, then the latest version of that element that has been delivered by any other developer or changes made directly in the integration stream
- If the element has not been modified, then the version selected by the project's baseline foundation.

Figure 8-4 shows the relationship between streams in a project with multiple developers. The triangles on the bottom represent development streams, each stream has foundation baselines and a set of activities. The activities are delivered into the common project integration stream indicated by the triangle at the top of the project. The Rebase operation is used to update the foundation baselines of the development stream.

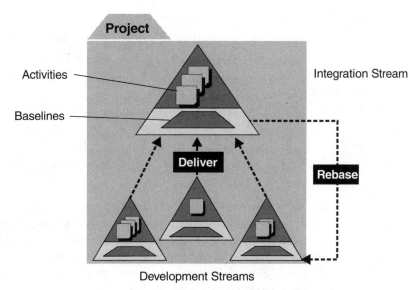

FIGURE 8-4 Project/view/stream relationship

8.3   Making Changes

The real work happens when you modify files and directories to implement a specific activity or task. The following sections discuss how changes are made in the context of the UCM model.

8.3.1   Working with Activities

One aspect of the UCM model is that it is activity-based (see the Activities section in chapter 4). This means all the versions you create when modifying elements must be associated with some named activity. You do this at checkout time.

If your project is using only ClearCase, you create these activities when you begin working. They act as kind of a supercomment for your work. ClearCase activities are designed to be lightweight and involve low overhead. If your project is using ClearCase and ClearQuest, then the UCM model uses Clear-Quest entities (e.g., defects and enhancement requests). Therefore, activities will usually already exist, be assigned to you, and be available on your to-do list when you start work. The complexity of an activity when ClearQuest is in use depends on the processes put in place for defect tracking and change request management (see chapter 11, Change Request Management and ClearQuest).

Either way, your responsibility is to ensure that the changes you make to a file are recorded against the appropriate activity. If you don't, the real benefits of activity-based CM cannot be realized. You will not be able to deliver complete, consistent changes automatically. You will not be able to see accurately what changes are included in an update to your workspace. Testers will not be able to see easily what changed from one build to the next. Release notes cannot be generated accurately and automatically.

It is up to you to ensure that the change set is accurately recorded against the correct activity. ClearCase UCM has made this process straightforward, using either the checkout dialog or the command line. In either case, the activity you select is remembered and used as the default for all subsequent checkouts until you change it.

> **WARNING:** The most common mistake made when associating changes with activities is to make two different changes in a file and then check in that file. In that case, you have just included two different changes in one element version. The UCM model does not allow you to associate two activities with one file version, so you would inaccurately record that this version includes changes for only one activity. The appropriate approach is to make one change, check in the change, check out the file again, and make the second change, thereby associating each checkout with the appropriate activity.*
>
> _____
>
> *Some SCM systems do allow you to associate two changes with a single version. However, once this is done, these two activities (changes) cannot be separated in an automated fashion. It becomes impossible to automatically include one of the changes in a build without the other. Because of this issue, the UCM model does not support associating multiple changes with one file version.

8.3.2   Modifying Files and Directories

To make changes you must be in a ClearCase view. When you check out a file, you must specify which activity you are working on. If your project is using ClearQuest, you will find pre-assigned activities available to be chosen from a pull-down to-do list query (which is part of the Check Out dialog). If your project is not using ClearQuest, then ClearCase will ask you to specify what you are working on by providing a brief description (e.g., "Fixing missing parameter to the readdata() function call"). Subsequent checkouts will present the activity you specify as the default. Figure 8-5 shows the Windows Check Out dialog. Notice you have the option of selecting an activity from the drop-down list, creating a new activity, or browsing other activities.

Once you have checked out, you can modify elements using any appropriate tool (e.g., an editor). Elements can be checked in and checked out again as many times as necessary when working on multiple activities or even when you

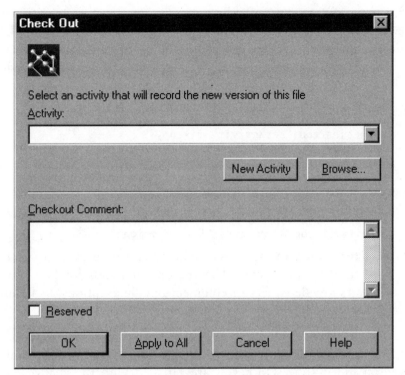

FIGURE 8-5 Check Out dialog example

want to store an intermediate version of the element in the VOB. The Checkin operation does not make the changes visible to other developers. This only happens during delivery.

8.3.3 Working from the Command Line

To create a new activity and make changes from the command line, you do the following (this example is for a project that is not using ClearQuest for change request management):

1. *Set your development view.*

```
prompt> cleartool setview john_hw_rel2
prompt> cd /vobs/hw_source
```

2. *Make an activity.*

```
prompt> cleartool mkactivity -headline 'fix copyright'
-instream john_hw_rel2  fixcopy
Created activity "fixcopy"
```

Here the user specifies the one-line description for the activity with the
-headline option (this is used when displaying the activity in the GUI). The
stream where the user wants to create the activity is specified with the -instream
option. The activity name (which is used to refer to the activity from the command line) is the final argument fixcopy.

3. *Set this new activity as the default for the current view.*

```
prompt> cleartool setactivity fixcopy
Set activity "fixcopy" in view john_hw_rel2
```

4. *Check out.*

```
prompt> cleartool checkout -nc example.c
Checked out "example.c"
Attached activities:
  activity:fixcopy@/projects "fix copyright"
```

Notice the activity that was set is remembered and used to associate the new
version with the fixcopy activity. The -nc option stands for "no comment."
ClearCase offers a wide variety of comment-handling options, including ways
to prevent users from not entering a comment.

5. *Edit, compile, and unit test.* At this point, the files you have checked out
are writable. Using your editor, you make changes to those files, compile them,
and perform unit testing. Once you are satisfied with the changes, you can
check in the files.

6. *Check in.*

```
prompt> cleartool checkin -cact
Checked in "example.c"
Attached activities:
  activity:fixcopy@/projects "fix copyright"
```

The -cact option is a shortcut that will check in all files that are checked out to
the current activity.

The final step, delivering the activity, is covered in the next section.

8.4   Delivering Changes to the Project

At some point, you will complete work on one or more activities. Because you
are working in isolation, you need to take additional steps to make the changes
you have made available to the project integrator. The process of making your
changes available is called a "delivery."

Delivering a change is a multistep process:

1. Check in any outstanding checked-out elements.
2. Rebase from the project's latest recommended baselines.
3. Run the ClearCase Deliver command.
4. Build and test the delivery.
5. Complete or cancel the delivery.

After delivery, your changes can be incorporated into the next project baseline and project-level build. The steps that make up a delivery are described in the following sections.

8.4.1   Check In Any Outstanding Checked-out Elements

When you deliver an activity, only the latest checked-in element versions will be delivered. Remember that you can check in multiple times without your changes being seen by other developers. You must check in changes in order to deliver them. If you deliver an activity and it has outstanding checkouts, the changes in the checked-out files will not get delivered.

There are a number of ways to search for outstanding checkouts. First, the Deliver operation will warn you that you have outstanding checkouts (see Figure 8-6). Second, you can use the list checkouts GUI to find checkouts. Third, you can go to the activities change set either from the ClearCase Project Explorer or from ClearQuest (if your project is using ClearQuest) and check in from the Change Set tab (see Figure 8-7).

From the command line, you can specify a few options to the Checkin command. The -cact option will check in all outstanding checkouts against the default activity set in the view. Alternatively, you can specify a specific activity. In this case, ClearCase will check in all outstanding checkouts that exist for that activity. The following examples show these command line options.

```
prompt> cleartool checkin -cact
prompt> cleartool checkin <activity selector>
```

▶ **Note:** It is still possible to deliver an activity that has outstanding checkouts if the project's policy allows this (see Deliver with Outstanding Checkouts Allowed in chapter 6). This is primarily used when you need to deliver intermediate changes for an activity on which you are not yet finished working. The Deliver operation will deliver the work you have checked in, ignoring any change in the checked-out files.

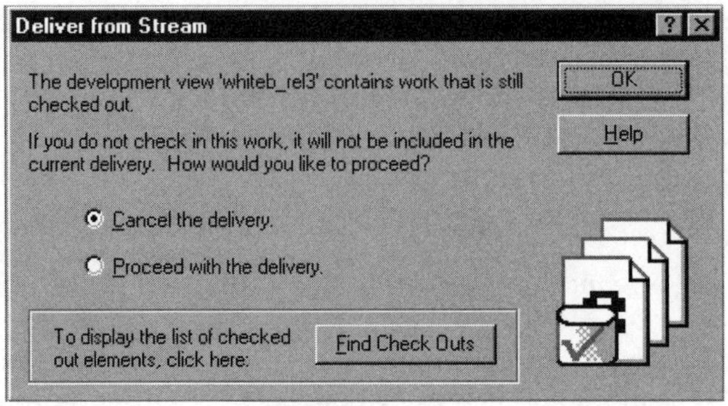

FIGURE 8-6   Deliver outstanding checkouts warning dialog

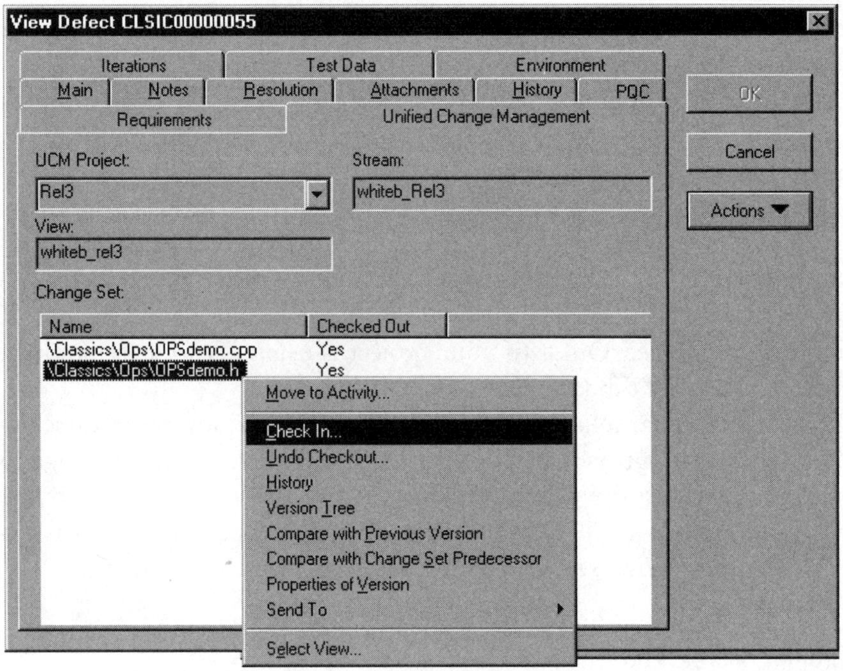

FIGURE 8-7   Activities properties—showing checkouts

8.4.2 Rebase from the Project's Latest Recommended Baselines

You should always consider whether to rebase your development stream prior to delivery. Rebase (described later in this chapter) updates your development stream and view with changes that have been delivered by other project members and incorporated into baselines. By rebasing before delivering, you are integrating your changes with other developers' changes in your own private working environment. This usually makes deliveries go more smoothly and means less integration work will need to be performed in the integration stream.

While it is good practice to rebase prior to delivery, you may be required to rebase to the project's latest recommended baseline if your project leader has set this project policy (see Rebase to Recommended Required in chapter 6).

8.4.3 Run the ClearCase Deliver Command

ClearCase has a Deliver command that is used to deliver the work done to satisfy one or more activities. This command can be issued from the ClearCase Home Base (see Figure 8-2), the ClearCase Project Explorer, or a number of IDEs such as Visual Studio. A delivery can also be started from the command line via the following command:

```
prompt> cleartool deliver
```

By default, all the activities in your development stream that have undelivered changes will be delivered. You can deselect activities in the GUI (see Figure 8-8). From the command line, you can specify a particular set of activities as

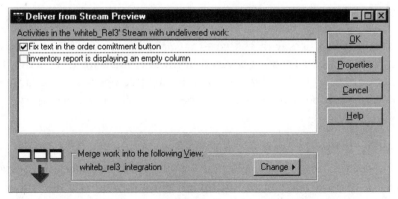

FIGURE 8-8   Deliver activities—Graphical user interface

part of the Deliver command. You can also see what activities would be delivered without actually performing a delivery using the following code:

```
prompt> cleartool deliver -preview
```

▶ **Note:** As with many ClearCase command line operations, you can specify the -graphical switch to the Deliver command if you want to use the GUI for this particular operation.

▶ **Note:** When you are working on two or more activities in the same development stream and modifying the same elements for both activities, you may be required to deliver the set of activities together. For example, you are working on two activities: A and B. You start working on A and check out a file named system.h. You make changes to system.h and check it in, creating version A1. Without delivering A, you start working on activity B. In the course of working on activity B, you also check out and check in system.h creating version B1. Since you are working on both of these activities in the same development stream, version B1 includes the previously made A1 changes. In this example, you would be allowed to deliver activity A by itself. You would also be allowed to deliver A and B together. However, ClearCase would not allow you to deliver just B since the B1 version of system.h also includes a partial piece of the A1 change. This is part of how the UCM model ensures you deliver a consistent set of changes.

The work performed by the Deliver operation occurs in your integration view. In this view, the elements you have modified in your development view will be checked out, and your changes will be merged from your development stream to your integration stream.

In most cases, this step will happen automatically. In some cases, you may have to resolve conflicts with changes that have been made by other developers on your team. This situation is covered in the Dealing with Conflicting Changes section later in this chapter. Delivery is a restartable operation, so large or complex deliveries can be done over the course of days/logins if necessary.

8.4.4   Build and Test the Delivery

After the initial deliver step has finished, you will have elements checked out in your integration view. These will be the same elements that make up the change set for the activities you delivered.

You should now verify your delivery before you commit it. What you do to verify a delivery will depend on your organization's policies. In general, you should ensure that your changes build in the integration view. It is also good practice to make sure that you unit-test your changes.

You might ask, "If I rebase before I deliver, do I need to do any testing?" The answer is, you should. There is a difference between testing in your environment after a rebase and testing in the integration view. Any activities that have been delivered by other developers, but have not yet been incorporated into a recommended baseline, will be seen in your integration view, but will not have been part of the rebase operation. The testing in the integration view is, basically, testing your changes with the absolute latest and greatest changes for your project.

In some companies, you are expected to make sure your changes work with the latest and greatest. In this case, you should build and perform unit testing in the integration view before proceeding. In other companies, an integrator is responsible for making sure everything works together. In this case, simply verifying that your changes build in the integration view is sufficient. It is always a good idea to review automated merges by comparing the checked-out versions with their predecessors; it can be done easily from the activities property sheet.

8.4.5   Complete or Cancel the Delivery

The final step is to either complete or cancel the delivery. Completing the delivery checks in all the changes to the project's integration stream. Once completed, a delivery cannot be undone. If you are not satisfied with the results of the delivery, you can cancel the delivery. Canceling a delivery cancels all checkouts in the integration view and removes any record of the delivery. You can deliver these changes later, after a cancel.

From the GUI, this can be done from the final Deliver dialog or by restarting the Deliver operation if the dialog has been dismissed. From the command line, use the following code:

```
prompt> cleartool deliver -complete
prompt> cleartool deliver -cancel
```

8.5   Rebasing Your Development Stream

Your development view selects a stable set of element versions. You will always see the same versions in your development view unless you do something to change them. Periodically, you need to update your development stream's configuration, thus updating the versions of the elements displayed in your view. This is done using a command called *Rebase*. Rebase updates your development environment, making changes other developers have made visible to you.

When you Rebase, you do not get the latest and greatest element versions. Those versions may be broken or may not even build together. Rather, you receive a stable set of baselines. The project integrator creates new project baselines, builds, and tests them. Once a set of baselines has reached a known level of stability (generally, this means it has passed some level of testing), the integrator declares the baselines as the recommended baselines (see chapter 9, Integration, Build, and Release, for more detail on the integrator's work). The recommended baselines are presented to you as the default when you rebase.

▶ **Note:** It is possible to override these default baselines, choosing either older or newer baselines. However, it is a good idea to accept the recommended baselines until you get familiar with ClearCase UCM.

Rebasing is a multistep process, as follows:

1. Run the rebase operation.
2. Build and test.
3. Complete or cancel the rebase.

These steps are described in the following sections.

8.5.1   Run the Rebase Operation

The ClearCase Rebase command can be issued from the ClearCase Home Base (see Figure 8-2), the ClearCase Project Explorer, or a number of IDEs, such as Visual Studio. A rebase can also be started from the command line using

```
prompt> cleartool rebase
```

When you rebase, you are updating the baselines you see in your development view. These baselines, of course, contain new activities delivered by you and other members of your project. You can see this set of activities and explore the changes you are accepting into your development stream by clicking Details on the Rebase dialog (see Figure 8-9). If you are using Rebase from the command line, you can do this by using the following command:

```
prompt> cleartool rebase -preview
```

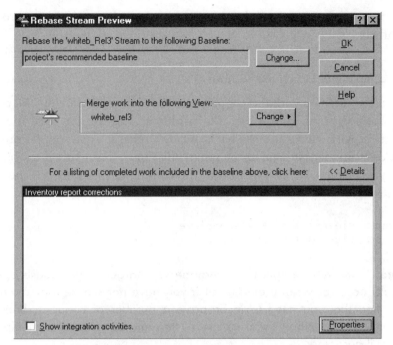

FIGURE 8-9   Rebase activities—Activity details

Note: As with many ClearCase command line operations, you can specify the `-graphical` switch to the Rebase command if you want to use the GUI for this particular operation.

In most cases, the Rebase operation will simply update your development streams configuration, and you will see new versions in your development view. Rebase also checks to see if there are any conflicts that must be resolved. That is, if there are any elements you have modified that someone else also modified. If this is the case, it will check out these elements and perform a Merge operation. The Dealing with Conflicting Changes section later in this chapter discusses this in more detail.

8.5.2   Build and Test

After the first step of the rebase is finished, but prior to committing the changes, you have the opportunity to build and test. It is a good idea to test if you can build the software in your development view, particularly if you need to resolve any conflicts.

8.5.3   Complete or Cancel the Rebase

After you are satisfied with the changes that have been made, you can complete the Rebase operation. If you ran into problems and do not have the time to resolve them, you can cancel (or back out) the rebase. These operations can be performed from the last page of the rebase GUI or by restarting the rebase operation if you dismissed this page. From the command line, this is done through the following:

```
prompt> cleartool rebase -complete
prompt> cleartool rebase -cancel
```

▶ **Note:** Some rebase operations may be very large. Large rebase operations usually occur between projects, but if you have not rebased for a while, you may find that you need to incorporate a number of changes. Rebase is a restartable operation so you can work through a rebase over multiple days/ logins if necessary.

8.6   Dealing with Conflicting Changes

When working in a serial development environment, only one person is allowed to change a file at a time. As we discussed in chapter 2, Growing into Your SCM Solution, this approach can cause development bottlenecks as well as make it very difficult to maintain multiple releases. ClearCase UCM supports parallel development—which means while you are working in your development view, you may be modifying the same files at the same time as another team member in his or her development view. Obviously, these changes must be merged or integrated at some point. With ClearCase UCM, this may happen during Deliver and Rebase operations. ClearCase provides specific tools to automate as much of this merging work as possible and tools to assist you in integrating changes when conflicts occur that cannot be automatically resolved.

8.6.1   Delivery Scenario 1 (No Conflicts)

Conflicts occur only when more than one developer works on the same file at the same time. If this never happens, you will never need to resolve conflicts.

Figure 8-10 shows a delivery scenario in which no merging is required. You have made a change to example.c, but no other member on your project team has modified the file. When you deliver, ClearCase simply copies the contents from your development stream to the integration stream. In ClearCase terms, this is called a *trivial merge*.

8.6.2　Delivery Scenario 2 (No Conflicts)

This case is similar to delivery scenario 1. There will be no conflict resolution required as part of delivery, and ClearCase will perform a trivial merge. However, in this case, another team member did modify the file example.c and, in fact, delivered his or her changes before you. The difference from scenario 1 is that you performed a Rebase operation before doing your delivery. The arrow shown in Figure 8-11 pointing from the integration stream to your development stream indicates a Rebase operation was performed. This is also a trivial merge for ClearCase.

8.6.3　Delivery Scenario 3 (with Conflicts)

In some cases, when you deliver, you will discover that someone on your project has modified the same element you have and has already delivered his or her changes. In this case, ClearCase will attempt to automatically merge these changes during the Deliver process. If it cannot do so, then you will be required to merge the changes using the ClearCase merge tool (see the Clear-Case Merge Tools section later in this chapter for details). Figure 8-12 illustrates this scenario.

8.6.4　Rebase Scenario 1 (No Conflicts)

When you rebase, you are essentially updating the baselines in your development stream. In most cases, the changes you accept will not have been made to the same elements you are working on and no merging takes place. Figure 8-13 shows what happens when you have not modified the example.c at all. Your development view will simply display the new version of the file.

8.6.5　Rebase Scenario 2 (with Conflicts)

In some cases, someone on the project will have modified and delivered a change to a file that you are also modifying. Figure 8-14 on page 188 illustrates this. In this case, ClearCase will attempt to automatically merge these files during the

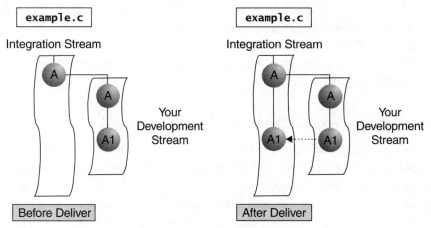

FIGURE 8-10   Trivial delivery scenario (no conflicts)

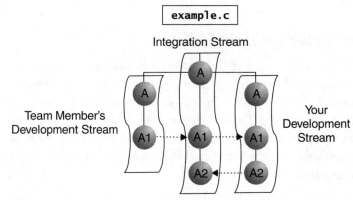

FIGURE 8-11   Trivial delivery scenario post-rebase (no conflicts)

rebase. If it cannot do so, then you will be required to merge the changes using the ClearCase merge tool (see the next section for details).

8.6.6   ClearCase Merge Tools

When a merge during Rebase and Deliver operations is not trivial (see Delivery Scenario 3 (with Conflicts) and Rebase Scenario 2 (with Conflicts) earlier in this chapter), ClearCase will attempt to merge the changes automatically. ClearCase can do this only for element types for which it understands the content. Out-of-the-box, ClearCase understands how to merge any ASCII text files, HTML

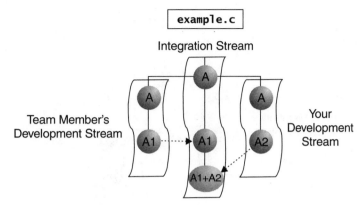

FIGURE 8-12   Delivery scenario with conflicts

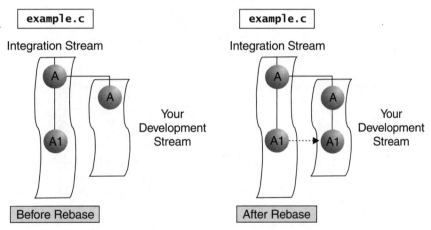

FIGURE 8-13   Rebase scenario with no conflicts

files, XML files, Rose Models, and Microsoft Word documents. For example, Figure 8-15 shows three text files and the automatically merged output. "Original" is the initial text file. "Contributor 1" is a modification of the original text file. "Contributor 2" is another modification of the original. "Result" is the automatically merged file that ClearCase produces.

While the merge algorithm supported in ClearCase is smart enough to understand insertions, deletions, and movement of blocks of text, it is important to understand that ClearCase does not know about the syntax of any language when it is merging. ClearCase understands only that it is a text file and

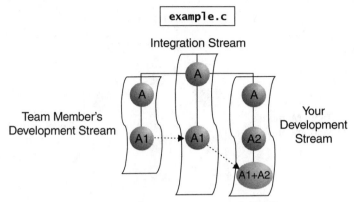

FIGURE 8-14   Rebase scenario with conflicts

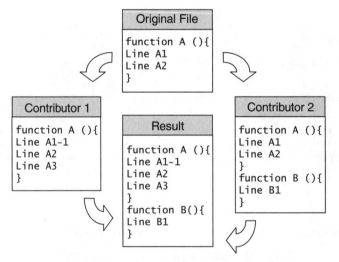

FIGURE 8-15   Automated merge example

performs the merge on this basis. Therefore, it is important to verify the merge after a deliver or rebase even when it has happened in a fully automatic way.

Of course, it is not always possible to fully automate the merge process. Figure 8-16 shows an example in which manual intervention is required. Once again, "Original" is the initial text file. "Contributor 1" is a modification to the original. "Contributor 2" is also a modification to the original. You can see that in Contributor 1 and Contributor 2 the same lines have been modified. In this case, you would choose one line or the other. In other conflicting scenarios, the right choice might be to include both lines or neither line. In fact, you might even need to do some additional coding to resolve the conflict.

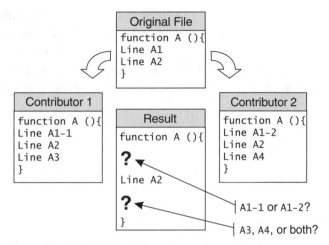

FIGURE 8-16   Manual merge example

FIGURE 8-17   Graphical merge tool

Performing a manual merge can be a difficult process without the right tools. ClearCase provides a graphic merge tool that greatly assists in this process. Figure 8-17 shows a screenshot from this merge tool. The lower panels show the original file, called the "common ancestor version." This version is computed for you by ClearCase. The other panels show the contributor versions. In this case, there are only two; but ClearCase can handle as many as 16 contributors (32 on Unix platforms). The top panel shows the results. With the navigation, contributor selection, and editing tools, the ClearCase merge manager makes it much easier to merge conflicting element changes.

Chapter 9　Integration, Build, and Release

It is the job of the integrator to take the work of the team and construct a single version of a software system or set of software components. It is also the integrator's job to take the work of the many teams and assemble a single version of a software system that can be tested against a set of requirements and ultimately released.

This chapter discusses merge and assembly, two types of software integration, and their application to the categories of software teams (see Five Project Team Categories in chapter 2). It also discusses how ClearCase branches are used for isolation and integration, using either your own branching strategy or Clear-Case UCM. Finally, it covers the baseline, build, staging, and release processes.

9.1　Software Integration

Integration is the process of bringing together independently developed changes to form a testable piece of a software system. It can occur at many levels, eventually culminating in a complete software system. The larger the software system and the larger the team working on that system, the more levels of integration are required to manage the software development effort. There are basically two types of integration relevant to SCM: merge and assembly integration.

9.1.1　Merge Integration

Merge integration involves the resolution of parallel changes made by different team members to common files and/or components. In this case, multiple people have modified the same set of system artifacts in parallel. It is therefore necessary to combine or, in ClearCase terms, merge these changes. In some cases, this can be automated with tools that understand the structure of the files. In other cases, the merge must be performed manually (e.g., if there are conflicting changes). It should be clear that merge integration requires some knowledge of the changes being made to the software system. In addition, more changes may be introduced to the software as part of performing merge integration (e.g., those changes required to resolve merge conflicts).

9.1.2   Assembly Integration

Assembly integration involves combining baselines of software components into a larger piece of the overall system. The Rational Unified Process defines integration as "the software development activity in which separate software components are combined into an executable whole" [RUP 5.5 1999]. Unlike merge integration, assembly integration does not modify the source code, but rather puts together the puzzle pieces of the software system (hopefully they all fit).

Assembly integration can occur at build time or runtime or both. With build-time assembly, you bring together two sets of source components, build them, and then link them together to form a testable executable. With runtime assembly you copy a set of prebuilt objects into a runtime environment, which can then be executed. A set of dynamically linked libraries (DLLs) from two different software components is a good example of runtime assembly integration.

The type of integration and the number of integration levels used are largely determined by the size of the software system and the size of the team. Integration choices also depend on whether the teams are organized around architecture or around features (see Organizing Large Multiproject Development Efforts in chapter 7). At some level, a system that has a well-defined software architecture uses assembly integration. A monolithic system is more likely to use merge integration all the way to the top.

9.1.3   Integration Scenarios for Teams of Differing Sizes

Let's take a look at some integration scenarios based on the team sizes defined in Five Project Team Categories in chapter 2.

Individual Integration

There are three integration scenarios for the individual: there is no integration required; integration for the individual happens all the time; or individuals develop separate pieces of the system independently and then perform their own assembly integration. In any case, integration for the individual is the easiest, usually just happens in the course of that person's work, and is relatively uninteresting.

Small and Modest Team Integration

Most small and modest-sized teams have one level of integration. Individuals work on their pieces of the software system, and at some point those pieces are integrated and tested as a whole (see Figure 9-1).

With monolithic systems and feature-oriented teams, each team member is allowed to make changes to any part of the software system that are required for the task they are trying to accomplish. This means that merge integration is usually used.

Major Team Integration

Major teams have two levels of integration. The first is done by each project team and is largely the same as that performed by small and modest-sized teams. The second level brings together the work of the teams.

Whether the team is architecture-oriented or feature-oriented usually dictates what type of integration is performed at the second level (see Organizing Large Multiproject Development Efforts in chapter 7 for information on team orientation). For architecture-oriented teams, the second level of integration is typically assembly integration. For feature-oriented teams, the second level is typically merge integration.

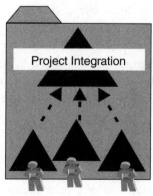

FIGURE 9-1   Merge integration for small and modest teams

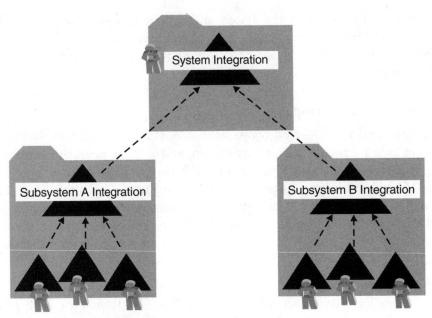

FIGURE 9-2   Integration for major teams

While terminology in this area is still rather varied, the first level of integration is often referred to as "subsystem" or "feature" integration. The second level is often called "system" integration (see Figure 9-2).

Extreme Team Integration

Extreme teams often require more than two levels of integration because of the size and complexity of the systems being developed. It is important to avoid monolithic systems for projects of this size and to have an architecture that will allow the use of assembly integration at the higher levels. If you allow more than 150 individuals to make modifications to all the source code in parallel, the advantages of parallel development will be lost in the complexity of trying to perform merge integration. Even if you are using feature-oriented teams, you should try to define the features in such a way as to isolate the changes to individual subsystems.

The way a system gets integrated and the number of levels of integration used can sometimes depend on the system architecture itself. Figure 9-3 shows an example of a system divided into six subsystems. Figure 9-4 shows how the teams and projects could be laid out for this example system and how integration could occur.

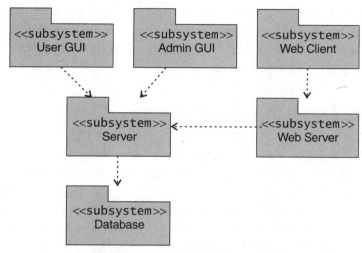

FIGURE 9-3   System hierarchy example

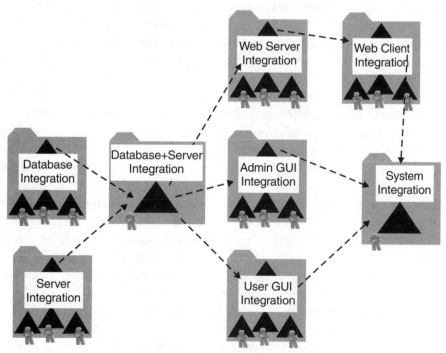

FIGURE 9-4   Integration for extreme teams

Even if extreme teams are feature-oriented, major features are often divided into a hierarchy of subfeatures. Teams independently develop subfeatures, which are integrated into a larger feature, which is then integrated with other major features of the overall system.

9.2   Isolation and Integration with ClearCase

Developer isolation is when developers are working in stable workspaces where changes other developers are making do not affect them nor do changes they make affect other developers. Similarly, teams can be isolated from other teams. Isolation is used to manage complexity. Problems or new features are divided up across teams and individuals. In order to work efficiently, teams and individuals isolate themselves from others' changes that may destabilize their workspace.

For example, Developer A may be making a change that requires alterations to a common interface as well as underlying code. If you tried to build and test the system after Developer A changed the interface, but before Developer A changed any calls to that interface, the system would be broken. So, if Developer B was not isolated from Developer A's changes, Developer B might be blocked from proceeding even if Developer B was working on a completely separate part of the system.

When you isolate work, at some point you must integrate. The difficulty is deciding when and how often this should take place—the developer isolation versus project integration dilemma. You are balancing a stable development environment against a better understanding of whether the pieces of the system being developed independently really work together. Infrequent integration means you discover integration issues late in the project causing significant and unplanned redesign work, which often results in a missed project deadline. Integrating too often causes unnecessary lost productivity. A destabilizing change that is integrated too early can cause an entire team to be unable to complete their work on time. Changes likely to cause destabilization should be isolated and unit-tested before being integrated. Deciding when and how often to integrate is how you tune the performance of your SCM process.

An improper approach to isolation and integration is probably the number one cause of SCM-related problems on a software project. How you apply your SCM tool does have a serious impact on how well your development organization performs. ClearCase supports a number of integration approaches, which are described in the next few sections. Only you can pick the right approach for your projects. This section covers the topic of using branching and merging to implement your own integration strategy and how the ClearCase UCM model supports integration. We begin by discussing two interesting integration approaches: no isolation and branch/LATEST development.

9.2.1   The Shared View—No Isolation

A view is typically used by one individual. However, in a case where you desire no isolation between team members, a single ClearCase view can be shared by multiple individuals. The best way to think about this is as a single copy of your source tree in which everyone works at the same time.

Everyone working in a shared view will be isolated from each other's changes only while a change is being made in an editor. Any commitment of a change to disk (e.g., a save) will make the change visible to others working in the shared view. Basically, this means you have almost no isolation between team members and integration is occurring automatically and constantly. When a file is checked out, it becomes writable by anyone working in that view. ClearCase checks out files to a view rather than an individual. Since the view is shared, anyone has access to it. Thus, developers cannot work on the same file in parallel.

Shared views should be used only for very small teams (no more than four individuals) on short-lived (less then a week) tasks. The task should require developers to see each other's changes as the changes are being made, possibly because of the critical nature of the task or some tricky interface changes.

If you use shared views as a general-purpose solution, you will experience many of the problems encountered in early SCM systems, as described in chapter 2, Growing into Your SCM Solution. However, there are times when a shared view is the right choice.

9.2.2   Branch/LATEST Development—Maximizing Integration

ClearCase supports a style of integration called *branch/LATEST development*, which is unique to ClearCase and offers some distinct advantages. For small and modest-sized teams, the branch/LATEST approach attempts to replicate the ease of integration enjoyed by an individual. Branch/LATEST development minimizes isolation and maximizes integration. Team members work on the same set of source files, but each individual on the team is isolated in his or her own view. Changes become visible to other team members at checkin time rather than file save time, as in the shared view approach.

Team members can work on the same files in parallel by using the reserved/ unreserved checkout mechanisms described in Concurrent Changes to the Same Project Files in chapter 2. Conflicting changes are integrated/resolved at checkin time.

Branch/LATEST development supports rapid integration because there is no explicit integrate or merge action required for team members to share each other's changes. A team using branch/LATEST development integrates "on the fly," similarly to the way an individual would. Branch/LATEST development has different isolation and integration characteristics depending on the type of view being used (see Workspaces: Snapshot and Dynamic Views in chapter 4).

Let's take a look at an example using both dynamic and snapshot views. Let's say we have a team of three developers: Xena, Hercules, and Godzilla. Xena and Hercules are using dynamic views, and Godzilla is using a snapshot view. Figure 9-5 shows what each individual sees in his or her view. Notice how the dynamic views access `file.c`, version 1 directly out of the VOB, while the snapshot view must load (copy) `file.c`, version 1 into local file storage.

Hercules checks out `file.c` to make a change, using a reserved checkout. In Figure 9-6, notice that the reserved checkout is seen only by him. Xena and Godzilla will not see the changes Hercules is making even when he saves them. The changes become visible only at checkin time.

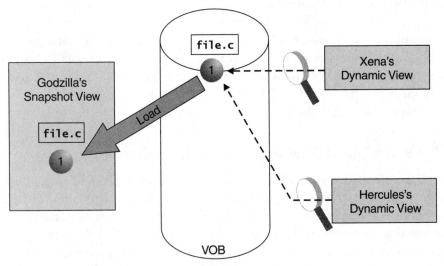

FIGURE 9-5   Branch/LATEST view—Initial situation

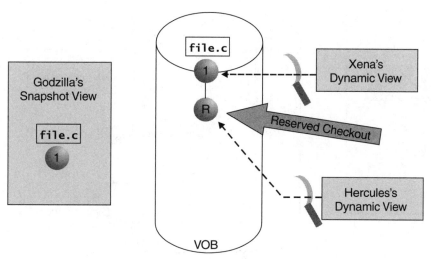

FIGURE 9-6　Change isolation using branch/LATEST

In branch/LATEST development, using the "checkin" operation is the way to declare that a change is ready to be seen by other developers on your team. Hercules checks in and creates version 2 of file.c. Automatically, through the ClearCase dynamic view mechanism, Xena will see this change in her view. Godzilla, on the other hand, is working in a snapshot view and does not see the change (see Figure 9-7).

With snapshot views, Godzilla has an additional level of isolation. In order to see changes made by Hercules, Godzilla must use the snapshot view Update command. A snapshot view update looks at the view's configuration and copies (or updates) any files that have changed. After the Update operation, all team members now see the changes that Hercules checked in (see Figure 9-8).

The advantage to branch/LATEST should be clear. It provides some level of isolation, but integration occurs without explicit integration operations or merge actions. This approach works well for teams of up to eight developers. Once the team size grows much beyond this, problems may occur, caused largely by the fact that developers need more isolation from each other than this approach provides. The drawbacks of branch/LATEST development are as follows:

- *No ability to checkpoint*
One of the disadvantages of branch/LATEST development is that developers cannot checkpoint their work. Checkpointing is checking in a file before a

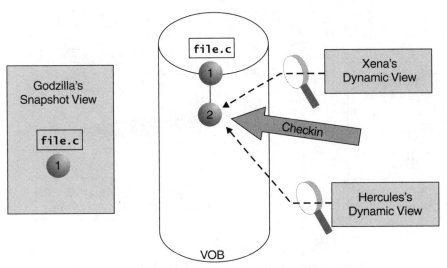

FIGURE 9-7   Checkin under branch/LATEST

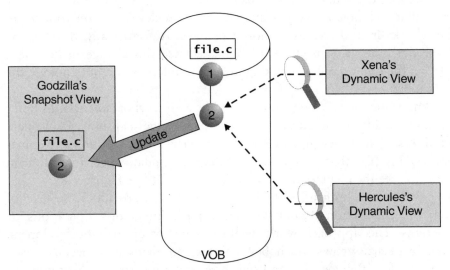

FIGURE 9-8   Final branch/LATEST view situation

change is complete in order to securely save an intermediate version. This is similar to creating a backup file, but is more secure since the version is stored in the SCM repository. In the branch/LATEST approach, checkin makes changes visible to other developers, so checkpointing an intermediate change is not desirable.

- *Unexpected integration at checkin time*

Since integration of parallel changes to common files occurs at checkin time with branch/LATEST development, developers may be required to do extra integration work when they finish their tasks. This can cause problems in certain circumstances. For example, you are working on a critical bug fix that you want to finish by the end of the day, and it is already 5:55 p.m. When you go to check in, you find out someone has modified and checked in some of the same files you changed during the day. You must resolve any conflicts between your changes and his or hers before you are allowed to check in.

- *Version skew*

"Version skew" is when your view selects file versions that are not compatible. An extreme case of this would be to see files from release 1 and some from release 2. A more common example of version skew may occur when using branch/LATEST development. You make changes to two files—an interface and its implementation—but forget to check in both files. While everything builds fine in your view, the partial change in another developer's view may cause the build to break or cause unexplained runtime errors. This is because his or her view selects the interface change you made and checked in, but not the implementation change you made but forgot to check in.

- *Decreased productivity*

There are a number of reasons you may see a decrease in productivity using branch/LATEST development. First, individual build times may increase. For example, if a developer checks in a change to a low-level header file, this change becomes visible to all dynamic view users immediately. This may cause each developer to rebuild the entire system. Second, developer builds may fail more frequently if developers are undisciplined about checking in changes (e.g., checking in changes that were never compiled). Finally, the rate at which new changes are being introduced by a development team may be too much for each individual developer to integrate automatically. For example, if 50 developers were using branch/LATEST development, the frequency of change would cause most developers to spend a lot of time getting their code to work with everyone's changes throughout the day, rather than focusing on the problems they are solving or the features they are implementing.

Branch/LATEST development is a clear advantage for smaller teams that require some level of isolation but also want to integrate as frequently as possible with the least amount of effort. However, for larger teams, more isolation is required, and branch/LATEST development cannot be recommended. The additional isolation needed by larger teams is achieved using ClearCase's branch and merge capabilities or through the use of the ClearCase UCM model.

9.2.3   Using Branches for Isolation and Integration

ClearCase provides rich branching and merging facilities, which have been used to implement a wide range of approaches to isolation and integration. Branches are used to isolate a change or class of changes for any given element. The ClearCase merge tools are used to find and integrate these isolated changes by moving changes from one branch to another and by helping the integrator resolve conflicting changes that may have occurred on individual branches.

The types of branches you use, how these branches relate to one another, and how you merge changes between branches are referred to as your *branching strategy*. When you define a branching strategy, you are really defining the isolation/integration strategy for your project. ClearCase UCM has its own branching strategy described in the Integration with UCM section later in this chapter. This section provides a brief introduction to branching strategies outside the context of UCM.

For the purposes of this discussion, branches are classified into two types: development and integration. This is the same as UCM's classification of streams. Development branches are those used to perform new development. Integration branches are those used to manage lines of development, typically serving as the starting point and the integration point for development branches.

The following are some typical uses of the development and the integration branches.

■ *Development branch per activity/task*
Each development task is performed in isolation and then merged/integrated into an integration branch, which usually represents a release. That is, each developer is isolated for each task he or she performs. This approach is similar to the ClearCase UCM activity-based approach (see the Integration with UCM section later in this chapter). It differs from UCM in that it uses the branch to capture the change set.

■ *Development branch per major feature/subproject*

Each major feature or subproject is developed on its own branch. This case differs from the branch-per-activity approach in that there is a small team of developers working on the feature or set of related features using the branch/ LATEST approach for the development of the major feature. As in the branch-per-activity approach, there is an integration branch usually representing a release into which the feature is merged/integrated.

■ *Development branch per team*

In this approach, each development team works in isolation on their own branch. The branching structure mirrors the team organizational structure and is not related to the work being performed by the team. This is typically not a good idea for two reasons. The organizational structure is more fluid, and changes made to the organization part way through the development cycle will require changes to the branching structure, which is never desirable and not always easy to do. The other drawback is it that is not easy to determine what work is being performed on that branch since the branch captures all of the work performed by the team.

The advantage of this approach is that team members are isolated from other teams, but not from themselves. The other advantage is that specific security can be applied (through ClearCase triggers) to the branch type, ensuring that only members of a particular team can make changes on that branch. Even with these advantages, this is not a recommend approach.

■ *Integration branch per subsystem*

In this approach, the branching structure mirrors the software architecture. The branch structure directly supports merge integration by allowing anyone anywhere to change the source and by using ClearCase merge tools to merge subsystem changes from a subsystem branch to a system branch. It also supports the ability to enforce ownership of changes to a given subsystem by restricting who can make changes on the integration branch. This approach is not very desirable for two reasons. The first is that architectural changes may require rearranging your branching structure, causing major headaches. The second is that this approach does not take into account parallel development of major releases, which is usually a requirement for teams that require a branch per subsystem. A better approach is integration branch per subsystem per release.

■ *Integration branch per integration level*

In this approach, there is a branch-per-integration level. For example, with three levels of integration, there might be a "development" branch, an "integration" branch, and a "production" branch. The advantage of this approach is that controls can be placed on the branches, allowing different organizational groups to control the different branches. For example, a test group could control the integration branch and allow only "approved" changes to be merged from the development branch.

This approach to branching models one of the original ways SCM was performed—by having different copies of the software system and moving files from one copy of the system to the next. This approach to branching is also the way many companies implement a promotion model for the source code.

Another advantage of this approach is that the graphical version tree browser for any given element makes it very easy to determine code quality levels. The disadvantage of this approach is that it does not take into account parallel development of major releases. A better approach would be a branch per integration level per release.

■ *Integration branch per release*

This approach is the classic reason branching is used. It supports parallel development of multiple releases simultaneously by isolating in its own branch changes for any given release. The most common example is maintenance work continuing on an existing release while development work proceeds on a future release. This allows a company to produce a minor or point release while still working on the major release. This approach provides isolation between the teams.

The disadvantage to this approach is that integration between the maintenance release and the development release must be planned in advance or it is likely to take place near the end of the major release's development cycle. This "Big Bang" approach to integration can cause significant delays to the release since integration problems are uncovered late. To avoid this, plan early integration points while the major release is ongoing. For example, plan an alpha release of the software and integrate the existing maintenance work at that point. Do this again for beta, and by the time you reach the final release, the major integration issues will already be resolved.

■ *Development branch per patch*

Another common reason for branching is to support a patch process. A "patch" is a single fix to a defect in a release that can be applied independently to that release, creating a variant of a given release, and so is similar to the development branch-per-activity/task approach.

By developing a patch on its own branch, you can integrate the patch into multiple releases at different times by using merge integration from a patch branch to a release branch. This allows these changes to be applied without the developer having to physically make the changes over and over again by hand.

■ *Development or integration branch per patch bundle*

A "patch bundle" is a grouping of individual patches that are applied as a whole. Service Packs from Microsoft for its operating systems are good examples of patch bundles. If all the patches were developed together by a single team, then the patch bundle branch would be a development branch and would behave similarly to the development-branch-per-major-feature strategy. If all the patches are developed on independent branches (using the development-branch-per-patch strategy) and then merged onto a single patch bundle branch, then the patch bundle branch would be an integration branch. These patch bundles, just like patch branches, should be merged into release branches at the appropriate time in the development cycle.

■ *Integration branch per system variant*

Sometimes branching is used to maintain different variants of a system. A "variant" is a slightly modified version of a specific release of a software system. For example, porting a system to a new operating system would create an OS-specific variant of the system (e.g., release 1.0 of a software system may have a Windows variant and a Unix variant). Variant branches can also be used to support customer-special versions of the software. A customer-special variant of a software system is one in which the system has been modified, built, and released for a specific customer.[1]

The primary disadvantage of the branch-per-variant approach is that it is hard to reliably merge changes from one variant to another. In general, only some of the changes in the branch for one variant should be applied to another variant, which means that every merge from one variant branch to another must be carefully inspected for whether a particular change should be merged, ignored, or handled in a different way in the destination variant. The longer the variant branches exist, the farther they diverge from each other and the harder it is to sucessfully merge between them. A superior approach is to divide the system into variant-independent and variant-dependent components and then to control variant selection at build time.

Typically, a combination of the branching approaches described here is used to implement a branching strategy, and much more detail on these approaches is necessary for a complete discussion of branching strategies. While ClearCase can be used to define your own branching strategy, the ClearCase UCM model offers an out-of-the-box approach described in the following section.

---

1. Care must be taken when doing customer specials as they are very resource intensive and must be maintained independently.

9.2.4   Integration with UCM

As we've seen, the issues of isolation and integration are critical to the efficiency of a software development project. ClearCase UCM provides a fairly flexible model for how a project performs isolation and integration. As well as the basic approach, UCM supports some alternative uses of the model that provide different isolation and integration characteristics. The following subsections explore the basic model and the variants.

The Basic Model—One Developer/One Development Stream

The ClearCase UCM model has some basic tenets that impose some structure on how isolation and integration are handled. These are as follows:

1. Each developer is isolated from other developers' changes.
2. Developers are responsible for integrating their changes with those of other team members.
3. Developers control when they see changes made by other developers.
4. Changes integrated into any stream are consistent.

First, in the basic model each developer is isolated from other developers. Unlike in branch/LATEST development or shared views, developers do not see each other's changes at save or checkin time. Each developer works in his or her own development view attached to his or her development stream. Branching is used to ensure that each development stream is isolated from changes going on in other development streams. The branching model can be described as "per stream, per project," where "project" can be defined in any way necessary to achieve the right isolation characteristics. For example, a project could be a release or the implementation of a patch bundle. And "stream" can be defined as a set of related activities that a developer must implement. Developers can work in one single stream for the life of a project, create a new stream if they need to work on two unrelated or conflicting tasks in parallel, or create a new stream when they have finished a major set of work and want to start afresh.

The reason for isolating developers is so they can focus on the task at hand without being disrupted by changes going on elsewhere in the project. This is the most efficient way for an individual to work as it avoids all the problems associated with the branch/LATEST model.

One developer may have multiple streams for any given project if he or she needs to isolate pieces of his or her own work. Developers make their changes available to other project members using a UCM operation called "deliver" (see Delivering Changes to the Project in chapter 8). They update their development environment using a UCM operation called "rebase" (see Rebasing Your Development Stream in chapter 8).

Second, developers are responsible for integrating their changes with those of other team members. They explicitly make their changes available to other project members by issuing a UCM command called "Deliver." The deliver process copies development stream changes to the project's integration stream. This is done on a per-activity basis and is a merge integration operation. That is, if there are conflicting changes made by two developers, resolution/integration is done during the deliver by the developer. Usually, UCM delivers can be called "push delivery" because the developer "pushes" the changes into the project's integration stream. See Delivering Changes to the Project in chapter 8 for more details on delivery.

If you do not want individual developers to be able to push changes into the integration stream, you can lock the integration stream to allow only certain individuals to make changes there and thus stop developer deliveries. This will require you to have some method for developers to notify the integrator that an activity is ready for delivery. The integrator can then go to the developer's stream (via the Project Explorer) and execute the delivery him- or herself. You may also be interested in the pull delivery option currently supported for remote development streams (see the Push Deliver versus Pull Deliver section later in this chapter).

Third, developers control when they see changes made by other developers. Developers make changes available to other team members by delivering those changes to the project's integration stream. The basic UCM model gives each developer control over when he or she will see the changes made by other members of the project team.

As discussed, when developers want to see changes made by other team members, they perform a rebase. Rebase also causes a merge integration, but this time from the integration stream to the development stream. Rebase uses assembly integration for read-only or unmodified components. See Rebasing Your Development Stream in chapter 8 for more details.

The UCM model then gives control of the developer's working environment to the developer. This is different from the branch/LATEST approach in which the developer's environment is dynamically updated as changes are checked in by other developers (see the Branch/LATEST Development—Maximizing Integration section earlier in this chapter).

The advantage to the UCM approach is that developers are often more productive because their environment is stable. The disadvantage is that it can become easy for a developer to remain isolated forever. By never rebasing the development stream, a developer could choose to never see changes made by other team members. In effect, this developer would drift further and further out of date with the latest source code changes. The result of this behavior on the integrator would be that changes being delivered by that developer would often not work with the latest software. This might mean it wouldn't build or would have problems in a runtime environment. When this happens, the integrator spends more time getting things to work, basically integrating this developer's changes for him or her.

To combat this problem, while still providing the developer control of the working environment, UCM provides a project policy that can be set. This policy is described in Rebase to Recommend Required in chapter 6. The purpose of this policy is to require the developer to rebase (update) to the project's recommended baselines prior to delivering any changes. In this way, developers can choose to remain isolated until they need to deliver a change. At that point, they are required to rebase their development stream to the latest baselines recommended by the integrator. The UCM approach provides an effective compromise between developer isolation and project integration.

Finally, changes that are integrated into a stream are consistent. UCM reduces the problem of version skew (see discussion of version skew in the Branch/LATEST Development—Maximizing Integration section earlier in this chapter) by using automation to ensure that changes moving between streams are consistent (either deliver, or out-bound changes, and rebase, or in-bound changes). Deliver operates on an implicit set of versions that are consistent in terms of the activity or activities being delivered. That is, when you issue a Deliver command, you specify an activity, not a set of versions. The primary purpose here is to make sure the new versions created to perform a logical activity are made visible in the integration stream as a whole. Rebase operations operate on baselines and therefore on a consistent set of versions that have been included in the baseline by the integrator. See the Baselining Software Components section later in this chapter for more on the steps the integrator performs to incorporate developer deliveries into new baselines.

Alternative Model 1—Multiple Developers/One Development Stream

One alternative to the basic UCM model is to have multiple developers working in one development stream, with each developer using his or her own view. This is good for a small (fewer than five) group of developers who must cooperate closely on some pieces of work. In that case, the developers are isolated from each other by means of the view. Each developer sees other developers' changes at checkin time for dynamic views and update time for snapshot views. Having multiple developers use a single development stream is how you get the same characteristics of the branch/LATEST development approach while using UCM (see the Branch/LATEST Development—Maximizing Integration section earlier in this chapter).

UCM has a few restrictions because of the activity-oriented nature of the model. First, each developer must be working on his or her own activity. This may require that a single logical activity be decomposed into smaller activities and assigned to each developer.[2] Second, if two developers make changes to the same files while working on two different activities, they introduce a deliver dependency between these activities causing the activities to be delivered together or in a specific order to ensure consistency.

The multiple developers/one development stream approach should be used in a UCM project when specific circumstances require close cooperation between a small group of developers.

Alternative Model 2—Multiple Developers/One Integration Stream

A second alternative to the UCM isolation/integration model is to forego the use of development streams altogether. In this case, each developer works in his or her own view, and all views are attached to the same integration stream. In effect, developers are working in the UCM model with isolation characteristics that are identical to those described in the Branch/LATEST Development—Maximizing Integration section earlier in this chapter. In short, they would see each other's changes at checkin time for dynamic views and at update time for snapshot views.

The advantage of this approach is that you still gain the benefits of UCM activities, components, and baselines without the overhead of Deliver and Rebase operations. The disadvantage is that developers do not have a stable working environment. This approach is recommended for smaller (fewer than eight) teams who want to integrate as early as possible and are willing to deal with changes occurring to their workspaces while they are developing. It is also recommended for technical writing teams primarily doing documentation in a format that does not support merging. See the Coordinating Documentation

---

2. If members of this small group *must* collaborate on one activity, then they would all use one view attached to one development stream. This essentially simulates the nonisolation characteristics described in The Shared View—No Isolation section earlier in this chapter.

Projects or Small Teams section in chapter 7 for more information on this type of project.

The pros and cons of the multiple developers/one integration stream approach are described in the Branch/LATEST—Maximizing Integration section earlier in this chapter.

Push Deliver versus Pull Deliver

One final note on UCM integration: UCM supports a slightly different model when it comes to remote development. Deliver has two forms: Push Delivery and Pull Delivery. With *push delivery*, a developer is responsible for integrating his or her changes into the project's integration stream where the integrator can create baselines and perform project builds. The developer "pushes" in the changes. With *pull delivery*, developers indicate that their changes are ready for integration, but it is the integrator who is responsible for integrating the developer's changes into the project's integration stream. The integrator "pulls" in the changes. ClearCase calls the pull delivery model a *posted delivery*.

Whether a delivery is push or pull depends on whether the development stream is mastered at the same site as the integration stream (see chapter 10, Geographically Distributed Development, for more details on mastership). For remotely mastered development streams, the delivery is considered a "pull" delivery.

9.3   Building and Baselining with ClearCase UCM

In a ClearCase UCM environment, an integrator is responsible for building, baselining, and smoke testing the software. This could be a part-time job for a development lead on a small project or a full-time job on a much larger project, or it may be performed by several individuals.

These are the steps the integrator must perform:

1. Lock the integration stream.
2. Baseline the software components.
3. Build the software components.
4. Execute any smoke tests available.
5. Promote the software component baselines.
6. Unlock the integration stream.

The following subsections discuss each of these steps, as well as automating this process and working with multiple projects.

9.3.1 Locking the Integration Stream

The first step is to lock the integration stream. This can be carried out most easily from the Project Explorer. Figure 9-9 shows the Properties tab from the integration stream for the "Rel3" Classics project. The Lock tab is displayed. Make sure you exclude yourself from the lock. As shown, the user "whiteb" is still allowed to make changes in the integration stream. Locking the integration

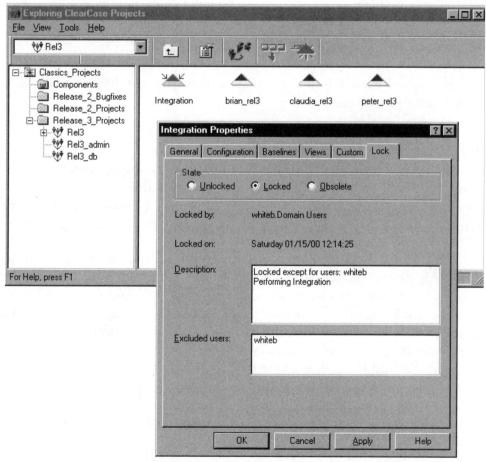

FIGURE 9-9 Locking the integration stream in the Project Explorer

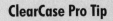

ClearCase Pro Tip

A big decision in SCM is whether to build, then baseline or baseline, then build. Either approach offers advantages and disadvantages. The easiest approach with UCM is to build first and baseline second.

Many times build problems arise that can be fixed easily by a quick change to a file. These fixes are so minor that it is desirable to "slip them into" the baseline. This was traditionally accomplished in ClearCase by sliding a label down to the new versions on some files. However, component baselines do not allow you to tweak their content. Once they are created, they cannot be changed. In order to fix a build problem, you must create a new baseline.

If your build times are short and you want to allow for minor fixes before you create a baseline, simply build first, then baseline afterward.

stream stops deliveries from occurring so that you can baseline and build against a stable code base.

9.3.2   Baselining Software Components

Baselining is a ClearCase UCM operation that creates new versions of components (see Component Management: Components and Baselines in chapter 4 for more on components and baselines). To create a new baseline, the integrator goes to the Project Explorer and selects "Make Baseline" on the context menu of the integration stream (see Figure 9-10).

The Make Baseline operation looks at all the activities that have been delivered. It determines which components on a particular project have been modified and then offers to create new component baselines for each of these components. In Figure 9-11, you see the Make Baseline dialog. First is the name of the baseline; second, whether the baseline is full or incremental; third, an indication of the project and stream in which the baseline is being created; fourth, the view that will be used to create the baseline; and, finally, a list of components that have had elements modified and delivered since the last baseline was created. In this case, only one component, Classics, has had any modifications.

Baseline creation can also be scripted or performed from the command line with the following:

```
prompt> cleartool mkbl
```

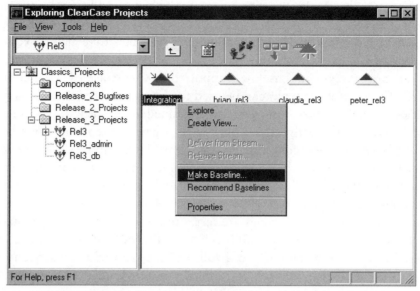

FIGURE 9-10   Make Baseline operation from the Project Explorer

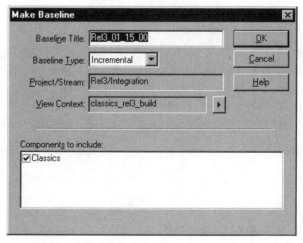

FIGURE 9-11   Component baseline selection
during Make Baseline

The command line Make Baseline offers a number of additional options that are not available in the GUI. For example, you can selectively pick from the delivered activities and make new component baselines that include your chosen subset of delivered activities.

There are two types of baselines supported by ClearCase UCM: incremental and full. These baselines types can be used to optimize performance. A baseline identifies a single version of elements contained in a ClearCase component either directly or indirectly. A *full baseline* is a baseline that directly records a version of every element contained in the ClearCase component. An *incremental baseline* is a baseline that directly records a version of elements that have changed since the last full baseline and indirectly records versions of elements by recording the last full baseline.

Initially, incremental baselines are faster to create. However, over time they begin to take as much time as a full baseline. At this point or before, you should convert an incremental baseline to a full baseline, and then subsequent incremental baselines will be faster. It is highly recommended that you convert important incremental baselines to full baselines. The conversion from incremental to full can be done as a background operation.

> ### ClearCase Pro Tip
>
> Using base ClearCase, you relate a set of versions by creating a label type and then attaching instances of that label to each element version (see Labels in chapter 4). To better understand incremental and full baselines, think in terms of labels. A full baseline is then a baseline where every single element of the component has had an instance of label type attached. An incremental baseline is a baseline where only those elements that have changed (since the last fully labeled baseline) have a label attached.

9.3.3 Building Software Components

Once the baselines have been created, you perform the build. Building is the first level of testing performed by the integrator. The purpose is to ensure that all the new changes made to the system will actually build together. The idea here is that one person (the integrator) debugs any build problems first, rather than allowing a build problem to cause all the developers' builds to break, as it could using the branch/LATEST development model.

Builds can be done using Clearmake, Make, or any other build utility. The UCM model does not provide any specific support for building nor does it hinder any approach to building the software.

If the system builds correctly, you can move on to running smoke tests or promoting the baselines to a higher level. However, builds often fail. For example, problems may occur when project builds have happened on multiple platforms while the developer has built only on one platform. Some build problems are easy to diagnose. Sometimes it is clear that the problem is specifically build related, and it can be easily fixed. For these problems, the integrator usually makes the changes him- or herself and continues to try to get a successful build. With UCM, the easiest way to do this is for the integrator to create an activity in the integration stream and make these changes. No delivery is required since the changes are made directly in the integration stream.

The hard build problems are often due to changes delivered by multiple developers and usually require some knowledge of the software internals to determine what needs to be done. In these cases, the integrator may engage one or more developers to help diagnose the problem. It may be necessary for a developer to make further changes to an activity that has already been delivered and redeliver the activity.

UCM supports the ability to deliver an activity multiple times. To allow the developer to redeliver a change, the integrator can modify the lock on the integration stream to allow this developer access while keeping other developer deliveries from occurring.

9.3.4   Executing Smoke Tests

Smoke tests are usually subsets of a system's full-regression test suite that can be executed automatically. Smoke tests verify the basic functionality of a software system. The purpose of running them is to increase the level of confidence in the software system by ensuring that a basic runtime system works. If the smoke tests are successful, an integrator can conclude that the changes that have been delivered and integrated are stable enough to be used by developers to rebase their development streams and so will promote the new baselines to the appropriate level.

9.3.5   Promoting Software Component Baselines

Baselines are assigned a promotion level. For every project, one promotion level is defined as the "Recommended" level (see Recommended Baseline Promotion

Level in chapter 6 for how this is set). The latest baselines in the project's integration stream promoted to that level will become the default set of baselines offered during developer rebase operations.

Integrators have a choice at this point. The easiest approach is to use the right-mouse context menu on the integration stream from the Project Explorer. This menu option promotes all the latest baselines in the project's integration stream to the recommended level (as defined by the project's policies). Alternatively, the integrator can select each baseline individually and promote it to the appropriate level.

Integrators should also demote baselines that have known problems. If a baseline fails to build, it should be moved to the "REJECTED" or other appropriate promotion level. This avoids accidental use of bad baselines.

9.3.6   Unlocking the Integration Stream

Once complete, the integration stream is unlocked. New activities can be delivered, and developers can rebase to the new baselines.

9.3.7   Automating the Nightly Build Process

If you perform automated nightly builds, the entire process just described could be scripted using the ClearCase command line interface. In particular, the commands `mkbl` (Make Baseline) and `chbl -level` (change baseline) would be used to create new baselines and promote them to a specific level. If you have an automated test suite that can programmatically determine whether the tests succeeded or failed, you can automate the smoke-testing portion of this process as well.

This approach is good for larger teams since it does not block deliveries during the day and allows developers to rebase in the morning to pick up the previous day's changes. Automating this process is particularly important at the end of a software development project when you want developers to regularly stay up to date with project changes.

9.3.8   Moving Changes between Projects

There are many scenarios where you will need to integrate changes between projects. Some are directly supported by UCM automation, such as when you are managing a current project and a follow-on project simultaneously or when you are integrating a patch release project into a new release project.

The UCM model supports these through the use of the Rebase operation between projects.[3]

In cases where rebase is not supported, the ClearCase merge tools can be used to easily find and merge changes between projects at either the baseline or activity level. The ClearCase project manager documentation describes this in more detail.

9.4 Staging and Release

Up until now, we have talked mainly about versioning of source code. Two other very important processes with respect to SCM are staging and release. *Staging* is the process of putting derived object files (executables, libraries, data files, generated header files, etc.) under version control. *Release* is the process of putting the runtime software into its final form and making it available to its intended users.

The primary purpose for staging is to store copies of the executable or runtime parts of the system so that they are secure and can be reliably recalled. The reasons behind staging and how staging is performed can be very different depending on the type of software system you are developing. In fact, it is very hard to generalize the process of staging.

The primary purpose of release is to make the software available to its end users. While staging is very hard to generalize, the processes surrounding a release are almost impossible to generalize. Every company has its own release processes that are almost always dependent on a number of factors, including but not limited to the following:

- The way the software will be delivered
- How the software is built
- How the software is staged
- How the company is organized
- How manufacturing occurs
- How many end users/customers exist
- How many releases are produced per year/month/week/day
- Whether the customers are internal or external to the company

---

3. Control of this is currently limited to the command line interface in ClearCase 4.0.

To be clear, you may stage a number of builds over the course of a software project and you may produce a number of candidate releases for installation-testing purposes, but there will be only one "official" build that was both staged and released.

Even though it is extremely difficult to generalize about the specifics of the staging and release processes, looking at a few examples should help clarify the concepts. Four broad categories have been chosen to highlight the differences in the staging and release processes: commercial software, embedded systems, Web sites, and internal software components. These are not intended to be an exhaustive list.

9.4.1 Commercial Software

Commercial software release is probably familiar to everyone involved in the software industry. For extremely small systems (e.g., those that produce a single executable that only runs on one platform), software can be tested easily, and installation involves just copying the executable onto a target machine. Most software systems are more complex. They have many working parts and must be installed on a target machine for final testing.

After a build is complete, the derived objects are staged. These version-controlled objects are then used to create an install area on the network, which can be used to install the software on a target machine and perform the testing. This testing is often referred to as "software system testing."

Near the end of the development cycle, a test CD-ROM is created from the staged derived objects, and the installation and testing is performed from the CD-ROM rather than over the network. Usually, there is a bit-for-bit comparison between the files and directories on the CD-ROM and those in the install area used for the system testing. If the CD-ROM is good, the software is ready to enter the release cycle. The CD-ROM becomes the "master" and is sent to manufacturing where it is mass-produced, packaged with documentation, shrink-wrapped, and shipped to the customer.

▶ **Note:** Many commercial software systems today are distributed from a Web site. No physical media is produced, but rather the software is downloaded from a Web site and installed on the target machine. The final testing is done by performing this download/install/test process. Release is performed by making the downloadable software available for customers on a Web site. No manufacturing takes place. This is obviously the future of software release for commercial systems.

9.4.2 Embedded Systems

Staging and release for embedded systems are different because the software resides in a hardware device. There is no CD-ROM produced and no installation performed. A good example is for a cell phone.

As for a commercial system, the software is built and staged. For most complex embedded systems, there is some level of software-only system testing. This is done using hardware emulators or test harnesses. After this software-only testing, the staged software is downloaded to the target machine (this time an embedded device) for final system testing.

When testing is complete, one of the staged builds is used by manufacturing to load the hardware. This can be done directly by downloading the software to the hardware device or, in other cases, by creating a hardware chip (just like producing a CD-ROM). This chip can then be mass-produced and used in the manufacturing of the final hardware device.

Some embedded systems have one and only one version of software. For example, a microwave has one version of the software for its lifetime. If you want some new features, you get a new microwave (even this example may be out-of-date soon). Many embedded systems have ways of upgrading the embedded software through any number of methods: floppy disk, CD-ROM, download through a serial port, download over the airwave, or chip replacement.

▶ **Note:** For embedded systems that allow software upgrades, it is particularly important to establish traceability from the hardware device to the software source code. That is, given a hardware device (e.g., cell phone), you can find out what release of the system is being used. From this release, you can identify the staged derived object files, and from those files, you can identify the right versions of the source code. Traceability from hardware to software source is often where some CM processes are lacking.

9.4.3 Web Sites

Staging and release of Web sites is entirely different from that of embedded and commercial software systems. You may not even think about a Web site in terms of "release" but in terms of "deployment" or "publishing." For basic Web sites with very little dynamic content, all the files that make up the site will already be under version control (at least they should be). Generally, the directory structure these files are stored in mirrors that of the live Web site. Typically, with these simple, static sites, there are really no build or staging processes.

However, this is changing on even simple sites with more dynamic content (e.g., Java applets).

For more complex sites, build processes will be involved. This is particularly true for e-commerce sites that have back-end database systems and for internal corporate sites that provide a Web front end to legacy systems. In these cases, staging is similar to that of commercial software systems: the built pieces of the system are placed under version control and managed along with the source code.

Whether you stage or not, there is still a specific release process. In the case of a Web site, releasing involves copying the files from where they are managed to the live Web site.

The release process for a static, content-only site is easy. Sites with only a few scripts and gizmos also have few problems. However, today many sites have a requirement to remain live 24 hours a day, 7 days a week. These sites are often very complex and have back-end databases, front-end content, and many scripts. One of the interesting release challenges is to figure out how to update these 24 x 7 sites with no downtime. It is like updating a software system database or user interface while the software is running.

The telecommunications industry has a somewhat similar problem with telephone switches. Phone switches must remain live constantly, just like Web sites. You can't turn them off and upgrade the software. So with many switching systems, the new software is installed while the switch is running. This is an incredibly complex process that is specific to each switching system.

For Web sites, the general solution used today is to provide multiple Web servers to handle the Web site load. Servers are taken down one at a time, upgraded, and brought back on-line. However, as Web sites get more complex, this may not always be possible, for example, when changes occur to a centralized database back end, making the the front end or middle-ware incompatible.

As the Web grows in complexity, Web development teams will experience the same problems software development teams have solved through staging and release processes. At the same time, Web teams will experience some unique problems. It will be interesting to see how tools and processes adapt over the next couple years to support these unique characteristics.

ClearCase can be used to manage Web content and support the release process if you mirror the Web site directory structure in your ClearCase VOBs. By mirroring the directory structure, you can use the ClearCase snapshot view load and update mechanism to get full copies of the files onto the live Web site.

Once the snapshot view is populated, ClearCase is essentially out of the loop for day-to-day Web access to those files.

The use of snapshot views has two advantages. The first is that updates made to the Web site are done incrementally. That is, only the files that have changed since the last snapshot view update will be copied. This incremental update reduces the time it takes to update a live site. It also reduces errors in a manual copy or the need to write scripts to do the deployment.

The second advantage of using snapshot views is the ability to roll back a Web site. Rolling back is returning a Web site to a previous state. Roll back is usually performed just after a site has been updated and critical problems are discovered. ClearCase snapshot view updates can perform a roll back for you, which is more efficient and less error-prone than trying to back out changes manually. ClearCase tracks changes in the directory structure, so rolling back a site will not only copy the right files to the site but also rename files, remove new files that were added, rename directories, and rearrange the directory structure automatically back to the way it was.

Configuration management is still largely an unknown discipline in Web content management and even in some Web application development projects. However, it will not be long before the need for CM is seen in the Web environment, even more so than in software development because of the extraordinarily rapid rate of change.

9.4.4   Internal Software Components

In this discussion, internal software components refer to components in very large software systems being developed by multiple project teams. Such organizations that arrange themselves along architectural lines may have, for example, a "platform" group, a "core" group, or a "database" group that provides the basic services other development teams reuse. Whatever it is called, that group must stage and release its components for internal development customers. A good example of what gets staged and released would be a library file and a set of header files that describe the public interfaces to the library. Other groups do not rebuild these components but rather link against them. In fact, in many cases it may be desirable that other groups not be able to see or modify the source code for these reusable components.

Staging is exactly the same as in a commercial software system. The build objects are placed under version control. Release is somewhat different, however: the other groups access the "released" software components directly from the ClearCase VOB. Internally, most teams working on a single software system will be using the same SCM tools. So, copying files to uncontrolled directories or shipping around a set of tarred/zipped archive files does not make sense. Different development teams can simply select the baseline of the staged components they are interested in, and these files will become visible in their working environments.

This approach works well for managing complexity in a large software system. It is also effective for groups that are geographically distributed. See Architecture-oriented Project Teams in chapter 7 and chapter 10, Geographically Distributed Development, for more information.

Chapter 10 Geographically Distributed Development

Geographically distributed development is the development of software systems by team members who are not located in the same geographic region. This could mean teams distributed at different sites in the same city or in different countries around the world. While this presents a number of challenges, many companies are finding sound business reasons to do it, including the global nature of their own company, use of third-party components, coordination with third-party software houses, and mergers and acquisitions.

A whole book could be dedicated to this topic. This chapter will briefly discuss the organizational, communication, and technical challenges that need to be overcome for success in distributed development. It covers the support provided by ClearCase and an add-on product, called ClearCase MultiSite.

This chapter will then explore how best to apply ClearCase to three common distributed development scenarios. The three scenarios are as follows:

- *Multiple teams: Producer/consumer*
Multiple project teams are located at different sites that share software components in a producer/consumer relationship. The consumer does not modify the components delivered by the producer.

- *Multiple teams: Shared source code*
Multiple project teams at different sites are modifying the same shared software.

- *Single team: Distributed members*

A single project exists with team members at different sites working on shared software components. This differs from the previous two scenarios in that the distributed members are not organized into a remote team. Rather, there are many individuals working remotely (perhaps from home).

10.1   Distributed Development Challenges

Developing a single software system with distributed teams is no easy task. There are organizational, communication, and technological issues that must all be addressed in order to succeed. This section covers these issues in general. Later sections cover specific approaches to doing distributed development and discuss how each approach relates to these three challenges.

10.1.1   Organization

Organization deals with how team members are grouped into projects, who is responsible for leading the team, how multiple teams are interrelated, who is responsible for making projectwide decisions, and, who ultimately, is responsible for the success or failure of the project. There are probably an infinite number of ways to organize development efforts into projects—an infinite number of ways to assign team members to these projects, to distribute those team members around the globe, and to divide the work between team members. Interestingly, the managerial structure within an organization may not reflect the project team organization. The first issue a project manager faces is how to organize the available members of the development staff into projects.

In distributed development environments, it is often the case that there are different cultures and different development styles. This is easily seen between sites located in two different countries, but it is also true within a country. These cultural differences introduce additional and sometimes subtle obstacles to attaining success.

The key facts that need to be determined and understood by all team members are the following:

- Who is responsible for the overall success of the project?
- Who is responsible for the managerial issues the project encounters?
- Who is responsible for the overall system architecture?
- Who are the team members on this project?

Distributed development efforts tend to be large in scope. So, in general, there will be many smaller projects collaborating on an overall project, which we'll refer to as the "superproject." All members of the collaborating teams should be able to answer the questions about the superproject just listed.

In my experience, many distributed development projects fail because they do not establish this superproject organizational structure between teams working at two or more sites. Without this infrastructure, the tendency for the project teams is to make independent architectural and technological decisions. Ultimately, this makes the system more difficult or impossible to integrate. Even if integration can be done, the lack of overall direction may make project boundaries visible to the end users through the look and feel and other subtle behavior of the resulting system.

10.1.2   Communication

The second challenge of distributed development is communication. Because the teams are geographically separated, communication is impaired. Even today with e-mail, fax, voice mail, and video conferencing, two teams who are not at the same location have far fewer communication channels. The value of the community environment established by people working in one site cannot be underestimated. It is, therefore, important to maximize the teams' ability to communicate while minimizing the amount of day-to-day communication necessary for teams to have with each other to succeed.

To do this, the teams must have a common vision of how the system will work, expressed in an agreed-upon system architecture. Randomly dividing the features to be developed between separate teams at different sites is rarely successful.

Establish a system architecture upfront. Then divide that architecture into separately developable components and assign each component to one co-located team. In this way, the communication channels must be strong during architectural definition and system integration, but during the development of each individual component, the only time the teams must communicate is when the component interfaces require clarification or modification.

10.1.3   Technology

Distributed development involves two technological tools: implementation technologies and development technologies. Implementation technologies are those used in the creation of the system being developed (e.g., the operating system,

GUI components, languages used, and database). Development technologies are those used to establish an effective distributed software development environment (e.g., the SCM tool, the defect-tracking tool, the compiler, and the IDE).

Implementation Technologies

The technology used in the software system should be clearly specified as part of the system architecture. It is certainly possible for different teams to use widely differing technologies to develop their component pieces of the system, but this may have significant effects on many aspects of the resulting system, such as usability, ease of installation, ease of administration, and look and feel. It is important to establish some agreement between teams on what technologies and standards will be used. When these technologies differ there should be sound business reasons for these differences and an understanding of how these technological decisions may impact the final system.

For example, let's say you have two teams developing a Web-based application. When it comes to choosing the language, one team wants to use Java, and the other wants to use Visual Basic (VB). They may each have sound reasons for their choices. It may be that one team has significant experience in Visual Basic and has developed a set of core components used to develop similar applications. The Java team might think that VB won't meet the functional demands they believe the system is likely to require. Left to their own devices both teams could develop separate components that communicated through an agreed upon interface. However, the look and feel and the portability of the overall system would be jeopardized.

So, within the system architecture definition, you should nail down the technologies used to implement the system early on and demand commonality, unless there are sound business reasons for deviating. The following are some things to consider.

- Target operating system and version
- GUI presentation and GUI tool kit
- Database and database version
- User-exposed application interfaces (e.g., COM and CORBA)
- Communications (e.g., TCP/IP, HTTP, WebDAV, and SOAP)
- Data interchange format (e.g., XML)

Development Technologies

The second technological decision facing distributed development teams is what technology will be used to build and manage the development of the software system. This is often referred to as the "software development environment." You must determine the tools and processes your software teams will use and also ensure that the tools you employ can support distributed development.

While it is possible and sometimes necessary to use different software development environments, the number of issues your distributed teams must face will be greatly reduced if you can choose one set of tools and processes. Arriving at consensus between distributed teams is almost always a painful process, but achieving this will minimize the number of issues the project will face otherwise.

For example, if you use two different defect-tracking tools, it becomes more difficult for the project manager to determine defect closure rates for the overall superproject. Even worse, if each team is using a different process for resolving defects, you must figure out how these processes relate. Communicating defects between teams requires knowledge of two defect-tracking tools and processes. Decisions such as what compiler (and what version of the compiler) to use can impact how easy it is to integrate, build, and release a system developed by multiple teams.

Try to achieve a common set of development technologies early on and demand commonality unless there are sound business reasons for deviating. The following are some things to consider.

- SCM tools and processes
- Defect tracking/reporting (tools and processes)
- Build technology (e.g., compiler and make)
- Project management tools

Finally, you must ensure that the tools you choose are capable of supporting distributed development. Many tools claim they can, but you need to carefully explore what capabilities they really provide as you cannot afford to discover deficiencies in your development tools near the end of a release cycle as you try to integrate the efforts of multiple teams.[1]

---

1. Note that if you are waiting until the end of the development cycle to integrate, then you are probably already in trouble.

In terms of software configuration management, here are a few things to look for:

- Is there a reliable, secure means of replication and synchronization of the data between sites that can be completely automated?
- The tools should make the fact that the team is distributed as transparent as possible. The more teams feel as if they are working at the same site, the better the communication and coordination will be.
- There must be a clear distinction between which site currently owns which parts of the shared data.
- Flexibility, flexibility, flexibility. Distributed development between two teams is great, but how about three teams? How about five teams worldwide that work in a round-robin fashion as the sun rises and sets?

10.2   How ClearCase Supports Distributed Development

ClearCase supports four technological solutions for remote developers. Each approach has its own characteristics that make it the right choice in different scenarios. The four options are as follows:

- *Remote access*—logging into the primary site from a remote location (e.g., home)
- *Web access*—using the Web and HTTP protocol to access the primary site
- *Disconnected use*—working disconnected from the network with a local view
- *Local access*—copying VOBs and keeping changes in sync so all work is done locally regardless of site

10.2.1   Remote Access

Remote use is simple. The remote developer logs into the primary site and works remotely. This scenario relies on establishing secure, reliable, and fast connections between the remote developer and the primary site. In this case, all aspects of ClearCase are readily available for use since the developer is technically working at the primary site. The drawback of this approach is that the network connections typically are of lower bandwidth, which may hinder developer productivity. The primary advantage is that little or no additional infrastructure is needed. Remote use is illustrated in Figure 10-1.

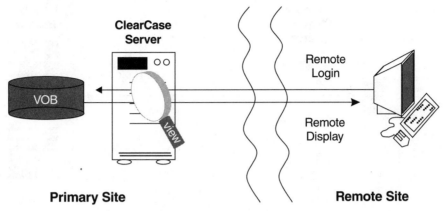

FIGURE 10-1   Remote access

10.2.2   Web Access

In this approach, a ClearCase Web client is used to access versioned elements and perform SCM operations. Once the files are retrieved from ClearCase, the network connection can be broken while the developer is working during the edit/compile/debug stage. Think of this approach as similar to electronic mail. You connect, get the files you need, send the files you've changed, disconnect, and continue working.

The primary drawback to this approach is that the ClearCase Web client does not allow you access to all of the ClearCase features that are available. Only the most common SCM operations can be used. Even with this disadvantage, however, this approach has a number of benefits. It requires less setup than the remote access approach because the HTTP protocol is often available outside a company's firewall, whereas arbitrary TCP/IP connections generally are not. In an emergency, a developer can access files from home or from another office. Another advantage is that ClearCase does not need to be installed on the client. Web access is illustrated in Figure 10-2.

Web access also works very well for occasional ClearCase users even when located at the same site. For example, if you have a number of users that need to browse design documents stored in ClearCase, rather than installing ClearCase on each machine, they can simply use a Web browser to access the files.

10.2.3   Disconnected Use

With the disconnected use approach, a user connects to the network from a remote site, loads a snapshot view, disconnects from the network, and then

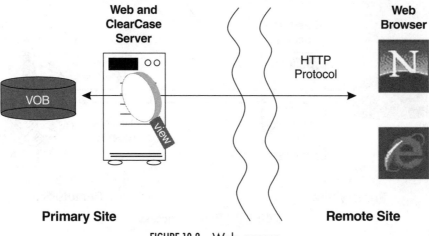

FIGURE 10-2   Web access

works on the downloaded files. Disconnected use is similar to Web access use in that the files are downloaded to a local machine. However, in this case, ClearCase is installed on the user's machine, and, while connected, the user has full access to ClearCase features. This approach could also be described as remote use while the network connection is down. It works only with snapshot views (see Workspaces: Snapshot and Dynamic Views in chapter 4). Disconnected use can be problematic for large systems with a large number of elements. Download/update time may discourage updates and cause developers to drift out of sync with project sources. However, the advantage of disconnected use is that it clearly supports the laptop user who is often away from the office. Disconnected use is illustrated in Figure 10-3.

10.2.4   Local Access

Local access removes barriers for the remote developer while adding some administrative requirements. In local access, the repositories are replicated and synchronized exactly as in the multiteam scenarios. The setup and administration of the replicas are the additional administrative cost. The benefits are that developers no longer need to think about whether they are working locally or remotely, connected or not. They work locally all the time, and performance is not reliant on network bandwidth. The data they produce and operations they perform are then replayed automatically and asynchronously back at the primary site. Similarly, actions and changes happening at the primary site are replayed at the remote site. In this way, developers do not need to consider

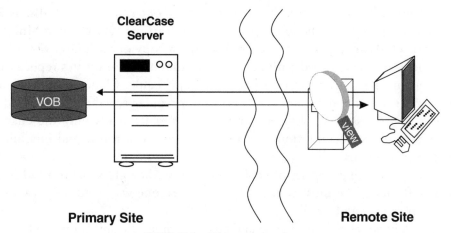

FIGURE 10-3   Disconnected use

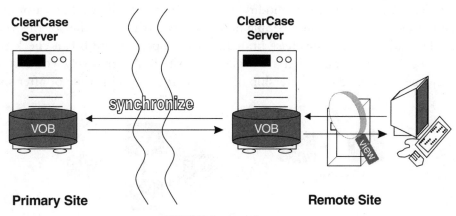

FIGURE 10-4   Local access

where they are located. Local use is illustrated in Figure 10-4. Local use is supported by a ClearCase add-on product called ClearCase MultiSite.

10.2.5   What Is ClearCase MultiSite?

This overview of ClearCase MultiSite is brief and intended to familiarize readers with the additional capabilities required to support MultiSite development. Setup and administration of ClearCase MultiSite is covered in the ClearCase documentation set.

In ClearCase, repositories are called *versioned object bases,* or VOBs, as discussed in chapter 4, A Functional Overview of ClearCase Objects. In a MultiSite scenario, VOBs are replicated or copied so that a copy of the VOB lives at each site. These copies are called *replicas*. The CM administrator creates replicas and then sets up the synchronization pattern and schedule. Changes made to one VOB are sent to the other and vice versa on a regular schedule. This could be nightly, hourly, or even every five minutes. MultiSite sends only the changes made between synchronizations, thus reducing network traffic and minimizing performance impact.

Like networking, the set of replicas and how they are synchronized is extremely flexible. The most common patterns are one-way read-only, two-way peer-to-peer, star, and circular (see Figure 10-5).

To avoid contention problems and ensure that synchronization can be completely automatic, MultiSite supports a notion called *mastership*. Each object in a VOB is mastered at a particular site. If you have mastership, you can modify the object. If not, you cannot modify it. So, for example, if you have a branch type mastered at site A, only people at site A can create branches of this type and check out elements on these branches. Developers at site B can check out only on site B branches, which are mastered at site B. Alternatively, you can set up schemes that hand off mastership of objects after a specific time or after spe-

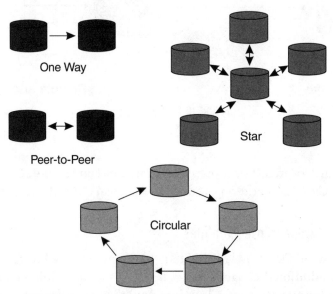

FIGURE 10-5   Common MultiSite replication patterns

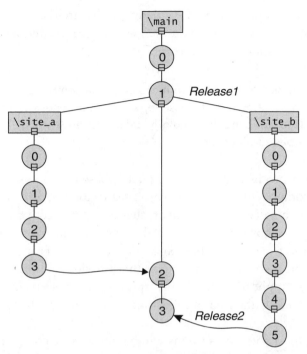

FIGURE 10-6   Branch mastership and integrating changes

cific operations. Changes between sites are integrated by merging changes from one branch to another (see Figure 10-6).

ClearCase UCM provides explicit support for MultiSite by removing the need for developers to understand the underlying branching structure. The following sections discuss three approaches to geographically distributed development and how ClearCase and ClearCase MultiSite can be used to support them. These are the producer/consumer, shared source code, and distributed members scenarios.

10.3   Multiple Teams: Producer/Consumer Scenario

In the producer/consumer model, the geographically distributed project teams produce and/or consume components of the overall system. Only the producer team may modify a component. Projects that consume components do not make any modifications to the components they consume.

Sharing is accomplished by first defining the architecture of the system. Once the architecture is defined, you then assign each component of the system to a single, locally situated project team.

▶ **Note:** If projects at a site develop more then one component, then the components chosen for that site, if possible, should be cohesive. They should also have very little coupling (particularly build dependencies) with components being developed at other sites.

The simplest producer/consumer model is based on a system composed of two software components with two project teams located at different sites. One project produces a software component; the second project consumes that software component, incorporating it into the final system. For example, let's say you have a project team in Sydney and another in San Francisco. The Sydney team is producing a software component that provides all the database services and isolates the application from any specific database technology. The San Francisco team builds the final application on top of this database component (see Figure 10-7).

Of course, most software systems will be much more complex. A simple but more realistic example might be a multitier architecture in which there is one or two commercially available databases, a database abstraction layer, a middle tier that captures the business logic, and a client layer that provides the user interfaces (see Figure 10-8).

A very large software system may have hundreds of components, all being provided by different third-party suppliers or other groups internal to the company. Each of these groups may be working at different sites. It is also possible to have a producer/consumer supply chain where project B consumes a component produced by project A and project C consumes the component produced by project B (see Figure 10-9).

The producer/consumer approach to distributed development is very productive and has the least number of integration-related problems associated with it. Organizationally, each project team has a project leader, and the entire

FIGURE 10-7   Producer/consumer model

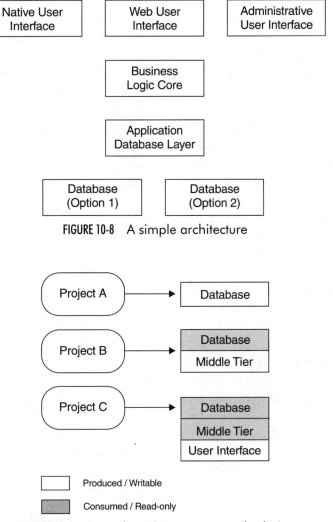

FIGURE 10-8   A simple architecture

FIGURE 10-9   A producer/consumer supply chain

team is located at a single site. This makes management of the project more efficient and effective.

The basic idea here is to minimize the number of dependencies between project teams. The key is to break these dependencies along architectural lines. To do this, there must be a well-defined system architecture, and the system must be decomposed into components. The architecture describes these components and their interfaces. These components are then assigned to project teams, who produce their components and consume components produced by other teams. Ultimately, there is one team that holds the responsibility for consuming all other components and integrating them into the final software system.

The key management and organization challenge inherent in the producer/consumer approach is establishing an effective means of defining and evolving the architecture and component interfaces. This is best done by establishing a cross-project/site architecture team. But, and this is a big but, there should be a clearly defined chief architect who has the authority to make the final decisions on all debated architectural issues. Likewise, it is usually necessary to establish a single program manager who has responsibility for overall management of all projects and can resolve personnel, organizational, process, and cultural issues that may come up between project teams. The big benefit of this approach is that once the architecture has been defined and the interfaces between major components clearly articulated, the various project teams can work in relative isolation to produce their components.

Technically, there are three issues involved from a software configuration management standpoint. First, you must be able to identify a version of a component. Since a component is made up of many elements, you must select one version of each element and identify it. ClearCase refers to this version of a component as a "component baseline." Second, you must have a means to reliably and efficiently deliver the components from one project team to another over a potentially low bandwidth or unreliable network. Third, you must ensure early and regular integration between components to eliminate the risk that a major design error exists in the architecture. This means that each project team should plan first to produce an early baseline of their component that stubs out the external interfaces. This baseline implements the interface without implementing the full functionality behind the interface. Consuming teams can use this to begin testing the interface and early functionality.

This third point leads to the final aspect of managing a distributed development project: iteration or integration planning. The overall program manager must establish an integration plan for all project teams. This plan must identify key project iterations (milestones), what component baselines must be delivered at each iteration, project dependencies, and what functionality will be demonstrable. This allows each team's project leader to plan his or her development accordingly. It also allows the overall project manager to encourage early integration, assess overall project status, and facilitate communication between the teams.

10.3.1   Supporting Producer/Consumer Teams

Supporting the producer/consumer model comes almost for free once you pay the cost of MultiSite administration. That is, once you have set up the VOBs, created the replicas, and established the automated synchronization, it all just works (he says with a smile). In order to implement a secure producer/consumer relationship, you should do one of two things: adopt the UCM model for both teams or use the correct configuration specifications and VOB layout.

10.3.2   How UCM Supports the Producer/Consumer Model

UCM provides direct support for the producer/consumer model. Let's take the simple example just described to explain how it works (see Figure 10-7). We have the Sydney team producing the database and the San Francisco team producing the rest of the application while consuming the database from the Sydney team.

The CM administrator configures the replication environment. First, he or she creates a replica of the project VOB containing the project and component information. Second, he or she creates a replica of the VOB that contains the database deliverables.[2] In this case, there are two projects: the database project and the system project. Both physically reside in a single, replicated project VOB. A database component would also be created.

When the system project was created in San Francisco, the project manager would see the database component and its available baselines on the pick list when declaring components for the system project (See chapter 6, Project Management in ClearCase, for more details). Once a component was selected, the project leader would indicate that this is a read-only component for the San Francisco–based system project team. ClearCase UCM handles the details from there, making the file versions visible and ensuring that they cannot be modified.

10.3.3   How Base ClearCase Supports the Producer/Consumer Model

If you are not using UCM, there are a variety of ways to accomplish a producer/ consumer model on your own. The two things you need to ensure are that the right versions of the files and directories are available and that they cannot be

---

2. This could be the database sources' VOB or a separate database deliverable VOB depending on the staging strategy, build strategy, and the relationship between the teams (see Staging and Release in chapter 9).

modified. As with UCM, the CM administrator must set up and replicate the VOBs containing the database files.

Once this is done, the administrator must ensure that the configuration specification (config spec) used by all San Francisco–based developers is set appropriately. This can be done by telling developers what config rules to set, providing a template for them to use, or writing some scripts to set it for them. Either way, the correct configuration specification rule would be as follows:

```
element  <VOB root path>/...  LABEL -nocheckout
```

where `<VOB root path>` lists the path to the root directory containing all the database elements and `LABEL` is the label type that has been applied to the appropriate versions of all the elements. The `-nocheckout` part of this rule declares that any versions of files selected by this rule should not allow checkouts, for example:

```
element  /vobs/database/...  RELEASE3 -nocheckout
```

You may list multiple rules to cover files not all stored in the same place or under the same root directory. You may also list subdirectories of a VOB.[3]

Three words of caution for setting up your own config specs to support this scenario. First, if you ever plan to adopt UCM, all elements in a component should exist under one root directory. Second, while you can specify a directory that is not at the VOB root, it will take a bit longer for ClearCase to search for and find the right versions. If you have too many of these rules in a configuration specification, it can affect dynamic view performance. Third, if you are working in a heterogeneous environment and use VOB-rooted paths in your config specs, the configuration specifications must be written differently for Unix and NT. For example, the database VOB might be mounted under /vobs/db on Unix. For Windows NT access, it is under \db, so dynamic views might access the VOB from z:\db. When a VOB is specified in a config spec, the Unix version would look like the following:

```
element    /vobs/db/...    RELEASE2
```

NT would look like the following:

```
element    \db\...         RELEASE2
```

---

3. Detailed configuration specification rule syntax can be found in the ClearCase product documentation.

ClearCase Pro Tip

An alternative to following strict tag conventions or maintaining two config specs is to use VOB-tag-neutral format. Instead of specifying the VOB tag in the config spec, you specify the VOB family ID number. This can be found by using the following:

```
prompt> cleartool lsvob -l <vobtag>
```

The VOB family ID number is found under the Vob family uuid: heading. It is a long string of digits.

```
prompt> cleartool lsvob -l /vobs/example
Tag: /vobs/example
...
Vob family uuid:  0c53996a.8faa11ce.a28f.00:01:72:33:a3:f6
...
```

VOB TAG FORMAT:

```
element/vobs/database/...    RELEASE2
```

VOB TAG NEUTRAL FORMAT:

```
element  [0c53996a.8faa11ce.a28f.00:01:72:33:a3:f6]/...    RELEASE2
```

10.3.4   Summary

The producer/consumer model is easy to establish and manage and has a strong likelihood of success given a common system architecture. You should do the following:

- Define a system architecture and assign architectural components to co-located teams.
- Assign a common architect, who is responsible for developing the architecture and making the final decisions on architectural issues.
- Assign a common overall program manager, who is responsible for defining an overall project integration plan and tracking the progress of each project iteration.

Each individual project team is responsible for producing the assigned component functionality for each project iteration. One system project is responsible for consuming, integrating, and testing the final deliverable system.

10.4   Multiple Teams: Shared Source Code Scenario

In the producer/consumer model, the consumer does not modify the components that are produced. Now let's examine the case where multiple teams are working on components that may be modified by any team at any site. When two or more teams are modifying the same set of source code in parallel, the development and integration processes are more complicated if your objective is to maintain a common code base and not diverge. Doing this when the teams are located at the same site is difficult. Geographically distributed teams make it even more complicated.

Because of this complexity, it is best to avoid the shared source code scenario if at all possible and use the producer/consumer scenario. In the real world, this is not always possible or practical. Therefore, optimally, some combination of the producer/consumer model and the shared source code model would be employed.

There are a number of legitimate situations in which you will need to support shared source code. There are also a number of legacy problems that can lead to the shared source code model as the only solution. Many of these problems are avoidable if detected early. A number of situations that may cause you to support shared source code with distributed teams are listed here. Some of these are similar, and often you will find more than one of these in play at any given site.

■ *The system architecture is monolithic or brittle.*

If the system architecture is monolithic or brittle, it becomes impossible to define components on any functional boundary. Because the system cannot be decomposed, the development teams cannot be assigned pieces of the system that do not have a high degree of coupling.

■ *The system is in maintenance mode.*

If the system is fairly old and most work being performed is maintenance work, it is often easier to think in terms of adding features even if those features span architectural boundaries. Sometimes maintenance team sizes are smaller, as compared to new development, and so dividing the work by components is not always practical.

- *The organization favors a feature-based approach.*

A feature-based approach is often applied during system maintenance. It assigns features to individuals or teams even if those features cross architectural boundaries. The individual or team is responsible for implementing the feature regardless of what code is touched. Organizations that favor this approach require developers to have a broad knowledge of the entire system.

- *It just happened that way.*

In many cases, shared code just happens. One team needs some of the code from another team and just takes a copy. In this case, each team modifies all parts of the code, but there are essentially multiple variants of the same code evolving in different groups. Inevitably, this will lead to costly project delays during integration or when the receiving teams want to incorporate further changes made by the original team.

- *There are remote porting/platform teams.*

This case is slightly different, and it is a very legitimate and unavoidable scenario for shared source code. In this case, both teams work on the shared source code. One team produces new functionality, and the second makes secondary changes. Typically, the second team is porting the product to a new platform, making changes to support a different language, or both.

This case comes close to a producer/consumer relationship, because it is largely one way. However, to optimize future porting efforts, it is often a good idea to incorporate changes made by the porting/platform team into the primary team's source code base.

- *You deliver source code to your customer.*

In this case, "you" may be a software house that delivers components to an outside party, which incorporates/modifies the components for use in its own products. In this case, your only concern is that you know your customer will need to integrate future changes from you with its own changes. Using a common SCM tool with a replicated repository will significantly reduce problems in the future, rather than following a throw-it-over-the-wall approach.

- *A third party delivers source code to you.*

This is similar to the previous point, but in this case you are on the receiving end of third-party source code that you will modify. Once again, it is to your benefit to encourage the third-party vendor to use the same SCM tool as you do. If not, then you need a way to capture and componentize the source code you are receiving so that you can treat the third party as a remote development team.

■ *There is no common core team.*

Ideally, when there is common core code used to build different products, there should be a separate team that develops and internally releases this core code. In many cases, there is no such team, so multiple product teams make modifications to the shared code. This case is easier to eliminate if the architecture is such that the interfaces to this common piece can be easily identified and the build dependencies can be reduced (e.g., a common library can be constructed).

Organizationally, in a shared source scenario, you can say that there is no relationship between system architecture and the teams developing the system. However, the farther apart the feature view of the system, the team organization, and the system architecture are from being aligned, the more likely your system and its architecture will become brittle and monolithic. This increases the cost of maintenance and your ability to add new features to the system.

Look closely for the shared source code scenario in hiding. For one large customer I worked with, the project teams were organized architecturally. There was a core team, a database team, a server team, and several application teams. However, any team was allowed to modify any source. This meant that the application teams could modify the source in the core. Basically, this was a shared source code scenario in hiding.

Supporting shared source code scenarios provides a great deal of flexibility for your organization at the cost of requiring significant tooling and additional integration work. It is vital that the overall project leader do integration planning, defining points in time when the shared source is to be integrated. In shared source development, this integration is likely to take longer than it does in a producer/consumer model. Additionally, if it is not planned, the code streams can often diverge for a long time. The longer they diverge, the more difficult integration becomes.

For example, at a large telecommunications firm, two project teams produced two different products starting from a common core set of source code. Once each team had a separate copy of the original source code, it quickly diverged. At one point, one team needed new functionality in the core that had been developed by the other team. It took three months for the entire development team to merge the core to a common code base and establish the necessary tooling and processes to ensure that they did not diverge again. This was a full three months of development time lost, which could mean missing a critical market window in this industry.

The shared source code scenario need not conform to any specific architecture. That is, if you have a monolithic system or a system in maintenance, you can simply divide the work by feature/fix among the teams. This is at the cost of lost architectural integrity and a more complex integration cycle. Architectural integrity can be compromised unknowingly since all source code can be changed. Integration is more complex because of feature-level integration. Generally, how each feature of a release is to work with other features is not well specified; therefore, problems are often caught only at integration time.

The shared source code scenario cannot be easily established without the right technical infrastructure. ClearCase MultiSite provides the support to make shared source development possible. The key technological aspects are replication and sychronization of the repository (VOB), explicit mastership of data and elements, and the means to diverge and merge the code base in a practical way. Of course, you need these capabilities regardless of whether or not your teams are located at the same site.

ClearCase MultiSite supports multiple distributed teams working on the same source through mastership. Mastership, as discussed earlier in this chapter, means that certain pieces of data are owned by certain sites. When it comes to version control, this means that one site may own a branch of an element, and another site may own another branch of the same element. Parallel changes at the sites get integrated through the Merge process.

The following sections discuss setting this scenario up for two different projects: one using ClearCase UCM and one using base ClearCase. If you have only a few developers at your remote site and they are not organized into a separately managed project, then see the Single Team: Distributed Members Scenario section later in this chapter.

10.4.1 How UCM Supports Shared Source Code

With ClearCase UCM, developers can deliver changes to the project integration stream and rebase their development stream with changes made by others on the project. This is described in Single Team: Distributed Members Scenario later in this chapter. This section discusses two collaborating projects where one team is remote, but both teams are working on the same source.

Using ClearCase UCM, it is possible for two or more projects to modify shared source code at the same time. Each UCM project is isolated from other projects' changes in the same way as developers are isolated from each other's changes within a project. UCM uses a per-project/per-stream branching strategy. So, when you have local and remote projects, both projects will have their own project integration branch. To integrate changes between projects you would merge changes between projects' integration streams using base Clear-Case merge functionality or rebase between integration streams where it is supported.

10.4.2   How Base ClearCase Supports Shared Source Code

If you are using UCM, you can still use base ClearCase to support the shared source code scenario. This is done using branches.

With ClearCase MultiSite, a branch can be mastered by only one replica at any time. This means that each site must have mastership of at least one branch in order to check in changes for elements in the replica. The temptation is to create a sitewide branch. This approach can be limiting, as we will see shortly.

Let's explore an example. Say you have 10 developers in a remote site in the U.K. and 20 developers at the primary site in Washington. The overall project everyone is working on is code-named "teatime," and you are working on release 3. The U.K. team is responsible for adding some new GUIs, which will require database work, and the Washington team is responsible for implementing support for a new database, which will also require database work. You divide these teams into two projects.

You could create two branches washington and uk. However, once you have more projects underway and more releases to support, this approach will break down. A per-project, per-release, per-site approach is recommended. So, the two branches would be teatime_rel3_washington and teatime_rel3_uk. You should establish one branch as the primary branch where final integration will take place or have a third branch that is used for integration and stabilization. This could be the main branch or a project-only branch such as teatime (see Figure 10-10).

Integration between project teams is done in a pull fashion. The project that masters the main project branch can periodically integrate changes from the other project branches using the FindMerge operation or the ClearCase merge manager.

This branch per-project, per-release, per-site approach allows each team to work in isolation with a coordinated, planned integration schedule that can be automated and supported by ClearCase MultiSite.

10.4.3   Summary

In the shared source code scenario, multiple teams modify the same shared sources. This approach to distributed development is more difficult and has sig-

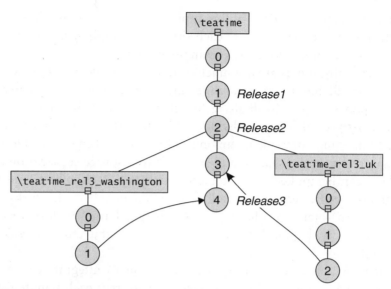

FIGURE 10-10 Branching for shared-source, distributed, collaborating projects

nificant integration issues. In some cases, it must be supported (e.g., with mono-lithic systems and remote porting teams). The organizational and architectural constraints for success are relaxed, but this is at the cost of integration time and architectural integrity. Robust technological support and a focus on multiteam integration planning are essential to success.

10.5   Single Team: Distributed Members Scenario

This scenario is a bit different from either of the other scenarios. It deals with a single project team that has distributed team members. Typically, there are fewer developers involved and less remote management structure in place than with either of the multiple team scenarios. For example, if you have 20 develop-ers at one site and 50 developers at another site, you are likely to have project management at each site. However, if you have 20 developers at one site and 3 developers at a remote site, then you may have project management only at one site (i.e., the three remote developers report into the same management structure as the others).

So, in this scenario, you will have a shared architecture and project manage-ment located at one site. The site you pick should contain the majority of your development team members. The remote site should contain only a small group of developers.[4] Another variant of this approach is to have multiple remote sites with only one or two developers at each site. For example, you may be running a project where each developer is working from home.

Architecturally, things are not much different from the previous two scenarios. You must define a system architecture, divide it into components, and assign components to individuals rather than teams. This approach reduces contention between different individuals for the same source files. However, completely dividing components among individuals is rarely possible in practice. Some code must be shared, and so the shared source scenario on an individual level can be applied to these pieces. This approach is best implemented by assigning specific features to individual team members. It works well on projects in a maintenance phase (see Organizing Large Multiproject Development Efforts in chapter 7 for a discussion on architectural versus feature orientation).

Whether or not code is shared, you will want to integrate changes much earlier and much more often. In fact, you want to treat each remote developer as if he or she is not remote at all. That is, he or she should deliver his or her changes in the same way as other team members, and those changes should be incorporated into the nightly build.

It is inefficient to establish a producer/consumer–style relationship at the individual developer level. You want the development team to be cooperating closely and integrating early and often. This means that the technology you choose must facilitate this kind of support.

This scenario may become more widespread in the near future, as wide area networks improve and good software development people become harder to attract. Companies that support remote development, by allowing the practice and by providing the infrastructure, will be able to attract talented staff who do not wish to relocate or commute into the office.

You can use any of the four approaches described in the How ClearCase Supports Distributed Development section earlier in this chapter to support distributed team members. If you are using local access and ClearCase MultiSite, other interesting aspects are discussed next.

---

4. It is difficult to give concrete guidelines as to how many developers can be at a remote site before you need to establish a remote team and adopt one of the preceding scenarios. If pressed, I would say once a remote site has more than five developers, you should consider establishing a technical lead to handle coordination and day-to-day interactions. More than 10 developers and I would move to a multiteam approach.

10.5.1 How the UCM Model Supports Local Access

ClearCase UCM provides support for local use. Once the project VOB and source VOBs have been replicated to the remote site, the remote developer can join a project exactly as if he or she were working at the primary site. ClearCase UCM handles the details. The remote developer's development stream is mastered at the remote site, and the remote developer can create activities and make changes as necessary.

Once changes have been made, the remote user performs a Deliver operation. The delivery process is slightly different for remote users. The deliver is performed using the pull model rather than the default push model used by developers at the primary site (see Push Deliver versus Pull Deliver in chapter 9). In pull deliveries, the remote developer marks a set of activities as "ready for delivery." The project integrator at the primary site then pulls the changes into the project integration stream. This approach removes the SCM details of branching and merging from the developer and automates the merge step as part of the delivery operation.

10.5.2 How Base ClearCase Supports Local Use

Just as for multiple teams, the remote user can create branches that are mastered at the remote site. These are usually referred to as private branches and may either be per user, per site, per activity (or task), per project, or a combination of those things depending on the integration approach you choose to take (see Using Branches for Isolation and Integration in chapter 9). The ClearCase UCM model basically uses a per-project, per-stream branching scheme. These four branching styles are discussed later, after we set up an example scenario.

Let's say you have 3 developers in Boston and 20 developers at the primary site in San Jose. The project everyone is working on is code-named "fuji," and you are working on release 2. In San Jose, the primary site, you have a project branch `fuji_rel2`, which will be used to integrate all the project changes. You replicate the VOBs to Boston, and now you want to set up the right branches and configuration specifications for the remote users.

Branch by Project or by Site

In this scheme, you could set up a remote project branch or a remote site branch. So, for example, you could set up a site-specific branch called `boston`. However, using a site-specific branch isn't recommended. It works fairly well if there are developers working on one project and you are supporting only one release of the product being developed. However, once you have multiple projects underway and you are maintaining earlier releases while developing newer releases (classic parallel development), this approach breaks down.

As described earlier, if you have multiple projects, then you might use just a project branch such as `projectA_rel2`. However, in this case, we have one project in which we want all the developers to participate. So, you should set up a per-project, per-site, per-release branch, for example, `fuji_boston_rel2`. In this example, the Boston developers start from a specific project baseline identified by a label created on the `fuji_rel2` branch and do their work on the `fuji_boston_rel2` branch (see Figure 10-11).

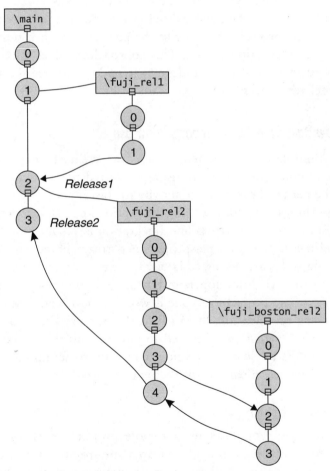

FIGURE 10-11   Branching by project and by site

This approach requires integration steps. The San Jose integrator needs to merge changes from only one remote branch, `fuji_boston_rel2`, into the project branch `fuji_rel2`. Similarly, the remote developers need only merge out from one branch to update their work with work that has gone on at the primary site.

The disadvantage of this approach is that the remote users will need to work closely together to coordinate their changes since any checked-in changes will be visible to all remote users. Since there is a small group of remote users, this is usually acceptable and desirable. However, sometimes this is not a workable solution depending on the type and frequency of the changes being made. The other approach is to use a per-user or per-task branching scheme.[5]

Branching by User

In this approach, there is no single remote branch for our three Boston developers. If you use a per-user branching scheme, then there would be three branches. For example, if one of our remote users was Lorie, then the branch for Lorie's development could be `lorie_dev`. However, once again, just a per-user branch is probably not a good idea unless there is only one project and one release in your team's future (let's hope this is not the case). A better approach is per project, per user. So, the user branch would be `fuji_rel2_lorie`.

Using branch by user, each remote user (and maybe even each user at the primary site) would work on his or her own branch. At certain points in time (usually new project baselines), users would merge out from the project branch `fuji_rel2` to their development branches. Once they had completed some work, the integrator would merge from the development branches into the project branch (see Figure 10-12).

A couple things to note on integration: The integrator must be able to find and merge from all the developers' branches. This is best handled by a good branch-naming convention and some tooling around the ClearCase FindMerge operation. While this complicates the integration merge, it does give all developers some control over what changes they see and allows them to deliver their work at a given point and time separately.

---

5. Additionally, you could use a per-user or per-task branching scheme off of a per-project, per-site branch. But generally, the additional level of branching is too complicated for only a handful of remote developers. It is more applicable and beneficial for the remote teams of 10 or more.

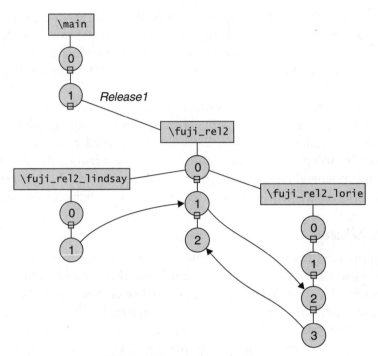

FIGURE 10-12   Branching by user

Additionally, you need to have a way to tell the integrator that the work is ready. This can be done in a number of ways and should be set up in a way that best suits your organization. For example, it could be via e-mail. Another way would be for the developer to apply a label to the versions that are ready to be merged. Once again a good label-naming convention and scripts around Find-Merge can automate this process for the integrator. Another approach is to use attributes on the versions to indicate status.

Another thing to note about the per-project/per-user model is that developers must integrate all the activities they are working on at the same time unless they create another branch. Say you are working on feature A and an emergency bug fix gets assigned to you, so you fix bug X. Then, when the integrator merges from your development branch, he or she will get both bug X and feature A—that is, unless some automation has been written to support pulling these out separately as is the case with ClearCase UCM. However, if you are not using UCM, a good approach to solving this problem in base ClearCase is to use per-activity branching.

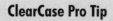

> **ClearCase Pro Tip**
>
> If you are automating the branch-by-user process, there is one other bit of automation that you should consider. In the approach just described, the developer's branch will live on for the life of the project. The more files that users modify, the more time and complexity will be involved in the merge-out operation. This problem can be solved by renaming the branch type and creating a new branch type with the former name, after the changes have been merged into the project branch. This forces a new development branch to sprout the next time that a file changes; and if the developer does not modify that file again, it will appear as if there are no changes made by the developer. The rename should be to something meaningful in order to show the branch history in the version tree. So in our example, you might rename the branch to `fuji_rel2_lorie.1`, `fuji_rel2_lorie.2`, and so on.

10.5.3 Branching by Activity

As in per-developer branching, per-activity branching creates no single remote branch for our three Boston developers. If you use a per-activity branching scheme, then there will be one branch for each activity developers are working on. This leads to a very bushy version tree. For example, if our remote user Lorie is working on feature A, then the branch for Lorie's development would be `feature_a`. In this case, it is not necessary or desirable to include a project extension, because this scheme gives you the flexibility to include or not include this feature in the release 2 fuji project.

Since these branches live only for the time it takes to develop the feature or bug fix, they are usually not updated with other project changes. When developers finish their work, they inform the integrator, and the integrator merges the activity branch into the project branch (Figure 10-13).

It is even more important in this branching by activity model than in the user branching scheme that there be a way to indicate that the branch is ready to be merged (in other words, that the activity is complete). Since there is no branch-naming scheme in play here, a different approach is required. There are a couple of ways to do this. One is to attach an attribute to the branch type and then lock the branch type. This attribute can describe the status of the activity, for example, "ready-to-integrate." Another approach is to attach a known label type, such as "READY_TO_INTEGRATE," to the versions on each activity

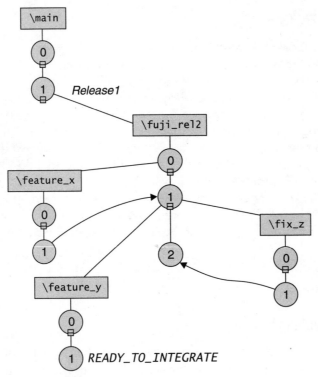

FIGURE 10-13   Branching by activity

branch. This approach makes setting up the correct config spec in the integration view easy. Either approach requires fairly simple scripting, so developers don't need to know the implementation details.

10.5.4 Summary

In some cases, the number of developers at a remote site does not warrant establishing a separate project management structure. In these cases, the remote developers must have the technical support in the SCM tool to allow them to participate in the project remotely. ClearCase supports remote developers in four ways: by remote access, Web access, disconnected use, and local access. As a project leader, you need to determine the optimal approach for your remote team members and how best to integrate their changes.

10.6   Other Uses for ClearCase MultiSite

ClearCase MultiSite can be applied in three other ways. Although not originally designed for these purposes, it has been adopted to solve backup, product delivery, and platform interoperability problems. Since MultiSite is an add-on product to ClearCase, some of these uses may be cost-effective only if you are already using MultiSite to support distributed development.

10.6.1   MultiSite for Backup

The data you store in your SCM system is critical to your company, especially if your company's business is dependent on that software (e.g., integrated software vendors, defense, e-commerce, and mission critical IT applications). You must back up your VOB data.

To back up a VOB, a system administrator locks the VOB, backs up the files associated with it, then unlocks it. The locking time is dependent on the size of the VOB but will require some downtime. One of the benefits to using MultiSite as a backup strategy is that you can back up the replica, thus leaving the primary VOB unlocked and available 24 hours a day. The cost associated with this strategy is that recovery takes longer since you need to use MultiSite in the recovery process rather than just simply recovering the original VOB files.

The frequency of VOB backups depends on your strategy but generally occurs nightly. So, another benefit of using MultiSite is that you can set up an hourly synchronization between the master and the backup replica. In a recovery scenario, you will then have all but the last hours' worth of changes without the overhead of doing hourly backups.

10.6.2   MultiSite for Delivery

MultiSite has also been employed as an automated delivery vehicle. Using MultiSite to replicate the data for and synchronize two sites that often exchange files and information means that a user can just check in a new version of a file and, after the synch time, the changes will automatically be available at the remote site. If the information is important, then this mechanism is more secure and reliable then using ftp to simply copy the files from one site to the other.

10.6.3   MultiSite for Platform Interoperability

ClearCase supports interoperability between Windows NT and Unix development environments. In particular, an NT client can access Unix VOBs and use

Unix views. Setting this up properly can require additional file system software, such as an SMB server on Unix or an NFS client on Windows if you are using dynamic views.

For optimal performance, MultiSite can be used to simulate a homogeneous environment by creating a replica on a Unix platform and another on an NT platform. In this case, each side can be better isolated from one another, and the additional steps needed to communicate between NT and Windows go away since the VOB exists locally on both platforms. This strategy works particularly well if you have one team developing the Unix version of a product and one developing the Windows version against a shared source.

Chapter 11 Change Request Management and ClearQuest

This chapter provides a brief introduction to a topic that is closely related to SCM, that of change request management (CRM). An effective and comprehensive change management solution can be achieved only through the application of the appropriate tools and processes in both disciplines. This chapter introduces CRM and the software product Rational ClearQuest and discusses how ClearQuest extends the UCM model to support CRM.[1]

11.1 What Is Change Request Management?

Change request management is the recording, tracking, and reporting of requests from any stakeholder to change a software system. It includes the decision-making processes an organization uses to decide what changes to make and the resolution processes used to make them.[2]

Change request management is a central part of a complete change management solution. Without recording, change requests may be lost or remain

---

1. CRM is a very important part of a complete change management solution and an entire book could and should be devoted to the topic. Regrettably, I have only scratched the surface. Refer to Humphrey [Humphrey 1989], Whitgift [Whitgift1991], and the Rational Unified Process [RUP 5.5 1999] for additional information.

2. The acronym CRM is also used in the related, but different, domain of customer support. In this domain, it stands for customer relationship management. This chapter uses CRM to refer to defect and request management in the software development domain.

unknown. Without tracking, existing change requests may be forgotten or remain unaddressed. Without reporting, project managers may have a difficult time assessing project status, determining the level of product quality, and conveying project status to upper management.

Rational Unified Process [RUP 5.5 1999] defines change request management as a process that "addresses the organizational infrastructure required to assess the cost and schedule impact of a requested change to the existing product. Change Request Management addresses the workings of a Change Review Team or Change Control Board." Change request management is like the central nervous system of your software development process and is integral to good software development practice. CRM processes and tools manage data that is essential to project stakeholders and the smooth operation of a software project. Other development disciplines related to and supported by change request management are requirements management, testing, release management, customer support, and project management.

11.2   What Are Change Requests?

Rational Unified Process defines a *change request* as "a general term for any request from a stakeholder to change an artifact or process. Documented in the change request is information on the origin and impact of the current problem, the proposed solution, and its cost" [RUP 5.5 1999]. CRM processes are often closely related to a company's internal organization, and terminology in this area is far from standard. However, change requests are often divided into two major categories: enhancement requests and defects.[3]

Enhancement requests specify a new feature of the system or a change to the "as designed" behavior of a system. *Defects* are "an anomaly, or flaw, in a delivered work product. Examples include such things as omissions and imperfections found during early lifecycle phases and symptoms of faults contained in software sufficiently mature for test or operation. A defect can be any kind of issue you want tracked and resolved" [RUP 5.5 1999]. While much of the data maintained for enhancement requests and defects is similar, these two types of change requests are often handled very differently in the CRM process.

---

3. The types of change requests used to manage change vary widely from company to company and even internally between projects within the same company. The types described here, defect and enhancement request, represent only the most basic kinds of change requests.

11.3   The Change Request Management Process

When implementing CRM, you must make a number of decisions. Typically, defining a CRM process involves a number of stakeholders in a number of different functional organizations (e.g., project management, development, testing). The decisions you must make revolve around what types of change requests you will track, what data you will track for these change requests, and how you will track the change requests.

The types of change requests you choose to track could be as simple as defects and enhancements requests, described previously. For large organizations, change requests can become much more complex and multitiered. For example, you might define a type of request that represents an external customer requests. One or more external customer requests may spawn one or more engineering-level enhancement requests.

Once you have defined the types of requests you are going to track, the next step is to define the type of information you need to record throughout the life of the request. For example, if you are tracking defects, you might want to record things such as who submitted the defect, when was it submitted, what was the resolution, was it a duplicate of another defect, or during what phase in the lifecycle was the defect found and fixed.

The most important and often the most difficult thing to define for each change request is the process used to monitor the change request. This process is typically represented in CRM tools by a state transition model. That is, you define a set of states and a set of actions to transition the change request from one state to the next.

Change request types and state transition models vary widely. However, almost all CRM processes include (or should include) the following six stages.

1. *Submission:* requests to change a software system are recorded (submitted).

2. *Evaluation:* change requests are evaluated, categorized, and prioritized.

3. *Decision:* based on the evaluation, a decision is made as to which change requests to implement and in what order.

4. *Implementation:* changes are made to system artifacts, and new artifacts are produced with the goal being to implement the requested change. The software system documentation is updated to reflect the change.

5. *Verification:* the change request implementation is verified as either meeting the requirements or fixing a defect.

6. *Completion:* the change request is closed, and the requestor is notified.

The following sections take a look at each stage of change request management and compare and contrast the treatment of enhancement requests and defects in these stages.

11.3.1   Submission

During submission, requests to change a software system are recorded. Defects and enhancement requests usually differ in the origin of the request and the type of information collected. Enhancement requests come from a wide variety of sources. In many cases, they come from customers and arrive in engineering directly or indirectly through marketing or customer support. The key data captured for enhancement requests are the importance of the request to the customer, as much detail about the request as possible, and the identity of the original requestor (if submitted indirectly), so that engineering can ask for clarification. In some cases, enhancement requests come internally either from testing or in-house use. In these cases, make sure that product management is aware of these requests.

Defects also come from a wide variety of sources. Most are typically found, recorded, and resolved internally. The key data recorded during submission are how the defect was discovered, how to reproduce the defect, the severity, and who discovered the defect. As with enhancement requests, defects can also be discovered by customers. Customer-reported defects usually arrive in engineering indirectly through the sales force, marketing, or customer support. The key data recorded for these defects are the same as enhancement requests, plus the identity of the customer having the problem, the perceived severity of the problem for that customer, and which version of the software system the customer is using. This is needed for the second step of the process—evaluation.

11.3.2   Evaluation

During evaluation someone must look at all newly submitted change requests and make some determination as to each request's character. Is this really a defect or should it be an enhancement request? Is the severity assigned appropriate? Can defects be reproduced? What is its priority compared to other requests? Is this a duplicate of some other change request?

Most organizations follow different processes for evaluation depending on whether something is a defect or an enhancement request. For example, a defect must be reproduced and confirmed. Defects are generally prioritized based on the severity and the importance of fixing the defect. Typically, defects are evaluated by engineering.

Enhancement requests do not need to be confirmed, but do need to be prioritized in relationship to other enhancement requests and product requirements. During evaluation of enhancement requests, you are looking at things such as the number of customers that have made the same request, the relative importance of the customers that are making the request, the possible impact on market share and product revenue, and the impact on the sales force and customer support. Typically, enhancement requests are evaluated by product management.

11.3.3 Decision

The decision stage is when you choose to implement a change request, postpone its implementation, or never implement it. Defects and enhancement requests are almost always handled differently.

For enhancement requests, a product manager or analyst usually makes the decision to implement. Various factors affecting a software product come into play. How easy is it to sell? How does it stand up against competition? How easy is it to install and support? What are the existing customers demanding? What changes could be made to enter into new markets? How many development, testing, and documentation resources will be required to make this change? All the enhancement requests are weighed together, and decisions are made whether to implement each in a given release, postpone it, or never implement it based on the information gathered during evaluation.

The decision process for defects differs depending on two factors: the development lifecycle phase and the size of the development effort. Early in the development lifecycle, you want to maximize change to the software while maintaining control (see chapter 2, Growing into Your SCM Solution). To allow this, the defect decision-making process is often done informally early in the development lifecycle. This allows more changes to be made rapidly. Typically, a defect is assigned to a developer, and the developer decides what to do. If the defect can be reproduced, he or she tries to fix it for the current release.

Near the end of the lifecycle (sometimes called the endgame of a software release), you want to make only necessary changes. Uncontrolled change late in the development lifecycle is disruptive, introduces risk, and often causes slipped schedules and cost overruns. Later in the development lifecycle, most companies institute a formal review process for all defects. For example, developers may do the evaluations, but they are no longer able to make the decision to implement or not implement. The review process can be complex or very simple, such as getting approval from the project leader and/or testing organization. The idea is to ensure that only critical defects are resolved during the code stabilization and final regression-testing phases.

Larger organizations will usually have a formal change review process that includes a formal review board. These review teams are commonly called "change control boards" (CCBs). There may be more than one CCB in very large organizations. CCBs are usually cross-functional and are concerned with making the trade-offs between product quality and project schedule during the endgame.

Rational Unified Process defines a change (or configuration) control board as "the board that oversees the change process consisting of representatives from all interested parties, including customers, developers, and users. In a small project, a single person, such as the project manager or software architect, may play this role" [RUP 5.5 1999]. CCBs are typically concerned only with defects, although the occasional last-minute enhancement requests do show up.

11.3.4   Implementation

During implementation, system artifacts are modified or created as needed to satisfy a change request. In implementation, the differences between defect remediation and enhancement are more subtle. Typically, enhancement request implementation requires more design work than defect implementation since enhancements often involve a new feature or functionality. Defects, on the other hand, require setting up an environment where the defect can be reproduced and where the repair can be tested.

Some defects and enhancement requests are submitted against the documentation. In these cases, the documentation is changed during implementation. For enhancement requests, this means documenting the new features or functionality added to the system. For defects, this can mean doing nothing, changing the documentation if the fix to the defect affects user-visible behavior, or even deleting documentation (e.g., removing a documented workaround to a defect which has been resolved). Documentation changes may also be required when defects are not fixed at all. That is, a decision made to not fix a defect may require that a workaround be documented or that the defect be included in the release notes.

11.3.5 Verification

Verification is when final testing and documentation take place. Testing of enhancement requests usually involves verifying that the changes made satisfy the requirements behind the enhancement request (as recorded by the analyst). Defect testing is simply verifying that the developer's fix does indeed resolve the defect. This usually means trying to reproduce the defect using an official project build.

11.3.6 Completion

Completion is the final closure of the change request. This could be when the request is fulfilled or when a decision is made not to fulfill the request. The primary step during completion is to close the loop with the original stakeholder who submitted the request. This is particularly good practice if the change request originated from an external customer.

11.4 What Is ClearQuest?

ClearQuest is a Rational product that provides out-of-the-box support for the change request management process. ClearQuest is a complementary product to ClearCase. It can be integrated with Microsoft Visual Source Safe, another SCM tool, for projects that require more advanced change request management before they require more advanced software configuration management.

ClearQuest has three key parts: a user interface (the client); a back-end core, which provides an interface to the datastore[4]; and a designer used to create and customize the CRM processes. The user interface has variants that run on Windows, Unix, and the Web. The client has three key panels (see Figure 11-1). On the left side is the tree view of saved queries, charts, and reports. On the right side is the results panel divided into a master/slave display. One line is shown per request in the top panel (master), with the lower panel (slave) showing the details of the request selected in the top panel.

ClearQuest provides out-of-the-box record types for defects and enhancement requests. If your change request management processes are different from those provided, you can use the out-of-the-box types as a starting point or design your own record types from scratch. Rather than doing this definition in

---

4. ClearQuest 2.0 supports Oracle (on Windows or Unix), Microsoft SQL Server, SQL Anywhere, and Microsoft Access databases.

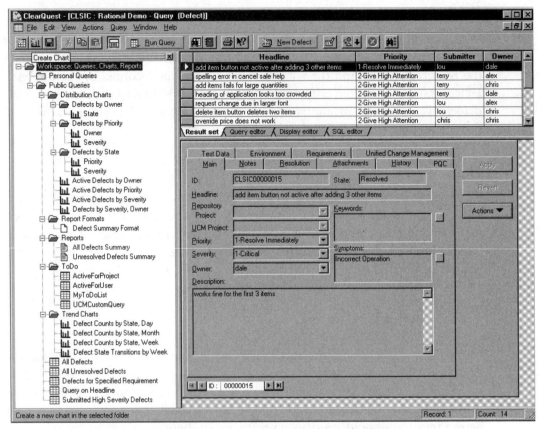

FIGURE 11-1   ClearQuest Windows display

some proprietary language, you have available in ClearQuest a design tool called the ClearQuest Designer. It allows you to modify all aspects of the schema, creating new record types and new fields, defining a state transition model, and controlling the layout of those fields in the submission and display forms. The ClearQuest Designer also supports basic version control for the CRM schema.

Figure 11-2 shows the ClearQuest Designer. The left panel provides a way to navigate to the various pieces of the CRM process. This example shows a folder that contains all the record types in the out-of-the-box schema. You can see three types: Activity, Defect, and Enhancement Request. The Defect record type is open, and under the folder "States and Actions," the state transition matrix is selected. The right panel shows the states and actions for the defect record type. This is where you define the state model for your record and the legal transitions, called "actions," that get you from one state to the next.

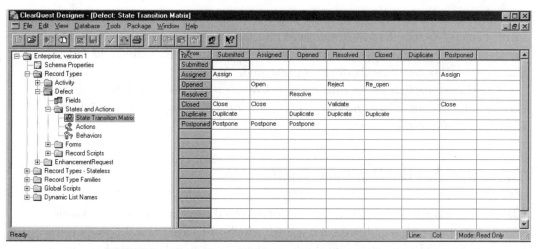

FIGURE 11-2   ClearQuest Designer example—Record types

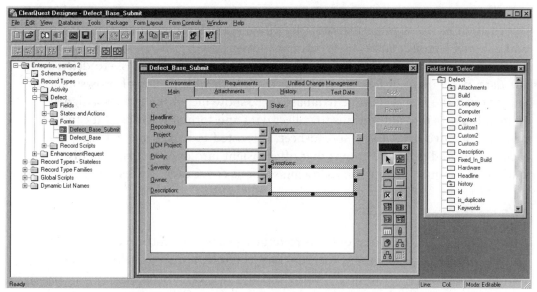

FIGURE 11-3   ClearQuest Designer example—Form editor

In another example, Figure 11-3, you can see the forms portion of the ClearQuest Designer. The left panel shows the defect record type. Under the forms folder, you see selected the "Defect_Base_Submit" form, seen in the middle panel. This is the standard form shown when someone submits a new record of type defect. This will most likely include fewer fields than the full defect form, named "Defect_Base." In the right panel is the form editor interface. This interface is like Visual Basic in that you can create buttons, fields, and labels, and so on, to lay out how the form is presented.

The ClearQuest Designer runs on Windows, but the resulting CRM schema can be used by all client interfaces. "Design once, deploy anywhere" is the ClearQuest marketing mantra.

11.5   How Do I Use ClearQuest Data?

ClearQuest records a significant amount of essential project data—for example, what requests for change have been made, which ones are critical, which ones are being worked on, who is working on them, and which defects have been fixed. This is all very good and very valuable information. However, the data in a change request management tool is useful only if there is an easy way to extract it in a form that allows you to use it. Project managers usually need this information to assess project status—determining the level of product quality—and to convey project status to upper management.

ClearQuest provides mechanisms—queries, reports, and charts—to deliver the data in a variety of forms. Queries provide a flexible means of browsing a subset of all the requests in the database (e.g., show me all the defects assigned to me). Reports provide a means to collect data and format it in a way it can be printed, included in an Excel spreadsheet, or posted to a Web site. Charts provide on-line and printable graphs that offer insight into data trends, data distribution, and request aging. The following sections cover each of these areas.

11.5.1   Queries

The purpose of a ClearQuest query is to return a subset of all the records stored so that you can evaluate those records. For example, a query could be "show me the defects assigned to me," "show me all open defects on Project X," or "show me all resolved defects in Release Y." A ClearQuest query is a set of search criteria defined by a filter that returns a list of records in a master-slave style display. That is, the top window (the master) shows the list of requests one per line, and the bottom window (the slave) shows the details of the request selected in the master window (see Figure 11-1).

Queries and how their results are displayed are constructed graphically by using the ClearQuest Query Creation Wizard. This tool walks you through the process of defining the query. The first step is to decide which data fields to display in the results window and how the data should be sorted. In Figure 11-4, you can see that the headline, priority, submitter, and owner fields have been chosen from all the fields available and will be shown in the master display. You can also see we have decided to sort this list by priority.

The second step in defining a query is to decide which records you are interested in displaying. This is done by choosing the fields and values for those fields in order to filter out the requests you do not want to see. In Figure 11-5, we have chosen two filter fields: priority and ucm_project. For priority, we have selected the top two priority values. Records with any other priority will not be displayed. We have restricted the value of the ucm_project field to one or more projects.

The results of this query are displayed in Figure 11-1. Queries can be saved both as personal queries for an individual or as public queries that become available to the entire project team. Saved queries are organized on the left side (tree view) of the main ClearQuest interface (see Figure 11-1). ClearQuest comes with a number of predefined queries.

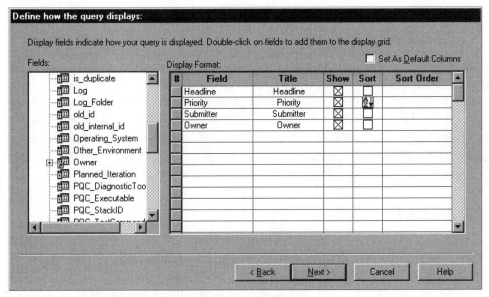

FIGURE 11-4 ClearQuest Query Wizard—Results definition

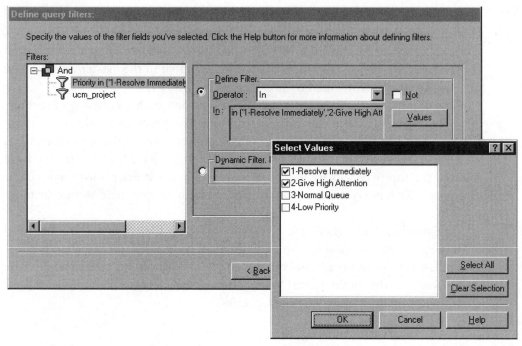

FIGURE 11-5   ClearQuest Query Wizard—Data filter

11.5.2   Reports

ClearQuest reports provide a means to collect a set of data and format it in a way that can be printed, exported, or posted to a Web site. ClearQuest includes one of the industry-standard report-generation tools, Crystal Reports, which allows you to create your own reports from scratch. Reports can be printed and exported into a number of formats such as Excel, HTML, Microsoft Word, comma-separated text, plain text, and Lotus 1-2-3. Figure 11-6 shows a change request summary report being exported to Microsoft Excel 5.0.

11.5.3   Charts

ClearQuest charts graphically represent data, both on-line and in printable form, making it easier to analyze. ClearQuest provides three different types of charts: distribution, trend, and aging. As with ClearQuest queries, there is a Chart Creation Wizard that will walk you through the process of creating your own charts. Charts can then be saved and rerun as needed.

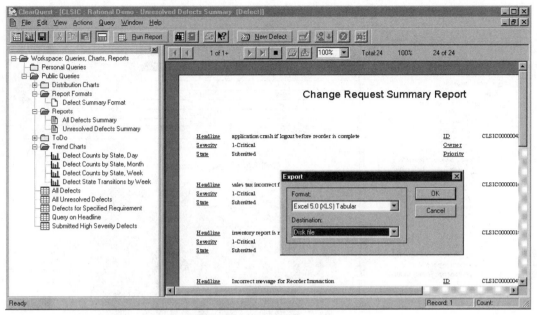

FIGURE 11-6   Example report

Distribution Charts

Distribution charts are used to categorize data and see how a given data sample is distributed across different categories. For example, charts can be used to balance the work load across team members and to get a look at the number of defects by category, such as priority or severity.

Figure 11-7 shows an example distribution chart. In the left panel you see the public queries and the "Distribution Charts" folder. This example screen shows the "Defects by Owner and State" chart. In the top right panel is the data set being used. The lower right panel shows the chart itself. Each bar represents a developer along the *x* axis. The *y* axis shows the number of defects. Bars are color-coded by state. The first bar shows defects that have not been assigned or have been closed. You can quickly see two things in this chart. First, there is a lot of unassigned work, which indicates unknown risk for the project. Second, Alex, Dana, and Devon do not have any open requests they are working on. Get to work, and assign the new requests to those three slackers!

Trend Charts

Trend charts are used to display how change requests are moving through the system over time. As defined by the ClearQuest documentation, "trend charts

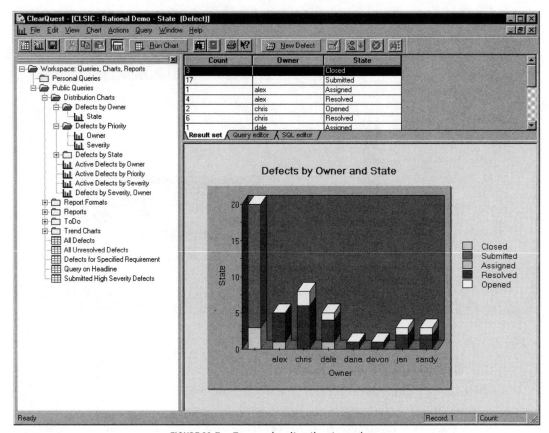

FIGURE 11-7   Example distribution chart

show how many records were transitioned into the selected states by day, week or month." Defect tracking is quite good in and of itself. However, trend charts provide the project manager with critical information that helps him or her objectively judge the status of a project. Trend charts can provide a picture into the endgame of a project by showing the rate of new defect submissions compared to the rate of defect resolution.

Figure 11-8 shows an example trend chart. Once again in the left panel are the public trend chart queries. The trend chart pictured is "Defect Count by State by Week." Again, the upper-right panel shows the data on which the chart is based. The lower-right one shows the chart. The x axis is time by week. The y axis is number of defects. Each line presents the state of the defects. You can quickly see that as the weeks have gone by the number of new defects "submitted" has risen from 20 to 40. The incoming defects have definitely leveled out

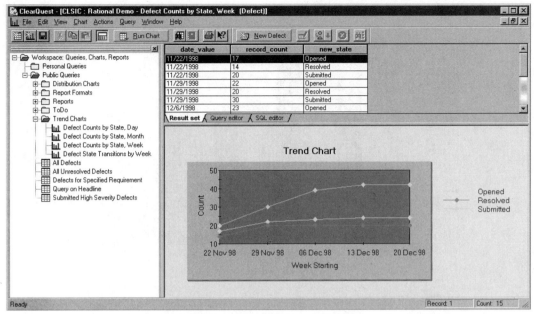

FIGURE 11-8   Example trend chart

so it could be that testing has completed or is blocked. Of more concern is that the number of bugs that have been resolved per week is not going up at all. Until you see the number of submitted defects moving downward and the number of resolved defects moving upward, you are probably far away from a good quality release.

Aging Charts

Aging charts are used to see how long a change request remains in a certain state. They are useful primarily for identifying change requests that are not getting any attention. For example, if a defect has been open for three weeks, it may indicate that it is a very hard problem, the developer has been working on other, higher-priority issues, or no one is looking at it. A change request that has been postponed for five years may be one you should consider filing away as never to be implemented.

Figure 11-9 shows an example of a custom aging chart created using the Chart Creation Wizard. The *x*-axis represents age in months. The *y*-axis represents the number of defects in a given state. The bars are color-coded by state. In this chart, you can see that none of the defects have been around more than

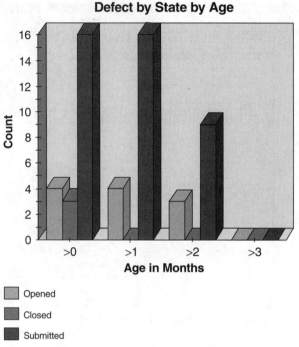

Defect by State by Age

FIGURE 11-9   Example aging chart

three months. However, you can also see that there are nine defects that have been in the submitted state for more than two months. Shouldn't someone take a look at these?

11.6   How Does ClearQuest Support UCM?

ClearQuest can be used to extend the UCM model (described in chapter 3, An Overview of the Unified Change Management Model) with support for change request management. The UCM process diagram (Figure 3-2 on page 55), shows two steps the project manager performs: assign and schedule work, and monitor project status. ClearQuest is the technology that supports these steps. With ClearCase alone, activities have only a name, a one-line description, and a change set. ClearCase maintains the essential configuration management information, but not the change request management information. To support change request management, additional data must be maintained, for example, state, assigned user, a long description, priority, severity, and so on. In a UCM environment, it is ClearQuest that provides these capabilities. If you are interested in an integrated change management solution, you will need both ClearCase and ClearQuest.

With ClearCase UCM alone, activities are used as the mechanism to track a change set (see Organize and Integrate Consistent Sets of Versions Using Activities in chapter 1). The primary difference between using ClearCase alone or in combination with ClearQuest is the level of process centered around the activities.

If you are using ClearCase UCM by itself, activities are created at the point of use. That is, individual developers, working in their development stream, create activities when they check out files. These activities consist of a one-line description and so appear to the developer as kind of a meta-comment for a change spanning multiple files. Modifying Files and Directories in chapter 8 goes into this in more detail. The bottom line is that ClearCase stand-alone with UCM does not support the process for activities you need if you want to do change request management.

With ClearQuest, activities are submitted, evaluated, decided on, implemented, validated, and completed. They can be of any record type that you define. So, they can be defects, enhancement requests, features, incidents, tasks, and so on. This is accomplished by adding UCM required fields from the Clear-Quest Designer to a given record type. Many of the predefined record types come pre-UCM–enabled. Figure 11-10 shows the additional tab, called Unified Change Management, and fields added when you apply the UCM package to a record type in the ClearQuest Designer.

An additional difference between using ClearCase by itself and using Clear-Quest is that ClearQuest adds the notion of a developer's to-do list. This is a list of activities assigned to a given developer for a given project. Automation keeps this list up to date, adding new activities as they are assigned and removing them as they are resolved. Additionally, ClearCase knows how to retrieve this to-do list and will display it for the developer where appropriate. For example, when you check out, the drop-down activity selection list is your own personal to-do list. There is no concept of a to-do list in ClearCase by itself.

So, when do you use ClearCase alone and when do you use ClearQuest? For small projects or projects that are process adverse, use ClearCase alone during the early phases of development when you want to encourage as much change as possible. Also use ClearCase alone if you are in an organization that already has a change request management system that you are not able to replace.

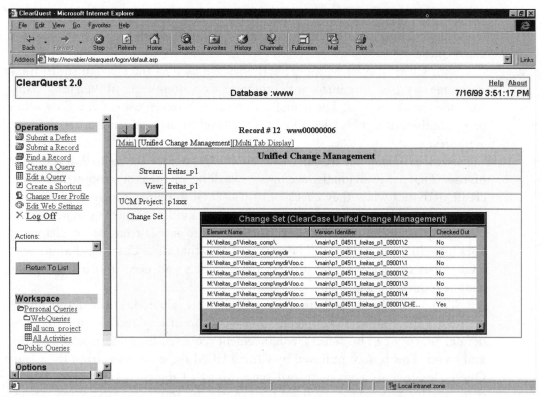

FIGURE 11-10   UCM fields in a ClearQuest record (Web interface shown)

Use ClearQuest when you are interested in change request management. I would suggest that during the endgame of any development project, ClearQuest should be used at least to do defect tracking. This will improve overall quality considerably. If you are uncertain, it is possible to enable and disable Clear-Quest for a project at any given time simply by changing the project policy setting.

Glossary

activity

1. A unit of work an individual may be asked to perform. Activities can be of different types. For example, a defect, enhancement request, or issue are all activities. This unit of work ties directly into the change request management system and processes. An activity can also be a child of another activity that appears in the project management system.

2. A ClearCase UCM object that tracks the work required to complete a development task. An activity includes a text headline, which describes the task, and a change set, which identifies all versions that you create or modify while working on the activity. When you work on a version, you must associate that version with an activity. If your project is configured to use the UCM-ClearQuest integration, a corresponding Clear-Quest record stores additional activity information, such as the state and owner of the activity [ClearCase 1999].

activity-based configuration management

The management of change to a software system based on higher-level activities (e.g., task, defect, enhancement) rather than individual file versions. This requires a SCM tool to track which file versions go to implementing a specific activity and then to present activities as key objects. The idea is to simplify complexity and ensure that when the system says a defect is included in a specific build, it has in fact been included.

administration VOB

A VOB containing global type objects that are copied to client VOBs on an as-needed basis when users wish to create instances of the type objects in the client VOBs. Administration VOBs are not a special type of VOB, but rather defined as relationships a VOB can have with other VOBs.

Note: Most of the definitions in this glossary are taken from one of three sources: ClearCase documentation [ClearCase 1999], Rational Software's Rational Unified Process [RUP 5.5 1999], or the IEEE's "Standard Glossary of Software Engineering Terminology" [IEEE Glossary 1990]. In some cases, these sources define a term differently. If the difference in definition aids understanding, both definitions are listed and the source is noted.

ALBD Server

Atria Location Broker Daemon. This ClearCase master server runs on each Clear-Case host. It starts up and dispatches messages to the various ClearCase server programs as necessary.

architecture

1. The set of significant decisions about the organization of a software system: the selection of the structural elements and their interfaces by which the system is composed together with their behavior as specified in the collaboration among those elements, the composition of the structural and behavioral elements into progressively larger sub-systems, and the architectural style that guides this organization, these elements, their interfaces, their collaborations, and their composition. Software architecture is concerned not only with structure and behavior but also with usage, functionality, performance, resilience, reuse, comprehensibility, economic and technology constraints and trade-offs, and aesthetic issues [Booch 1999] [Kruchten 2000].

2. The organizational structure of a system or component [IEEE Glossary 1990].

3. The architecture of a software system (at a given point in time) is its organization or structure of significant components interacting through interfaces, those components being composed of successively smaller components and interfaces [RUP 5.5 1999].

assembly integration

The software development activity in which separate software component baselines are combined into an executable whole. See *integration*.

attribute

A meta-data annotation attached to an object, in the form of a name/value pair. Names of attributes are specified by user-defined attribute types; values of these attributes can be set by users. Example: a project administrator creates an attribute type whose name is QAed. A user then attaches the attribute QAed with the value "yes" to versions of several file elements.

attribute types

An object that defines an attribute name for use within a VOB. It constrains the attribute values that can be paired with the attribute name (for example, an integer in the range 1 to10).

backward delta

A delta storage approach that stores the latest version of the file in its entirety and stores only the delta of the previous versions.

baseline

A ClearCase UCM object that typically represents a stable configuration for one or more components. A baseline identifies activities and one version of every element visible in one or more components. You can create a development stream or rebase an existing development stream from a baseline.

branch

An object that specifies a linear sequence of element versions.

branch/LATEST development

A branching strategy in which team members work in isolated views, but check out and check in on the same branch. Changes become visible to other team members at checkin time rather than file save time. Branch/LATEST development minimizes isolation and maximizes integration.

branching strategy

A strategy for isolation and integration of changes on a software project through the use of branches. A branching strategy defines the types of branches you use, how these branches relate to one another, and how you move changes between branches.

build

The process during which a build program (e.g., clearmake) produces one or more derived objects. This may involve actual translation of source files and construction of binary files by compilers, linkers, text formatters, and so on.

build audit

The process of recording which files and directories (and which versions of them) are read or written by the operating system during a build.

build avoidance

The ability of a ClearCase build program called clearmake to fulfill a build request using an existing derived object, instead of creating a new derived object by executing a build step.

change request

A general term for any request from a stakeholder to change an artifact or process. Documented in the change request is information on the origin and impact of the current problem, the proposed solution, and its cost. See also *enhancement request, defect*.

change request management

The recording, tracking, and reporting of requests from any stakeholder to change a software system. Change request management includes the decision-making processes an organization uses to decide what changes to make and the resolution processes used to make them.

change set

A list of related versions associated with a UCM activity. ClearCase records the versions that you create while you work on an activity. An activity uses a change set to record the versions of files that are delivered, integrated, and released together.

Some in the SCM industry distinguish between two terms: change package and change set. The difference is subtle and has to do with the implementation. A change set is defined as the actual delta that compose the change even if it spans files. A change package is a grouping together of a set of file versions. ClearCase uses the term change set to denote a change package.

checkout/checkin

The two-part process that extends a branch of an element's version tree with a new version. The first part of the process, checkout, expresses your intent to create a new version at the current end of a particular branch. The second part, checkin, completes the process by creating the new version.

Performing a checkout of a branch does not necessarily guarantee you the right to perform a subsequent checkin. Many users can check out the same branch, as long as they are working in different views. At most, one of these can be a reserved checkout, which guarantees the user's right to check in a new version. An unreserved checkout affords no such guarantee. If server users have unreserved checkouts on the same branch in different views, the first user to perform a checkin wins. Other users must perform a merge if they wish to save their checked-out versions.

checkpointing

The ability of developers to check in an intermediate version of a file they have been working on without this change being made visible to other team members. The ability of developers to checkpoint their work depends on what branching strategy an organization uses. For example, a branch/LATEST strategy does not allow checkpointing.

clearmake

A 'make' compatible build tool that is part of the ClearCase product and that provides build audit and build avoidance features.

component

1. A physical object in the CM system containing files and directories that implement one or more logical packages. A ClearCase component is a set of files and directories contained under a common root directory. ClearCase components are versioned, shared (reused), and released as a single unit. A large system will typically consist of many components. A small system may be contained in only one component.

2. A ClearCase object that groups a set of related directory and file elements within a UCM project. Typically, you develop, integrate, and release the elements that make up a component together. A project contains at least one component, and it can contain multiple components. Projects can share components [ClearCase 1999].

3. A nontrivial, nearly independent, and replaceable part of a system that fulfills a clear function in the context of a well-defined architecture. A component conforms to and provides the physical realization of a set of interfaces. A physical, replaceable part of a system that packages implementation and conforms to and provides the realization of a set of interfaces. A component represents a physical piece of implementation of a system, including software code (source, binary, or executable) or equivalents such as scripts or command files [RUP 5.5 1999].

component-based development

The creation and deployment of software-intensive systems assembled from components, as well as the development and harvesting of such components.

component subsystem

A stereotyped subsystem representing the logical abstraction in design of a component. It realizes one or more interfaces and may be dependent on one or more interfaces. It may enclose zero or more classes, packages, or other component subsystems, none of which are visible externally (only interfaces are visible). It may also enclose zero or more diagrams that illustrate internal behavior (e.g., state, sequence, or collaboration diagrams) [RUP 5.5 1999].

concurrent changes

Changes made by two or more developers to the same files at the same time. The SCM tool must also support the merging or integration of the changes thus recombining the work that was done in parallel. Concurrent change on a large scale made by two or more teams is referred to as parallel development.

configuration

1. A labeled or baselined set of versions that form a consistent set.
2. The set of versions selected by a view.

configuration and change control

An element of configuration management, consisting of the evaluation, coordination, approval or disapproval, and implementation of changes to configuration items [IEEE Glossary 1990].

configuration control

An element of configuration management, consisting of the evaluation, coordination, approval or disapproval, and implementation of changes to configuration items after formal establishment of their configuration identification [IEEE Glossary 1990].

configuration identification

An element of configuration management, consisting of selecting the configuration items for a system and recording their functional and physical characteristics in technical documentation [IEEE Glossary 1990].

configuration management

A more general definition than software configuration management, applying both to hardware and software configuration management. See *software configuration management*.

configuration record

A bill of materials for a derived object, indicating exactly which file system objects (and which specific versions of those objects) were used by the rebuild as input data or as executable programs and which files were created as output.

configuration specification

A set of configuration rules specifying which versions of VOB elements a view selects. The config spec for a snapshot view also specifies which elements to load into the view.

configuration status accounting

An element of configuration management, consisting of the recording and reporting of information needed to manage a configuration effectively [IEEE Glossary 1990].

defect

An anomaly, or flaw, in a delivered work product. Examples include such things as omissions and imperfections found during early lifecycle phases and symptoms of faults contained in software sufficiently mature for test or operation. A defect can be any kind of issue you want tracked and resolved. See also *change request*.

deliver

A ClearCase operation that allows developers to share their work with the rest of the project team by merging work from their own development streams to the project's integration stream. If required, the deliver operation invokes the Merge Manager to merge versions.

delta

The physical change made between one version of a file and the next.

derived object

A ClearCase specific name for the output files produced during a software build using clearmake.

development stream

A ClearCase UCM object that determines which versions of elements appear in your development view and maintains a list of your activities. The purpose of the development stream is to let you work on a set of activities and corresponding versions in isolation from the rest of the project team. The development stream configures your development view to select the versions associated with the foundation baselines plus any activities and versions that you create after joining the project or rebasing your development stream.

development view

A view associated with a UCM development stream. A development view is used to work on a set of activities and corresponding versions isolated from the rest of the project team. You then can share changes made in a development view with the rest of the project team by delivering activities to the project's integration stream. A development view can be either a dynamic view or a snapshot view.

dynamic view

A type of view that is always current with the VOB. Dynamic views use the MVFS to create and maintain a directory tree that contains versions of VOB elements. Dynamic views are not supported on all ClearCase platforms.

element

An object that encompasses a set of versions, organized into a version tree. Elements can be either files or directories.

enhancement request

A type of stakeholder request that specifies a new feature or functionality of the system. Enhancement requests specify a new feature of the system or a change to the "as designed" behavior of a system. See also *change request*.

entity

A record in a ClearQuest user database. Every entity is based on a specific entity type. Entities based on UCM-enabled entity types can be automatically associated with activities.

entity type

A metadata object that appears in a ClearQuest schema that describes the structure of a type of record, including its fields, states, actions, and forms.

follow-on project

A project that starts from an existing on-going project. A follow-on project inherits the on-going project's component baselines as its starting configuration.

forward delta

A delta storage approach that stores the first version of a file in its entirety and the other versions as deltas.

foundation baseline

A property of a stream. Foundation baselines specify the versions and activities that appear in your view. As part of a rebase operation, foundation baselines of the target stream are replaced with the set of recommended baselines from the source stream.

full baseline

A baseline created by recording all versions below a component's root directory. Generally, full baselines take longer to create than incremental baselines; however, ClearCase can look up the contents of a full baseline faster than it can look up the contents of an incremental baseline.

implementation view

An architectural view that describes the organization of the static software elements (code, data, and other accompanying artfacts) of the development environment in terms of packaging, layering, and configuration management (ownership, release strategy, and so on).

hyperlinks

A logical pointer between two objects. For example, a predefined hyperlink type of "Merge" defines merge relationships between versions on different branches. A hyperlink can have a from-string and/or a to-string, which are implemented as string-valued attributes on the hyperlink object.

A bidirectional hyperlink connects two objects in the same VOB or in different VOBs and can be navigated in either direction: from-object to to-object, or to-object to from-object. A unidirectional hyperlink connects two objects in different VOBs and can be navigated only in the from-object to to-object direction.

incremental baseline

A baseline created by recording the last full baseline and versions of elements that have changed since the last full baseline was created. Generally, incremental baselines are faster to create than full baselines; however, ClearCase can look up the contents of a full baseline faster than it can look up the contents of an incremental baseline.

in-line delta

An approach to delta storage where no copy of the file is stored in its entirety, rather only deltas are stored.

integration

1. The process of bringing together independently developed changes to form a testable piece of a software system. Integration can occur at many levels, eventually culminating in a complete software system.

2. The software development activity in which separate software components are combined into an executable whole [RUP 5.5 1999].

integration stream

A ClearCase UCM object that enables access to versions of the project's shared elements. A project contains only one integration stream. The integration stream maintains the project's baselines and configures integration views to select the versions associated with the foundation baselines plus any activities and versions that have been delivered to the integration stream.

integration view

A view associated with a UCM project's integration stream. An integration view is used to build and test the latest versions of a project's shared elements. It can be either a dynamic view or a snapshot view.

iteration

A distinct set of activities with a baselined plan and valuation criteria resulting in a release (internal or external).

label

An instance of a label type object that supplies a user-defined name for a version. A label is attached to a version of an element.

label type

A named tag that can be used to identify a consistent set of element versions. For example, you could create a label type called "RELEASE1" and attach instances of the label type to all the versions of the elements that make up the first release of a software system.

license server

A host whose albd_server process controls access to the licenses defined in its license database file.

main branch

The starting branch of an element's version tree. The default name for this branch is "main."

mainline project

A UCM project that serves as an integration and release point for multiple subprojects.

mastership

The ability to modify an object or to create instances of a type object.

merge

The combining of the contents of two or more files or directories into a single new file or directory. Typically, when merging files, all the files involved are versions of a single file element. When merging directories, all contributors to the merge must be versions of the same directory element.

merge integration

The resolution of parallel changes made by different team members to common files, directories, and/or components. In some cases this can be automated. In others, manual decisions must be made (e.g., when conflicting changes have been made to the same files).

metadata

Data associated with an object, supplementing the object's file system data.

multiversion file system (MVFS)

A directory tree that, when activated (mounted as a file system of type MVFS), implements a ClearCase VOB. To standard operating system commands, a VOB appears to contain a directory hierarchy; ClearCase commands can also access the VOB's metadata. MVFS also refers to a file system extension to the operating system, which provides access to VOB data. The MVFS is not supported on all ClearCase platforms.

package

A collection of metadata (fields, actions, forms, etc.) that can be added to a schema. In the UCM model, adding the UCM package to a schema will allow entities based on that schema to be automatically associated with activities and collect change sets.

parallel development

1. Concurrent changes made to individuals files and/or an entire software system by two or more individuals or teams. Parallel development also includes the ability to merge the changes that have been made in parallel.

2. The concurrent creation of versions on two or more branches of an element [ClearCase 1999].

posted delivery

See *pull delivery.*

project

1. A ClearCase UCM object that contains the configuration information needed to manage a significant development effort, such as a product release. The project is used to set policies that govern how developers access and update the set of files and directories used in the development effort. A project includes one integration stream, which configures views that select the latest versions of the project's shared elements, and typically multiple development streams, which configure views that allow developers to work in isolation from the rest of the project team. A project may be ClearQuest-enabled so that its activities will be associated with UCM-enabled ClearQuest entities [ClearCase 1999].

2. An endeavor performed by people, constrained by limited resources, and planned, executed and controlled. A project is a temporary endeavor undertaken to create a unique product or service. Temporary means that every project has a definite beginning and a definite end. Unique means that the product or service is different in some distinguishing way from all similar products and services. Projects are undertaken at all levels of the organization. They may involve a single person or many thousands. They may require fewer than 100 hours to complete or more than 10,000,000. Projects may involve a single unit of one organization or may cross organizational boundaries as in joint ventures and partnering. Projects are often critical components of the performing organization's business strategy [PMI 1996].

project VOB (PVOB)

A VOB that stores UCM objects, such as projects, streams, activities, and change sets. Every UCM project must have a PVOB. Multiple projects can share the same PVOB. See *versioned object base.*

promotion level

A property of a UCM baseline that can be used to indicate the quality or degree of completeness of the activities and versions represented by that baseline. You can use promotion levels to define policy for a UCM project. UCM provides an ordered set of default promotion levels, and also supports user-defined promotion levels. The action of changing the promotion level of a baseline is called promoting or demoting the baseline.

pull delivery

With pull delivery, developers indicate that their changes are ready for integration, but it is the integrator who is responsible for integrating the developer's changes into the project's integration stream. See *deliver.*

push delivery

With push delivery, a developer is responsible for integrating his or her changes into the project's integration stream where the integrator can create baselines and perform project builds. See *deliver.*

PVOB

See *project VOB (PVOB).*

rebase

A ClearCase UCM operation that makes your development work area current with the set of versions represented by a more recent baseline in the integration stream.

recommended baseline

The set of baselines that the project team should use to rebase their development streams. In addition, when developers join a project, their development work areas are initialized with the recommended baselines. The recommended baselines represent a system configuration, or set of components, that has achieved a specified promotion level. A baseline becomes part of the set of recommended baselines when the project manager promotes it to a certain promotion level, for example, "TESTED."

registry server

The host on which all ClearCase data storage areas (all VOBs and views) in a local area network are centrally registered.

release

The process of putting the runtime software onto/into its final form and making it available to its intended users.

replica

An instance of a VOB, located at a particular site. A replica consists of the VOB's database, along with all the VOB's data containers.

reserved checkout
> See *checkout/checkin.*

schema
> Defines the metadata for entities and other information in a ClearQuest user database.

snapshot view
> A view that contains copies of ClearCase elements and other file system objects in a directory tree. You use an update tool or rebase operation to keep the view current with the VOB (as specified by the configuration specification).

software configuration management (SCM)
> A software engineering discipline that comprises the tools and techniques (processes or methodology) a company uses to manage change to its software assets.

staging
> The process of putting the derived object files (executables, libraries, data files, generated header files, etc.) under version control.

stream
> A ClearCase UCM object that determines which versions of elements appear in any view configured by that stream. Streams maintain a list of baselines and activities. A project contains one integration stream and typically multiple development streams.

subsystem
> 1. A generic name used to refer to a ClearCase component.
> 2. A model element that has the semantics of a package, such that it can contain other model elements, and a class, such that it has behavior. (The behavior of the subsystem is provided by classes or other subsystems it contains.) A subsystem realizes one or more interfaces, which define the behavior it can perform. A subsystem is a grouping of model elements, of which some constitute a specification of the behavior offered by the other contained model elements [RUP 5.5 1999].

trigger
> A monitor that specifies one or more standard programs or built-in actions to be executed automatically whenever a certain ClearCase operation is performed.

trivial merge
> A merge between two branches where it is possible to automatically copy the contents of one file version on one branch to another using information contained in the version tree.

uncheckout
> The act of cancelling a checkout operation.

unified change management (UCM)

1. Unified change management (UCM) is Rational Software's approach to managing change in software system development from requirements to release. UCM spans the development lifecycle, defining how to manage change to requirements, design models, documentation, components, test assets, and source code.

One of the key aspects of the UCM model is that it ties together or unifies the activities used to plan and track project progress and the artifacts being changed. The UCM model is realized by both process and tools. The Rational products ClearCase and ClearQuest are the foundation technologies for UCM. ClearCase manages all the artifacts produced by a software project, including both system artifacts and project management artifacts. ClearQuest manages the project's tasks, defects, and requests for enhancements (referred to generically as activities) and provides the charting and reporting tools necessary to track project progress.

2. An out-of-the-box process, layered on base ClearCase and ClearQuest functionality, for organizing software development teams and their work products. Members of a project team use activities and components to organize their work [ClearCase 1999].

unreserved checkout

See *checkout/checkin*.

version

An object that implements a particular revision of an element. The versions of an element are organized into a version tree structure. Checked-out version can also refer to the view-private file that corresponds to the object created in a VOB database by the checkout command.

version control

A subset of software configuration management that deals with tracking version evolution of a file or directory.

version tree

The hierarchical structure in which all versions of an element are (logically) organized. When displaying a version tree, ClearCase also shows merge operations (indicated by arrows).

versioned object base (VOB)

A repository that stores versions of file elements, directory elements, derived objects, and metadata associated with these objects. With ClearCase MultiSite, a VOB can have multiple replicas at different sites.

view

A ClearCase object that provides a work area for one or more users to edit source versions, compile them into object modules, format them into documents, and so on. Users in different views can work on the same files without interfering with each other. For each element in a VOB, a view's configuration specification selects one version from the element's version tree. Each view can also store view-private files that do not appear in other views. There are two kinds of views: snapshot and dynamic.

view server

The daemon process that interprets a view's configuration specification, mapping element names into versions, and that performs workspace management for the view.

VOB

See *versioned object base*.

VOB server

The process that provides access to the data containers that store versions' file system data.

workspace

1. A private area where developers can implement and test code in accordance with the project's adopted standards in relative isolation from other developers [RUP 5.5 1999].

2. A generic SCM term for a ClearCase view. Sometimes used to refer to the combination of a view and a stream in a UCM context.

workspace management

The process of creating and maintaining a workspace.

Bibliography

[Beck 2000] Beck, K. *Extreme Programming Explained*. Reading, Mass.: Addison-Wesley, 2000.

[Booch 1999] Booch, G., Rumbaugh, J., and Jacobson, I. *The Unified Modeling Language User Guide*. Reading, Mass.: Addison-Wesley, 1999.

[ClearCase 1999] Rational Software. *Introduction to ClearCase—Release 4.0*. Lexington, Mass.: Rational Software Corp., 1999.

[Humphrey 1989] Humphrey, H. *Managing the Software Process*. Reading, Mass.: Addison-Wesley, 1989. *http://www.sei.cmu.edu/*

[Feiler 1991] Feiler, P. "Configuration Management Models in Commercial Environments." Pittsburgh: Software Engineering Institute, Carnegie-Mellon University, 1991.

[IEEE Glossary 1990] IEEE Standard 610.12-1990. "Standard Glossary of Software Engineering Terminology." New York: Institute of Electrical and Electronics Engineers, 1990.

[IEEE 828-1998] IEEE Standard 828-1998. "IEEE Standard for Software Configuration Management Plans." New York: Institute of Electrical and Electronics Engineers, 1998.

[IEEE 1042-1987] IEEE Standard 1042-1987. "IEEE Guide to Software Configuration Management." New York: Institute of Electrical and Electronics Engineers, 1988.

[Kruchten 2000] Kruchten, P. *The Rational Unified Process: An Introduction, Second Edition*. Boston: Addison-Wesley, 2000.

[Kruchten 1995] Kruchten, P. "The 4+1 View of Architecture." *IEEE Software* 12, no. 6 (November 1995): 45–50.

[Lakos 1996] Lakos, J. *Large-Scale C++ Software Design*. Reading, Mass.: Addison-Wesley, 1996.

[Leblang 1994] Leblang, D. "The CM Challenge: Configuration Management That Works." In *Configuration Management,* edited by W. Tichy. West Sussex, England: John Wiley and Sons, 1994.

[Oram 1991] Oram, A., and Talbott, S. *Managing Projects with Make*. Sebastopol, Calif.: O'Reilly & Associates, 1991.

[PMI 1996] Duncan, W., and PMI Standards Committee. *A Guide to the Project Management Body of Knowledge*. Newtown Square, Penn.: Project Management Institute, 1996.

[Royce 1998] Royce, W. *Software Project Management—A Unified Framework*. Reading, Mass.: Addison-Wesley, 1998.

[RUP 5.5 1999] Rational Software. Rational Unified Process. Cupertino, Calif.: Rational Software Corp., 1999. *http://www.rational.com/*

[Tichy 1994] Tichy, W. *Configuration Management*. West Sussex, England: John Wiley and Sons, 1994.

[Whitgift 1991] Whitgift, D. *Methods and Tools for Software Configuration Management*. West Sussex, England: John Wiley & Sons, 1991.

Index

M

Mainline projects, 154, 156–158
  final component baseline graph with/
    with no, 159
Major projects, 128
Major project teams, 25, 26
  and software integration, 193–194
Major releases, 163
  parallel development of, 160
Make Baseline
  command, 212, 216
  component baseline selection during,
    213
  dialog, 212, 213
  Makefiles, 59
"Make" tool (Unix), 35n.9
Make utility, builds done with, 214
Management changes, 22–23
Manual merge example, 189
Mapping
  between architecture and ClearCase
    components, 115
  between architecture and implementa-
    tion of architecture, 6
  of dynamic view to network drive, 76
  between organization of system and
    implementation of system, 59
  UML component, 60
Mastership, 232, 233, 243, 244
Media production, in build and release
    management, 47
Memory, and ClearCase performance, 107
Merge integration, 191–192, 207
  and team size, 193
Mergers and acquisitions, and geographi-
    cally distributed development, 223
Merges/merging, 243
  automated example of, 188
  and branching, 43, 45
  with ClearCase UCM, 184
  conflicts with, 192
  and integration, 197
  manual, 189
  trivial, 185
Merge tools
  ClearCase, 186–190
  and integration, 197

Metadata, 70, 90
Metadata types, 92
Microsoft Visual Source Safe, ClearQuest
    integrated with, 261
Microsoft Visual Studio, 63, 76, 108
Microsoft Word, 103
  documents, ClearCase merging of, 187
  element type, 88
  reports exported into, 266
Modest environment, 104, 105
Modest teams/modest project teams, 25, 26,
    128, 193
Modifiable components, 133, 143
Monolithic system architecture, and shared
    source code scenario, 240, 242
Multiple parallel release coordination,
    154–158
  follow-on project, 154–155
  mainline project, 156–158
Multiple teams
  producer/consumer scenario, 223,
    233–240
  shared source code scenario, 240–245
MultiSite. *See* ClearCase MultiSite
Multiversioned file system (MVFS), 74, 102–103

N

NFS, 102
Nightly builds, automating, 216
Notepad, 103
NTFS, 102

O

Object sharing, in ClearCase, 94
Off-line work, with snapshot views, 78
One-way read-only replica pattern, 232
Opaque data type, 91
Organization, and distributed development,
    224–225

P

Parallel building, clearmake support for, 94
Parallel development, 19, 25, 84, 115
  ClearCase UCM support for, 184
  versus serial development, 42
  support, 19, 42–43, 45
Parallel releases, 156, 157–158, 160

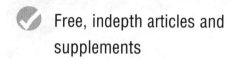
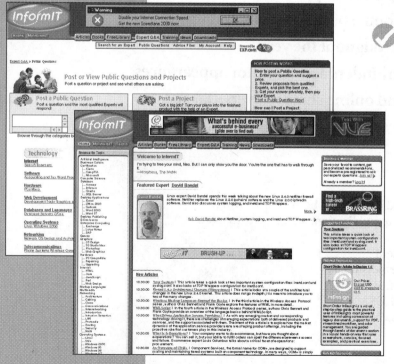

Register
Your Book

at www.aw.com/cseng/register

You may be eligible to receive:

- Advance notice of forthcoming editions of the book
- Related book recommendations
- Chapter excerpts and supplements of forthcoming titles
- Information about special contests and promotions throughout the year
- Notices and reminders about author appearances, tradeshows, and online chats with special guests

Contact us

If you are interested in writing a book or reviewing manuscripts prior to publication, please write to us at:

Editorial Department
Addison-Wesley Professional
75 Arlington Street, Suite 300
Boston, MA 02116 USA
Email: AWPro@aw.com

Addison-Wesley

Visit us on the Web: http://www.aw.com/cseng